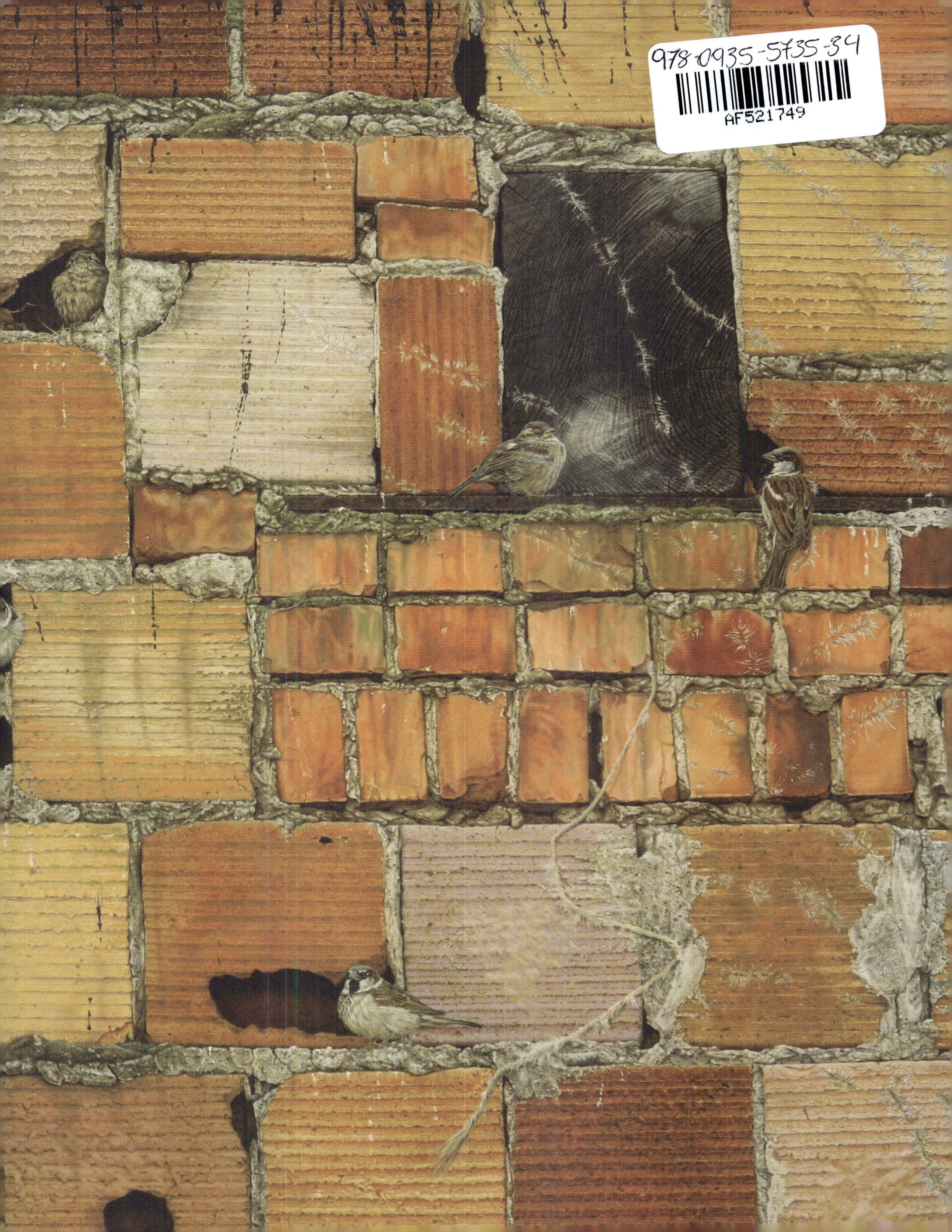

Birds in Art 2012

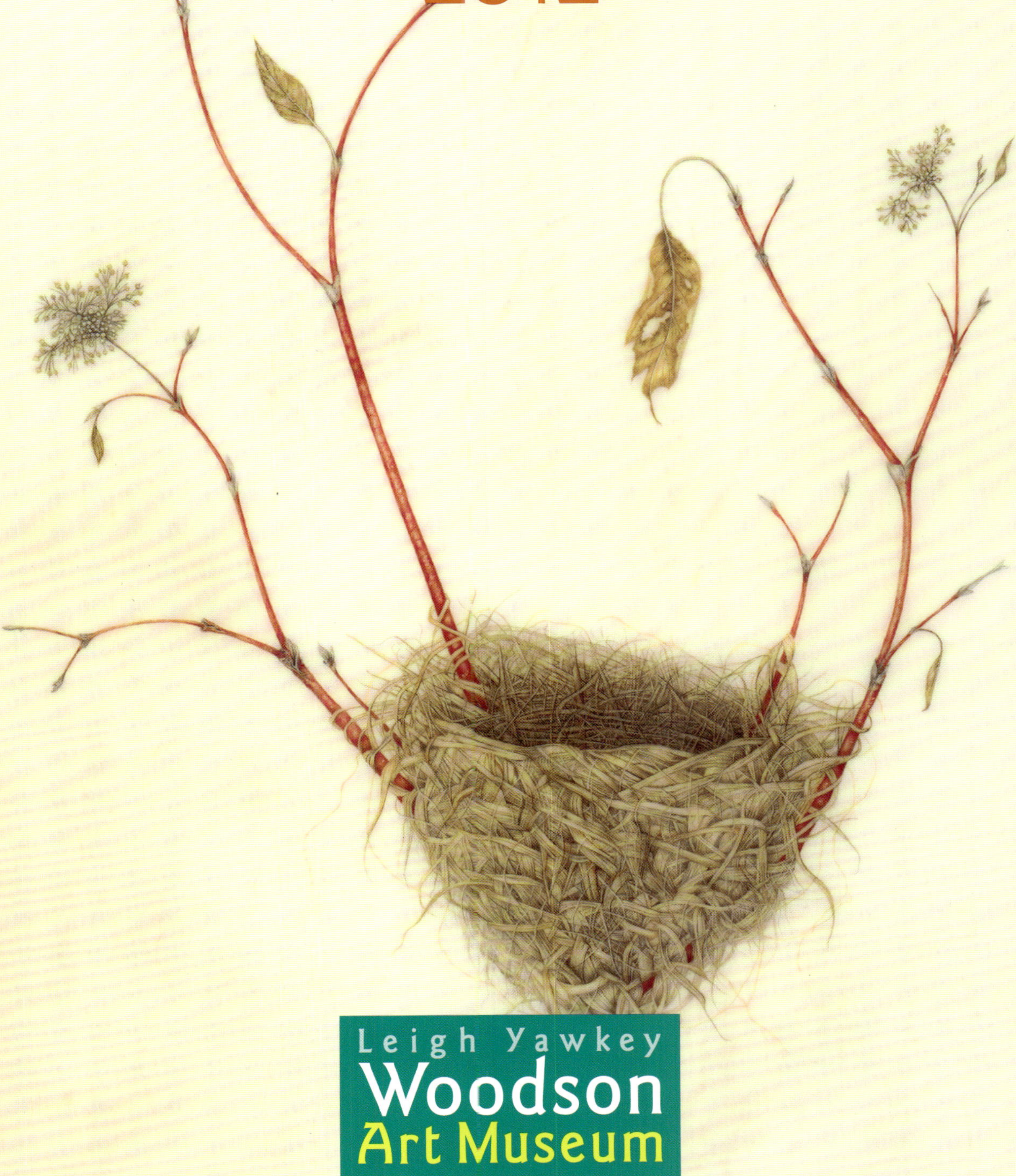

Leigh Yawkey Woodson Art Museum

Birds in Art® 2012 venues:

Leigh Yawkey Woodson Art Museum
Wausau, Wisconsin
www.lywam.org
715-845-7010
September 8 – November 11, 2012

The Wildlife Experience
Parker, Colorado
www.thewildlifeexperience.org
720-488-3300
December 1, 2012 – February 18, 2013

Newington-Cropsey Foundation
Hastings-on-Hudson, New York
www.newingtoncropsey.com
914-478-7990
March 9 – May 5, 2013

Frank H. McClung Museum, University of Tennessee
Knoxville, Tennessee
www.mcclungmuseum.utk.edu
865-974-2144
May 25 – August 18, 2013

Rockport Center for the Arts
Rockport, Texas
www.rockportartcenter.com
361-729-5519
September 14 – November 16, 2013

ISSN 1057-8110

The Wisconsin Arts Board with funds from the State of Wisconsin supports the Woodson Art Museum's exhibitions and programs. A City of Wausau Room Tax Fund Grant supports marketing efforts.

Accredited by the
American Association of Museums

Half Title Page
Kathleen E. Dunn
Chinatown, 2010

Title Page
Wendy Brockman
Remembrance, 2012

Contents

Foreword

Looking Back . . . Looking Ahead

Kathy Kelsey Foley
Director

A thirty-seventh anniversary may not typically be cause for celebration. For the Leigh Yawkey Woodson Art Museum and the 2012 *Birds in Art* exhibition, number thirty-seven is not only notable, but also auspicious.

Along with this edition of the Museum's flagship exhibition, we celebrate a major gift of forty-three paintings by Wisconsin legend Owen J. Gromme (1896-1991) and the completion of a significant building addition comprising gallery space and collection storage as well as visitor amenities.

BMO Harris Bank's gift of the Marshall & Ilsley Bank collection of Owen Gromme paintings brings a Gromme-Woodson Art Museum connection full circle. While many know Gromme as the "Father of *Birds in Art*," the circumstances and interconnectedness of influential Wisconsinites were unknown to me until recently.

A look back reveals that Museum founders John E. Forester and Alice Woodson Forester came to know Gromme in the 1960s through their friendship with John A. Puelicher, President of Milwaukee-based Marshall & Ilsley Bank. In 1965, Puelicher commissioned Gromme to undertake an ambitious painting project for the Bank.

As the Foresters and Alice's sisters, Nancy Woodson Spire and Margaret Woodson Fisher, and their families moved forward with their plans to establish an art museum in Wausau, they called on Owen Gromme for guidance. He suggested the theme for the museum's inaugural exhibition and served as the *de facto* curator for *Birds of the Lakes, Fields and Forests.*

No one could have imagined in 1976 that an exhibition born of a friendship that had its roots at a Milwaukee bank would spread its wings worldwide, continue to set the standard for avian-themed art, and prove critical in the decision to make the Woodson Art Museum the permanent home of Gromme's Marshall & Ilsley Bank paintings.

Birds in Art, as the Owen Gromme-organized exhibition came to be called, is one powerful catalyst!

How proud Owen and the Museum's founders would be today. In its thirty-seven year history, the exhibition has brought together artists, art enthusiasts, and bird lovers from around the world, creating a network of peers and friends that transcends geography and language to rally around the Woodson and to celebrate the best indoor birdwatching anywhere.

With the launch of the 2012 exhibition, we acknowledge and applaud the 125 artists whose work we enjoy in the Woodson Art Museum's galleries, in this accompanying catalogue, and throughout the subsequent four-venue tour.

For the record book, this year's exhibition boasts the following statistics. The work of 106 artists – nineteen of whom make their *Birds in Art* debut – was selected from entries submitted by 577 worldwide artists. Nineteen previously honored Master Artists are represented, including Guy Coheleach and Maynard Reece who had their Woodson debut in Owen Gromme's *Birds of the Lakes, Fields and Forests* and are distinguished by having participated in each subsequent exhibition. In total, the number of artists who have exhibited their work in *Birds in Art* since 1976 is approaching the one-thousand mark.

The challenge – and pleasure – of sorting and sifting through the entries was skillfully undertaken by Kevin Avery, senior research scholar at New York's Metropolitan Museum of Art; Maureen Bloomfield, editor in chief of *The Artist's Magazine;* and Deborah Woodiel, assistant director/museum educator at the Frank H. McClung Museum, University of Tennessee, Knoxville. To each of the jurors we express our gratitude.

Looking back at the genesis of John and Alice Forester's relationship with Owen Gromme fills in an important piece of the Woodson Art Museum's remarkable history. The Museum's highly regarded and growing collection, pacesetting programs and publications, and the friendships and memories that stem from *Birds in Art* are our building blocks for the future.

This future holds promise and unlimited potential as the Museum builds on momentum from the Gromme painting gift, expanded facilities, and enhanced services. I'm confident the hundreds of talented artists who comprise the *Birds in Art* family – past, present, and future – will continue to push the boundaries of art focused on the avian world as they strive to ensure their very best work finds its way to the Woodson Art Museum.

While I'm savoring the present and all that we've accomplished, I'm also looking ahead, ready to seize opportunities that present themselves. I know we'll be celebrating those next milestones in the blink of an eye.

Catalogue Notes

ARTWORK: Titles are captioned in bold italics; the date of the work follows. For bronze sculptures, edition size is provided; A/P signifies artist's proof. For graphics, the number of the actual print exhibited precedes the total edition number.

BIRD NAME: Common names are provided if they are relevant and not included in the title.

DIMENSIONS: All dimensions are in inches. Unframed dimensions are listed as height by width for two-dimensional works, and height by width by depth, generally including the base, for three-dimensional objects.

BIRDS IN ART: Year or years of an artist's inclusion are listed chronologically. For artists previously honored as a Master Wildlife Artist, this designation is noted.

W indicates an artist's inclusion in the Woodson Art Museum's permanent collection.

EXHIBITIONS: Titles are given for all but one-person exhibitions, when only the museum/gallery name, date, and location are listed. If an artist is represented in an exhibition more than one year (e.g., 2010-12), the reference is given only once followed by museum/gallery name and location. If an organization's annual exhibition does not have a distinct name, the organization name is given in italics followed by the date, venue if known, and location.

AWARDS: If received in conjunction with an exhibition, the citation signifies the artist's participation.

BIBLIOGRAPHY: Listings refer to articles and books authored and/or illustrated by or written about the artist. Self-published book references include title and date of first publication followed by SP. Online articles include title, publication name, and month/year of first posting followed by OL.

REPRESENTATIVES: Artists serve as their own representatives unless noted otherwise.

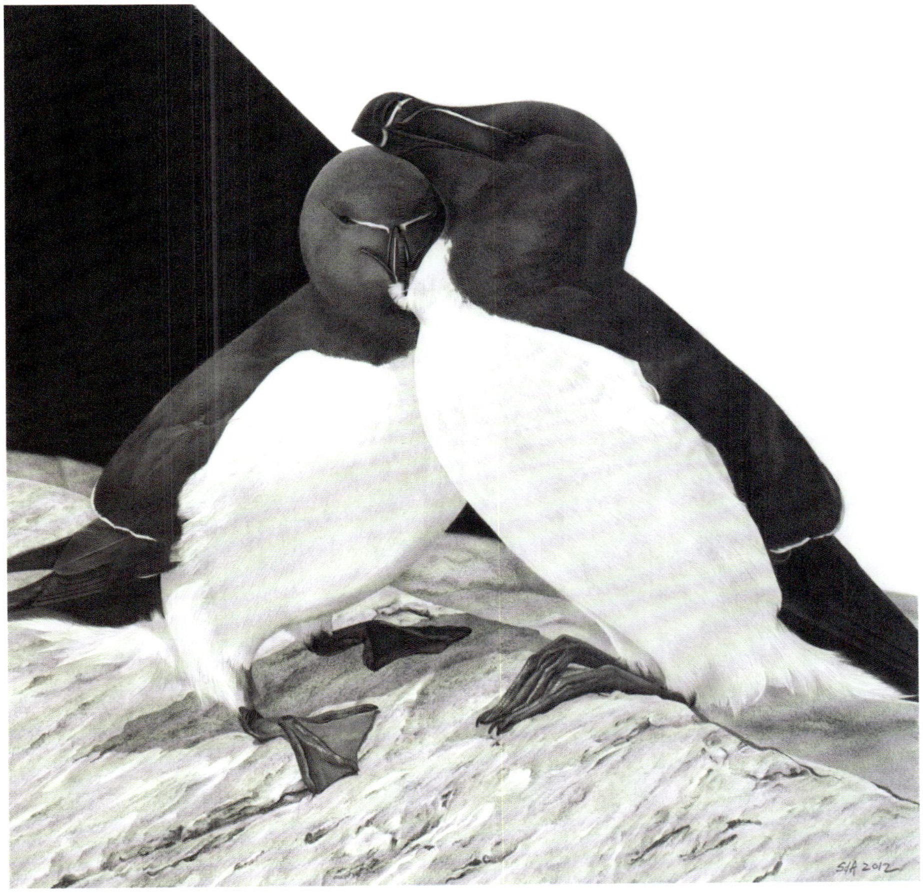

Renewing Their Bond,
2012
Razorbill
Graphite on Arches hot press paper
10 x 10

Collection of the artist

BORN: 1960, United States
RESIDES: Schenectady, New York
EDUCATION: B.A., Saint Lawrence University, Canton, New York
EXHIBITIONS: *Art and the Animal,* 2010, San Diego Natural History Museum, 2011, Dennos Museum Center, Northwestern Michigan College, Traverse City, and 2012, Hiram Blauvelt Art Museum, Oradell, New Jersey; *Art of the Animal Kingdom,* 2010 and 2012, Bennington Center for the Arts, Bennington, Vermont; *Artists for Conservation,* 2011, Spirit Gallery, Grouse Mountain, Vancouver, British Columbia, Canada
COLLECTIONS: Bennington Center for the Arts
BIBLIOGRAPHY: *Strokes of Genius 3: The Best of Drawing, Fresh Perspectives,* North Light Books, 2011

I had the good fortune to visit Machias Seal Island in the Gulf of Maine on a day when sea conditions allowed us to land on the island and observe and photograph nesting birds from blinds. It was a magical experience! Atlantic puffins surrounded us and even clattered around on top of the blind. There were lesser numbers of razorbills and common murres. I was drawn to the razorbills; their black and white coloration complements my preference for black and white mediums. I simplified the background by eliminating plant material and distant rocks, then added a wedge of black to emphasize the focal point and mimic the lines of this preening pair.

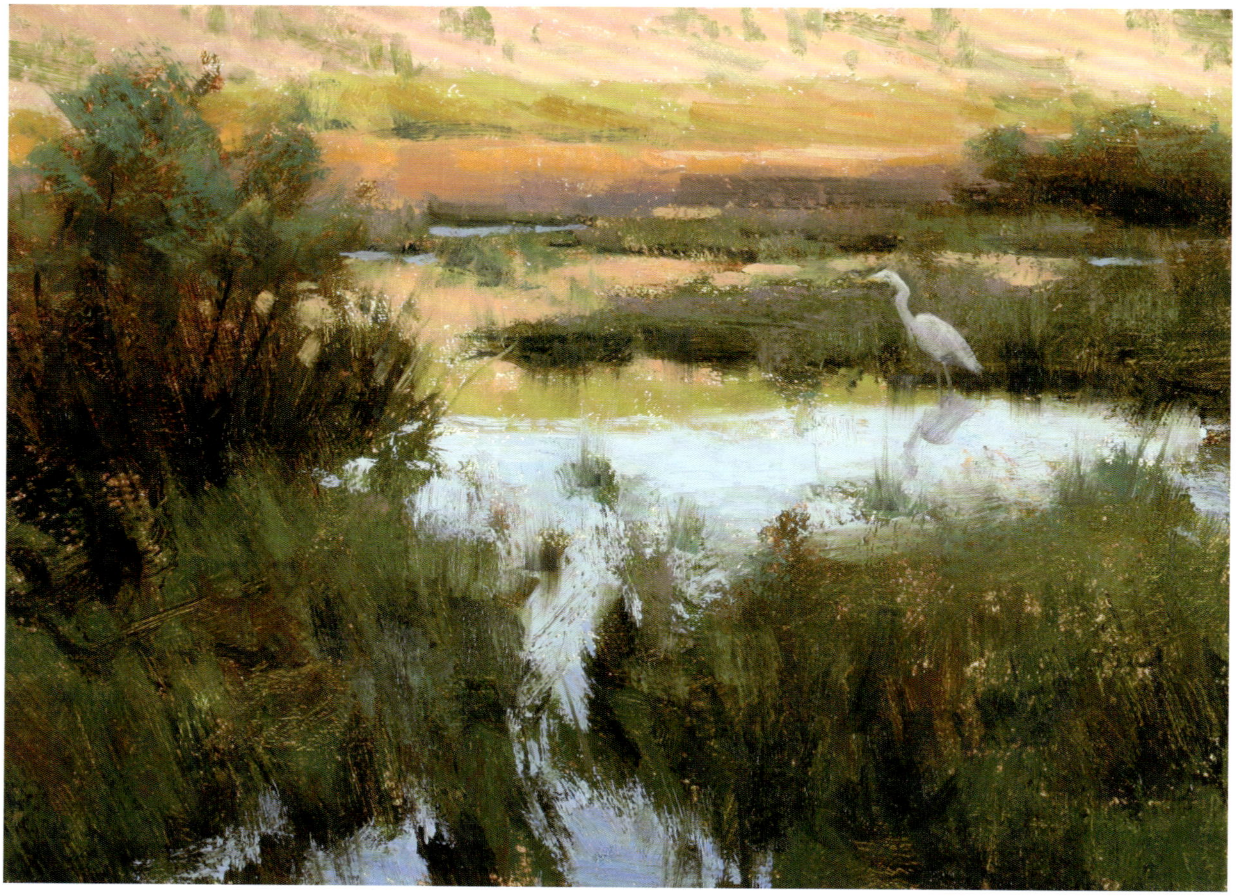

In the Stillness of the Morning, 2012
Great egret
Oil on linen
9 x 12

Collection of the artist

Birds in Art: 1990-91, 1994, 1997, 1999-00, 2002-04, 2006, 2008-09, 2011

W

BORN: 1965, United States
RESIDES: Golden, Colorado
EDUCATION: B.F.A., Rhode Island School of Design, Providence
EXHIBITIONS: *Small Works/Great Wonders,* 2010, National Cowboy & Western Heritage Museum, Oklahoma City; Mountain Trails Gallery, 2010-11, Jackson, Wyoming; *American Art Invitational,* 2010-11, Saks Galleries, Denver; Arizona-Sonora Desert Museum, 2012, Tucson; *Oil Painters of America National Exhibition,* 2012, Evergreen Fine Art Gallery, Evergreen, Colorado
COLLECTIONS: Arizona-Sonora Desert Museum; Bennington Center for the Arts, Bennington, Vermont
BIBLIOGRAPHY: "Coors Western Art Show," *Southwest Art,* January 2012
REPRESENTATIVES: Mountain Trails Gallery; Sage Creek Gallery, Santa Fe, New Mexico; Saks Galleries

A few years back while at Yellowstone National Park, I took a series of photographs in a flooded valley. The graphic qualities of the water and grasses were striking. Early morning shadows in the foreground intensified the contrasts, and the darker grasses generated wonderful shapes and light and dark passages. Good paintings have a compositional basis in abstract shapes and design. I often break down a composition into its most basic graphic elements before adding details. Here I felt a looser stylistic approach was necessary. The egret is almost incidental, as if a brief visitor to this piece of nature. The bird does, however, breathe life into the painting.

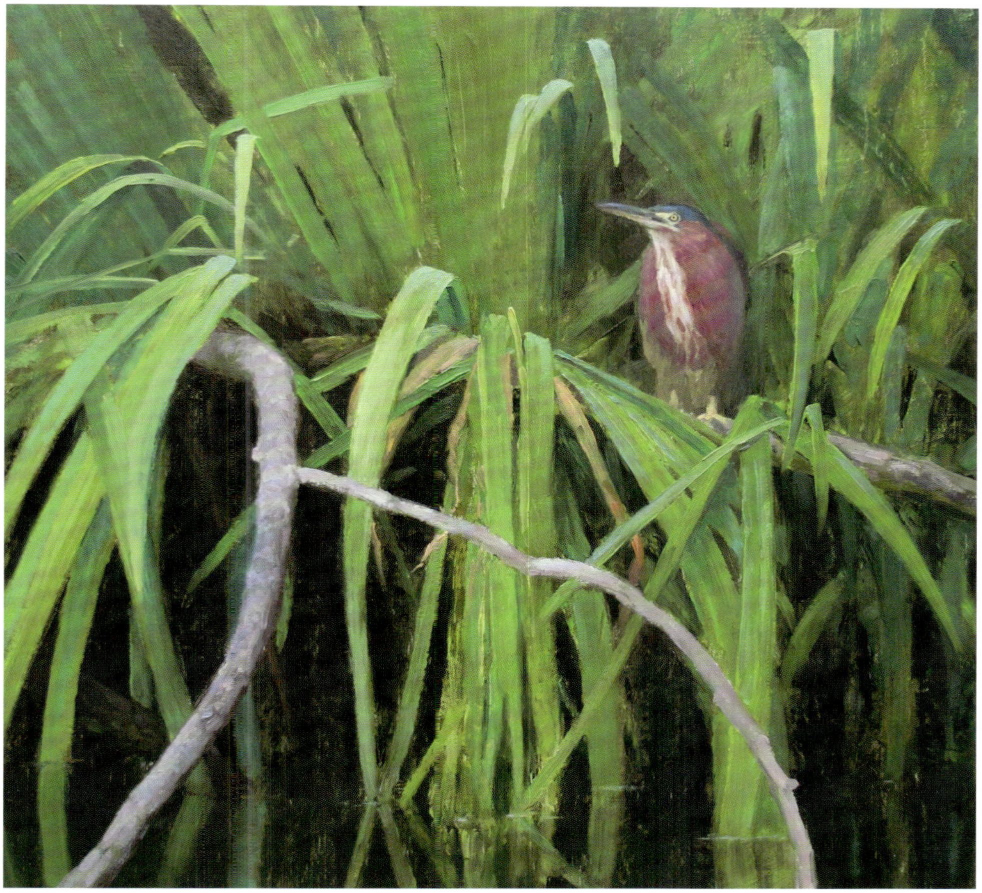

Green, 2012
Green heron
Oil on Belgian linen
18 x 20

Collection of the artist

Birds in Art: 1997, 2001, 2004, 2006-07, 2011

W

BORN: 1959, United States
RESIDES: Denver
EDUCATION: B.S., Texas A&M University, College Station
EXHIBITIONS: *Art and the Animal,* 2010, San Diego Natural History Museum; *Salon International,* 2010, Greenhouse Gallery of Fine Art, San Antonio; *Scottsdale Salon of Fine Art,* 2011-12, Legacy Gallery, Scottsdale, Arizona
AWARDS: President's Award of Excellence, 2010, *Oil Painters of America,* Legacy Gallery
REPRESENTATIVES: Breckenridge Gallery, Breckenridge, Colorado; Collectors Covey, Dallas; Legacy Gallery

Growing up, my field guides listed this bird as the green heron. At some point I realized the name green-backed heron also is used and is actually the overarching, descriptive name for a group of similar heron species. Based on the bird in this painting, one could argue it should be named the rust-fronted heron or red-breasted heron. In any case, green dominates – in my palette and in the bird's name. To me, it remains the endearing green heron.

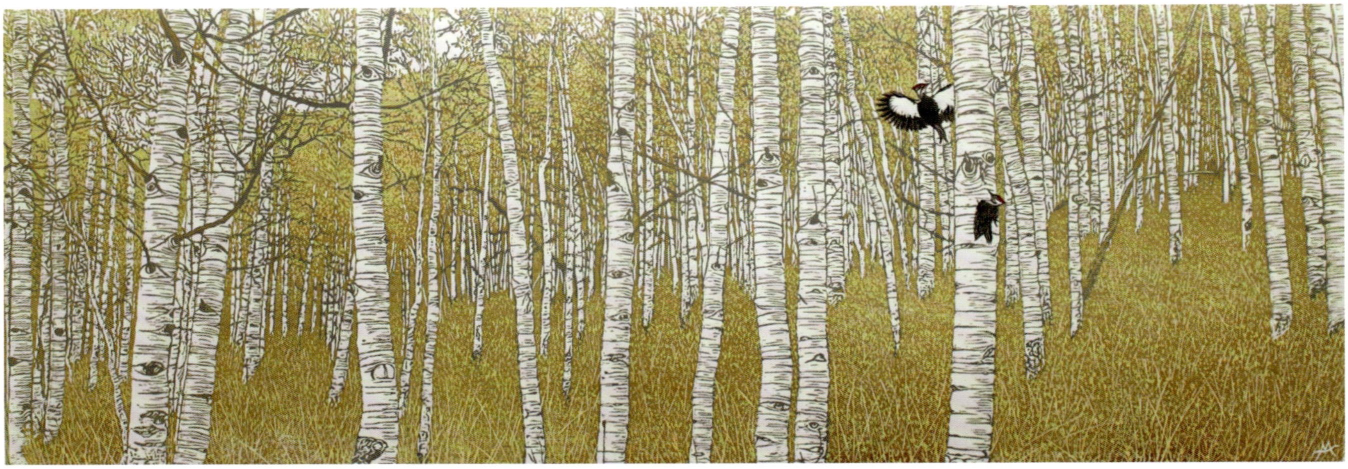

Pileated Woodpeckers
(1/18), 2011
Woodcut on Rives BFK paper
10 1/2 x 30

Collection of the artist

Birds in Art: 2011

BORN: 1979, United States
RESIDES: Stevens Point, Wisconsin
EDUCATION: B.F.A., University of Wisconsin, Stevens Point
EXHIBITIONS: *Visions,* 2010, and *Hand Pulled Prints,* 2011, Riverfront Arts Center, Stevens Point; *Natural Waters Run Deep*, 2012, Seasons on Saint Croix Gallery, Hudson, Wisconsin
COLLECTIONS: BioLife Plasma Services, Stevens Point
REPRESENTATIVES: Edgewood Orchard Galleries, Fish Creek, Wisconsin; Seasons on Saint Croix Gallery; Sivertson Gallery, Grand Marais, Minnesota

There is something about birch trees and pileated woodpeckers that lends itself to the woodblock printing process. While executing this print was tedious, the result was worth the effort. The black and white of the woodpeckers and the small flag of red on their heads – set against a northern Wisconsin stand of birch – give viewers a feel for the northwoods and the habitat in which pileateds live.

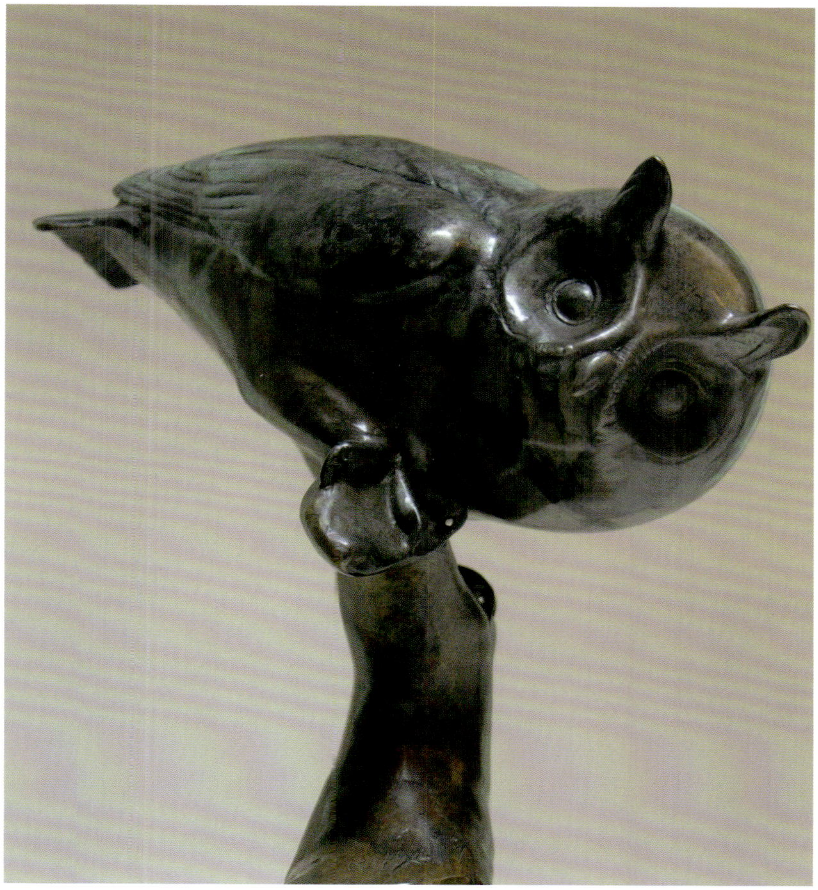

Inquisitive Owl (ed. 20), 2012
Western screech owl
Bronze
12 1/2 x 9 1/2 x 5

Collection of the artist

Birds in Art: 1985-87, 1992, 1998, 2000-11
Master Wildlife Artist: 2001

W

BORN: 1940, United States
RESIDES: Seattle
EDUCATION: M.A. and B.A., University of Washington, Seattle
EXHIBITIONS: *Contemporary Naturalism,* 2010, and *Romantic Contours, Modern Terrain,* 2011, Gerald Peters Gallery, Santa Fe, New Mexico; *Prix de West Invitational,* 2010-12, National Cowboy & Western Heritage Museum, Oklahoma City; Museum of Northwest Art, 2011, La Conner, Washington; Foster/White Gallery, 2011, Seattle; *Rendezvous Reunion,* 2012, Gilcrease Museum, Tulsa, Oklahoma
AWARDS: University of Washington Hall of Fame, 2011
COLLECTIONS: City of Seattle; Frye Art Museum, Seattle; Gilcrease Museum
COMMISSIONS: City of Redmond, Washington; Woodland Park Zoo, Seattle
BIBLIOGRAPHY: "Contemporary Naturalism," *Western Art Collector,* July 2010; "Corvid Man: Tony Angell Explores the Spiritual Power of Animals," *Wildlife Art Journal,* January 2011 CL; *Gifts of the Crow,* Simon & Schuster, 2012
REPRESENTATIVES: Foster/White Gallery; Gerald Peters Gallery

Given what we now know about the brains of birds, it's not a stretch to suggest they experience some of the same states of mind as humans. While crows may be the Einsteins of the avian world, after watching a family of owls near my home I'm convinced they also share some of our behavioral inclinations. I've observed screech owls apply their senses to strange sounds and subtle movements, seeking to find out what's behind these signals. In doing so, they move and assume postures that are, for me, invitations for sculptural interpretation. Inquisitive Owl *is the result of such a moment.*

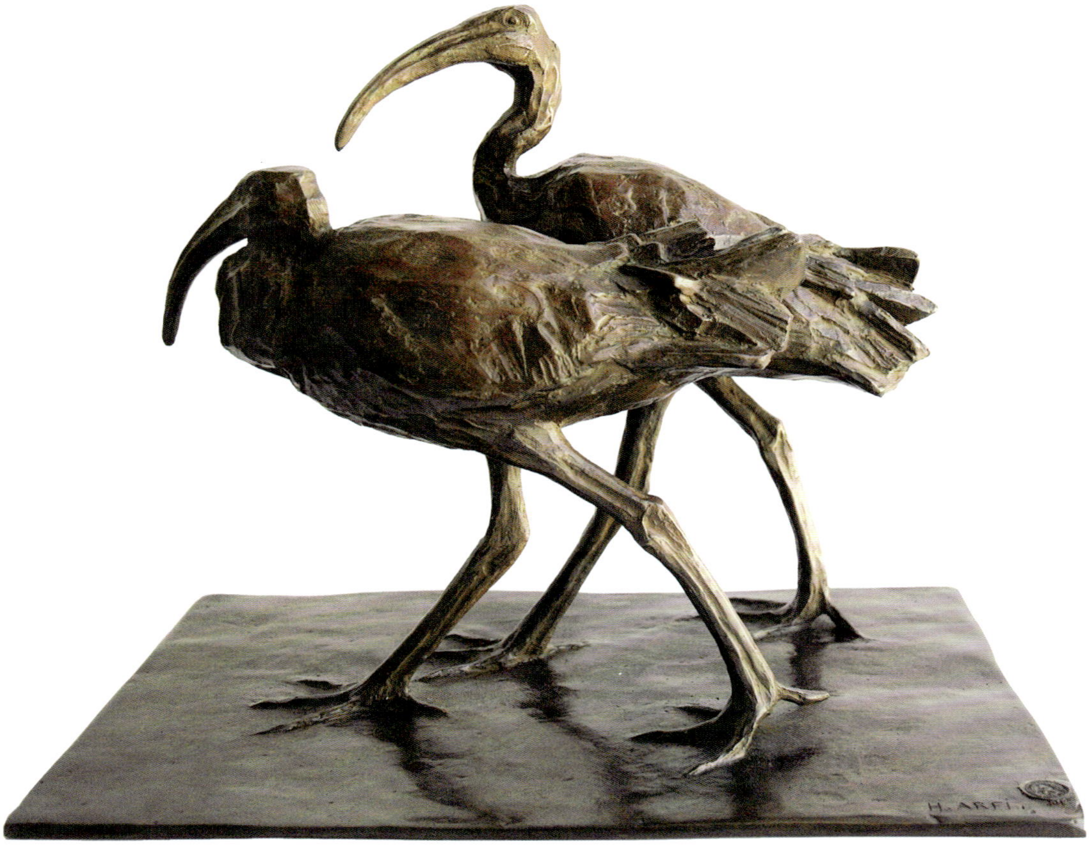

Sacred Ibises (ed. 8), 2012
Bronze
11 1/2 x 15 1/4 x 11

Collection of the artist

Birds in Art: 2005-08, 2010-11

W

BORN: 1957, France
RESIDES: Paris
EDUCATION: École Nationale Supérieure des Arts Appliqués Duperré and École Nationale Supérieure des Beaux-Arts, Paris
EXHIBITIONS: *250ème Anniversaire de l'École Vétérinaire de Lyon,* 2011, Musée du Service de Santé des Armées, Paris; *Salon National des Artistes Animaliers,* 2011, Hôtel de Malestroit, Bry-sur-Marne; *Salon des Artistes Naturalistes,* 2011, Salle des Fêtes, Fontainebleau; Galerie Vanaura, 2012, Versailles
BIBLIOGRAPHY: *Art Animalier: La Relève des Artistes Contemporains,* Éditions Abbate-Piolé, 2010
REPRESENTATIVES: Galerie 23, Damgan; Galerie Vanaura

The black and white sacred ibis was venerated in ancient Egypt. There, it was painted and sculpted as the symbol of Thoth, the god of wisdom and knowledge. The noble head with the long curved bill, the long legs contrasting with the roundness of the heavy body, and the black plumage ruffled by the wind – all contribute to the sacred ibis's graphic beauty and graceful curves and lines.

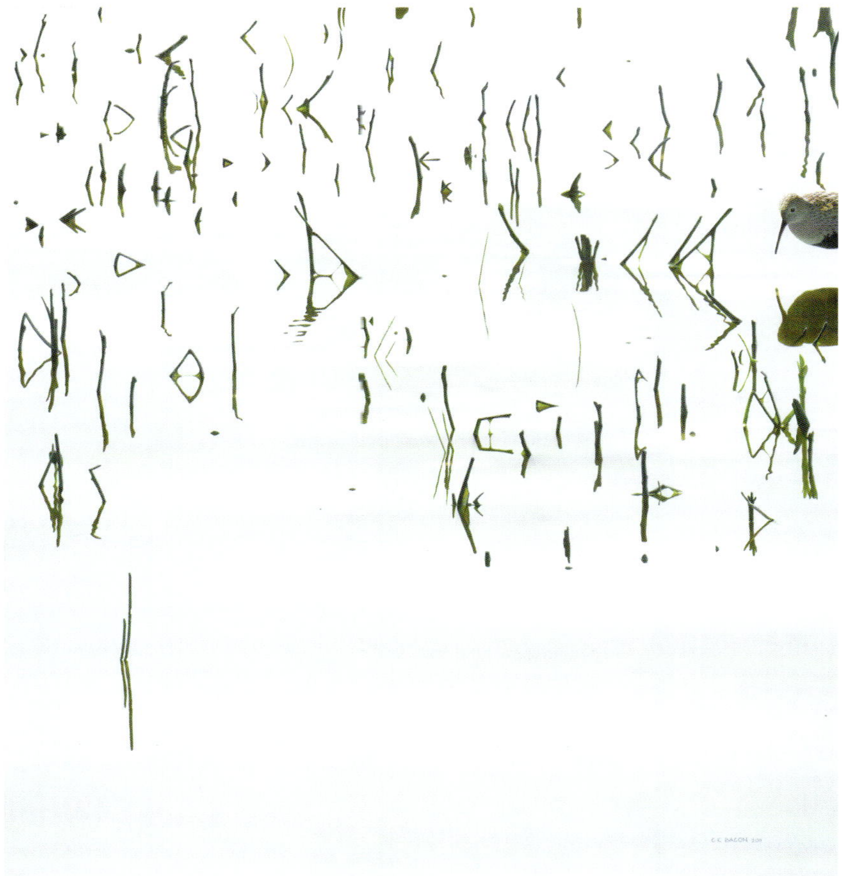

A Day in May, 2011
Dunlin
Watercolor and acrylic on rag board
26 x 24

Private collection

Birds in Art: 1987-91, 1993, 1995-00, 2003-11
Master Wildlife Artist: 2004

W

BORN: 1960, England
RESIDES: Burlington, Ontario, Canada
EXHIBITIONS: Burlington Art Centre, 2010, Burlington; *Change: An Artist's Perspective,* 2010, *International Year of the Forests,* 2011, and *Water,* 2012, Algonquin Art Centre, Algonquin Provincial Park, Ontario; *Art and the Animal,* 2011, Dennos Museum Center, Northwestern Michigan College, Traverse City, and 2012, Hiram Blauvelt Art Museum, Oradell, New Jersey
AWARDS: Queen Elizabeth II Diamond Jubilee Medal, 2012
COLLECTIONS: Canadian Society of Painters in Water Colour, Brampton, Ontario; Carpedia International, Oakville, Ontario; National Museum of Wildlife Art, Jackson, Wyoming
BIBLIOGRAPHY: "Artist Profile: Chris Bacon," *West of the City.com,* January 2011 OL; "Reflection Takes Wing," *The Artist's Magazine,* November 2011
REPRESENTATIVES: Spanierman Gallery, New York City

Each year in May, I visit Point Pelee National Park in Ontario, an important stopover for Neotropical migrants journeying north. Hillman Marsh last year held large numbers of plovers, dunlins, phalaropes, and other shore birds. As I soaked up the activity around me, the beautiful, almost abstract, patterns of the vegetation overtook me; it was as if I was trying to interpret a new language. All at once, the plovers took to the air in a huge, undulating collective mass, leaving the place vacant for a moment. Then a dunlin entered stage right; the representational and nonrepresentational were clashing for attention. I felt both excitement and anticipation for this visitor as it entered, charmed, and left the scene as it was.

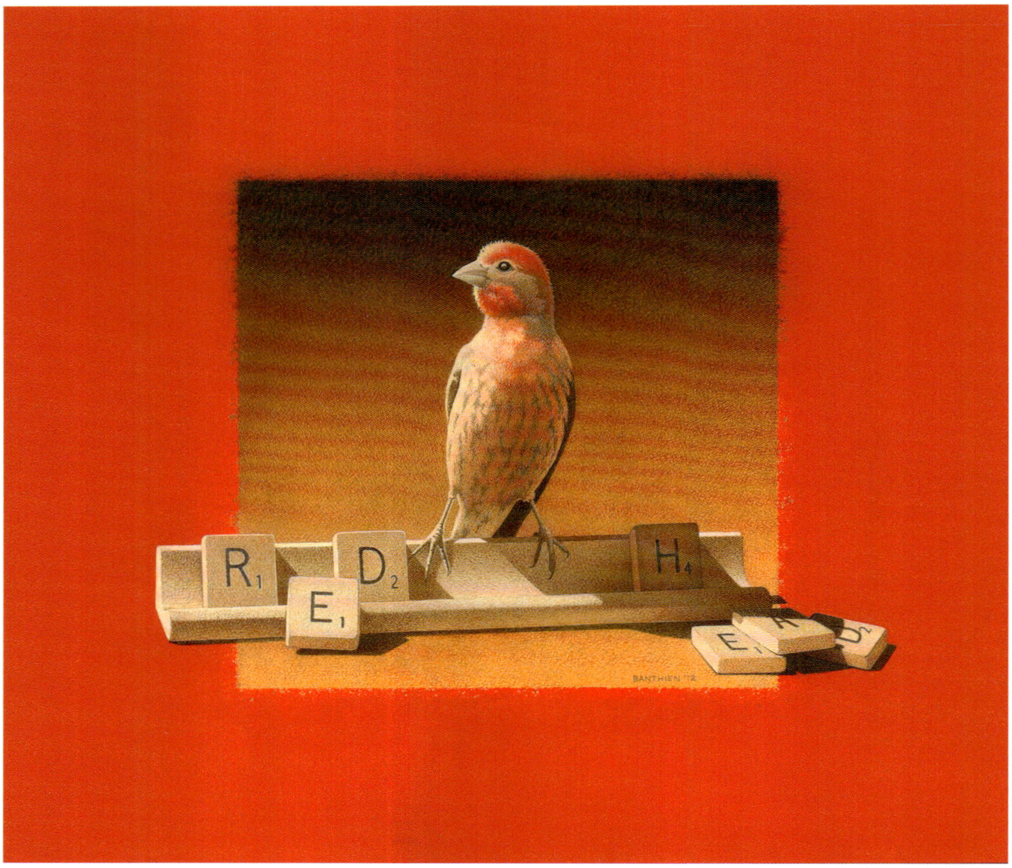

Scrabble, 2012
House finch
Acrylic on gessoed hardboard
12 x 14

Collection of the artist

Birds in Art: 1993, 1997, 2000-08

W

BORN: 1950, United States
RESIDES: Tiburon, California
EXHIBITIONS: *Art and the Animal,* 2010, San Diego Natural History Museum, and 2012, Hiram Blauvelt Art Museum, Oradell, New Jersey; Highlight Gallery, 2011, Mendocino, California; *Art of the Animal Kingdom,* 2011, Bennington Center for the Arts, Bennington, Vermont
REPRESENTATIVES: Highlight Gallery; Scrimshaw Gallery, Sausalito, California

Last year I saw an exhibition of Richard Serra drawings at the San Francisco Museum of Modern Art. There was one drawing in particular – a black, irregular four-sided shape on an off-white background – that just grabbed me. My mind jumped to seeing the background as brightly colored and as I turned this idea around, the irregular shape became a simple rectangle. Using some old cardboard and a paint roller, I experimented with different shapes and colors, and it shook up the way I see. I wanted to find a way to incorporate a bird into this color-field composition, and also to connect this creature to our everyday lives. That's where the Scrabble rack and tiles came from – simple shapes from our world that seemed to fit with the proud posture of the little house finch.

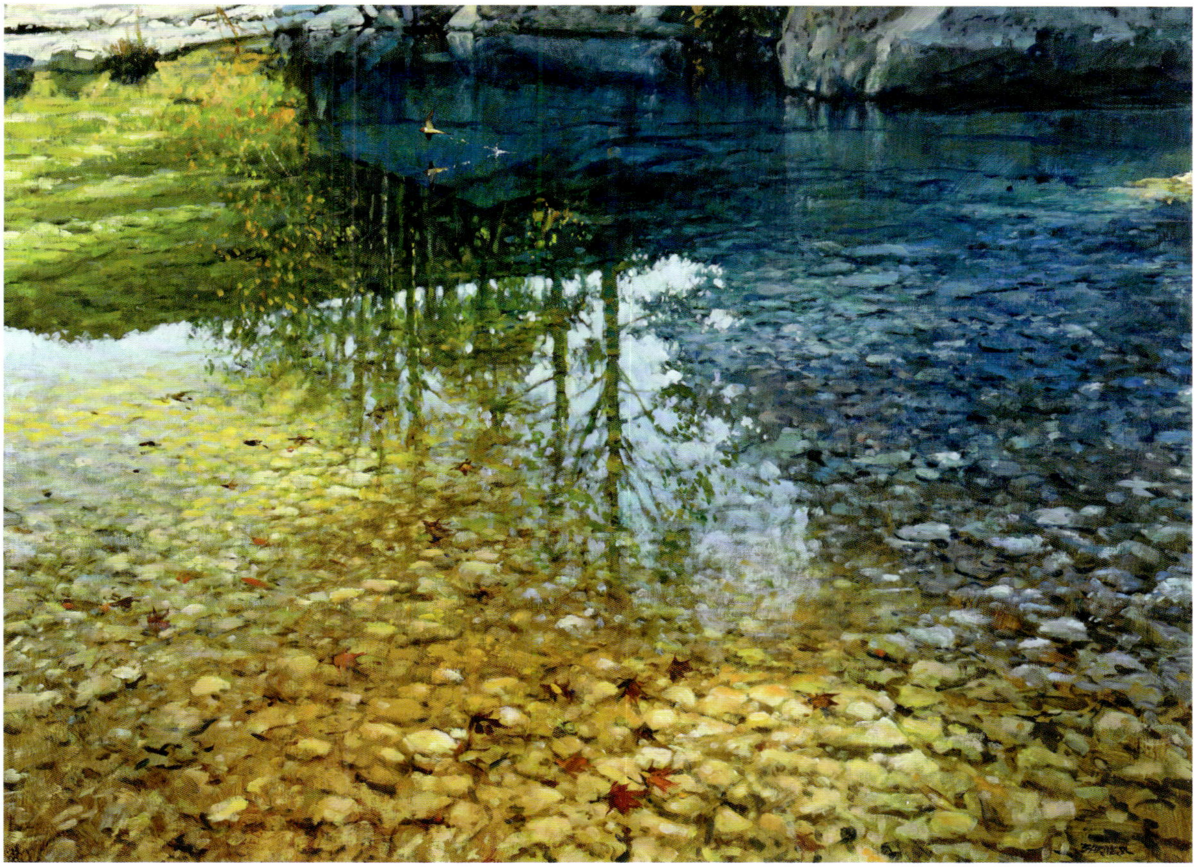

Lost Maples Refresh, 2012
Barn swallow
Oil on canvas
30 x 40

Collection of Nanci Barnes

Birds in Art: 1996, 1998-99, 2001-04, 2006-07, 2010

W

BORN: 1937, United States
RESIDES: Johnson City, Texas
EDUCATION: B.F.A., University of Texas, Austin
EXHIBITIONS: *Art and the Animal,* 2010, San Diego Natural History Museum; *Contemporary American Marine Art,* 2011, Cornell Museum of Art and American Culture, Delray Beach, Florida; *Art of the Dive: Portraits of the Deep,* 2012, Fishing Hall of Fame & Museum, Dania Beach, Florida
BIBLIOGRAPHY: "An Artist in His Elements," *Fine Art Connoisseur,* May/June 2012
REPRESENTATIVES: InSight Gallery, Fredericksburg, Texas; J. Russell Jinishian Gallery, Fairfield, Connecticut; Meredith Long & Company, Houston

This small spring-fed pond at Lost Maples State Natural Area in the Texas hill country was one of the remaining pockets of water after our devastating drought of 2011. Painting reflective or transparent water always challenges me, especially when doing both. It's like being able to partially look through a mirror. We have a family of barn swallows that claimed a spot on our porch for the last three years, and they dive-bomb the creek in the afternoon for a drink or a bath. While they weren't present at Lost Maples, I had no doubt they would show up later in the day.

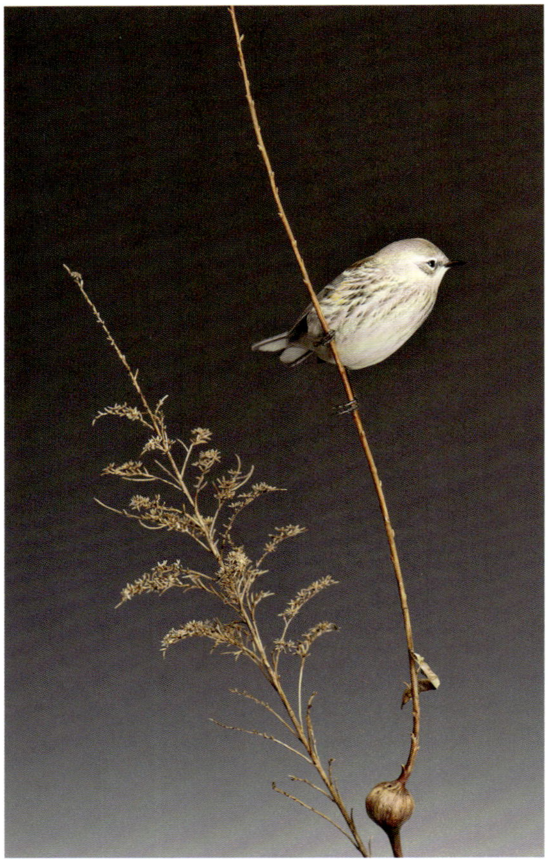

Yellow-rumped Warbler and Goldenrod, 2011
Acrylic on basswood, brass, and bronze
36 x 12 x 12

Private collection

Birds in Art: 1980-11
Master Wildlife Artist: 1991

W

BORN: 1957, United States
RESIDES: Stahlstown, Pennsylvania
EDUCATION: B.F.A., Carnegie-Mellon University, Pittsburgh
EXHIBITIONS: *Forty Years of Art, Nature, and Tradition,* 2010, Ward Museum of Wildfowl Art, Salisbury University, Salisbury, Maryland
AWARDS: Second in World, 2010, Best in World, 2011, and Third in World, 2012, *Ward World Championship Wildfowl Carving Competition,* Ocean City, Maryland
COLLECTIONS: Audubon Society of Western Pennsylvania, Pittsburgh; Mass Audubon Visual Arts Center, Canton, Massachusetts; Ward Museum of Wildfowl Art
BIBLIOGRAPHY: "Years in the Making," *Wildfowl Carving,* Winter 2010; "Birds in Art," *Wildfowl Carving Competition,* 2010-12; "South Hills Natives Carve Own Outdoor Niche," *Pittsburgh Tribune-Review,* July 24, 2011

It's hard to resist the strong color and bold pattern of spring warblers. I've chosen to portray warblers many times, always opting to present them in their most stunning plumage at the height of the breeding season. This time around I concentrated on the soft and subtle quality of winter plumage. It may not be as dramatic as spring dress, but it is just as beautiful and in many ways I find it even more appealing. As the years go by, I am drawn more to the whisper of a quiet, gentle beauty than to the 'Hey, look at me!' exhortation of something loud and flashy.

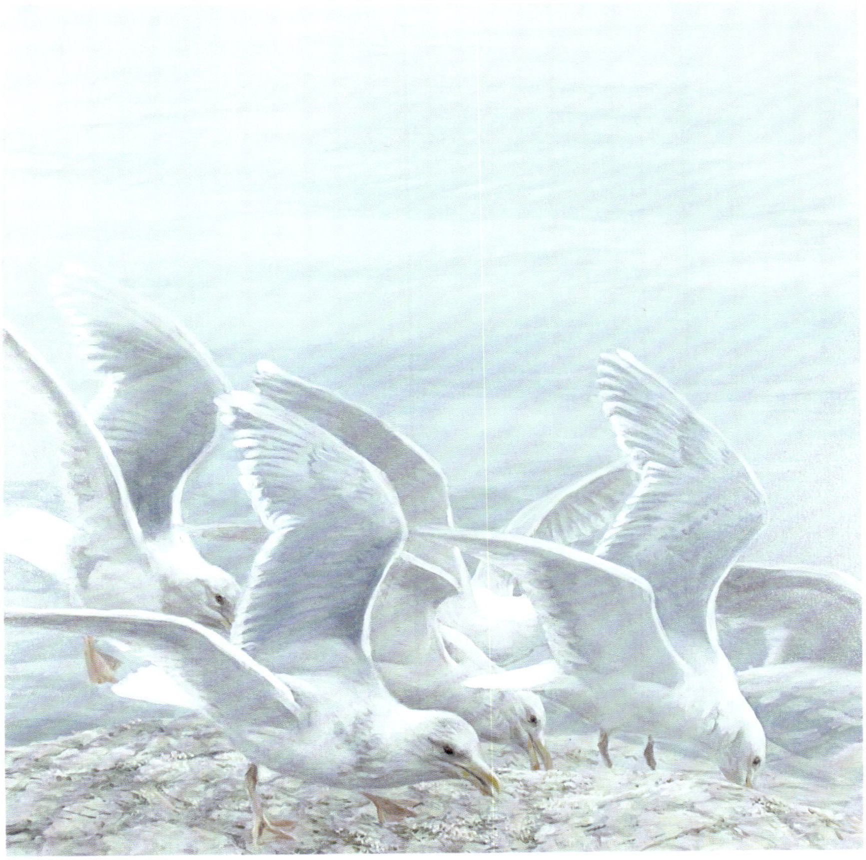

Glaucous-winged Gulls,
2012
Oil on canvas
36 x 36

Collection of the artist

Birds in Art: 1977-11
Master Wildlife Artist: 1982

W

BORN: 1930, Canada
RESIDES: Fulford Harbour, Salt Spring Island, British Columbia, Canada
EDUCATION: B.A., University of Toronto
EXHIBITIONS: *Change: An Artist's Perspective,* 2010, Algonquin Art Centre, Algonquin Provincial Park, Ontario; *Artists for Nature Jubilee,* 2012, Orangerie Landgoed Vollenhoven, De Bilt, Netherlands; *Art and the Animal,* 2012, Hiram Blauvelt Art Museum, Oradell, New Jersey
AWARDS: Honorary Doctor of Laws, 2010, Royal Roads University, Victoria, British Columbia; Society of Animal Artists Lifetime Achievement Award, 2010, San Diego Natural History Museum, and Hiram Blauvelt Art Museum Purchase Award, 2011, Dennos Museum Center, Northwestern Michigan College, Traverse City, *Art and the Animal*
BIBLIOGRAPHY: *Bateman: New Works,* Greystone Books, 2010; "The Great Robert Bateman," *British Columbia Magazine,* Winter 2010; "The Spectacular and Troubling World According to Robert Bateman," January 2011, and "Robert Bateman on the State of Wildlife Art," July 2011, *Wildlife Art Journal* OL
REPRESENTATIVES: Mill Pond Press, Venice, Florida

There is no such thing as a seagull. Check any field guide and you'll find fifty-one species of gulls, from the Arctic to Antarctica and most places in between. The common gull in coastal British Columbia is the glaucous-winged gull. It is much like the herring gull of the Atlantic but instead of black tips to the primaries it has a frosty silvery edging. When a food supply is available, gulls have a tendency to flock with a sense of vigor that verges on mobbing. Once a year a feeding frenzy takes place with the annual herring run. In appropriate locations along the coast of British Columbia, the herring come to spawn by the thousands. These areas turn into a mob scene with seals, eagles, many sea birds, and, of course, gulls gorging themselves on this nutritious bounty.

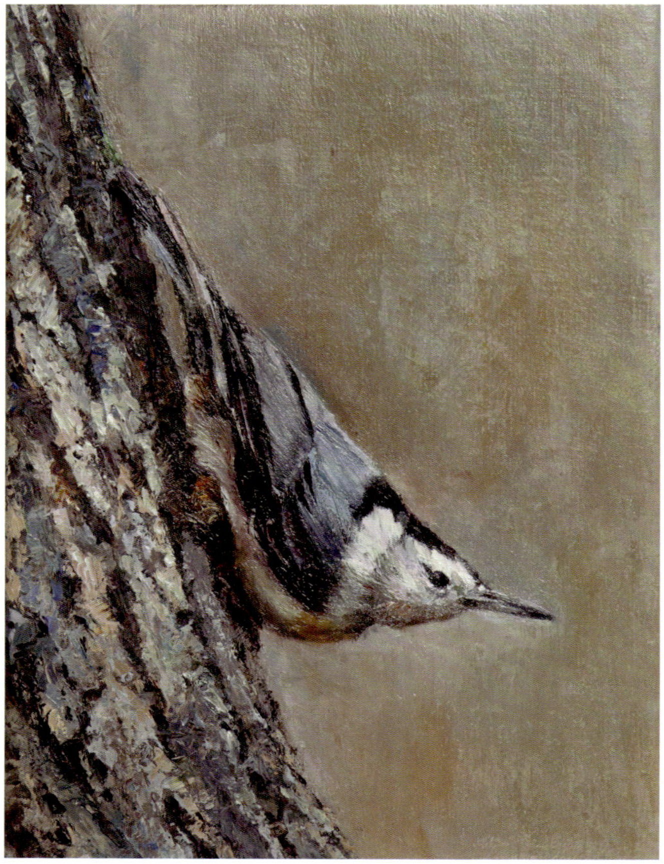

Limited Palette, 2012
White-breasted nuthatch
Oil on linen
11 x 8

Collection of the artist

BORN: 1960, United States
RESIDES: Lake Forest, Illinois
EDUCATION: B.A., University of Michigan, Ann Arbor
EXHIBITIONS: *Emerging Artists,* 2011, Art Center, Highland Park, Illinois

An encounter with a single nuthatch might seem insignificant. For me it's the kind of spontaneous, close interaction with nature that helps me better understand our environment and feel more deeply connected to it. Experimenting with a limited number of colors has made me more aware of their relational qualities and allows stronger color harmonies to develop. I painted the nuthatch's blues and grays and surrounding textures using blacks, grays, and greens to convey these cooler tones. My palette included only viridian green, cadmium yellow deep, cadmium red light, black, and white.

Julie Bender

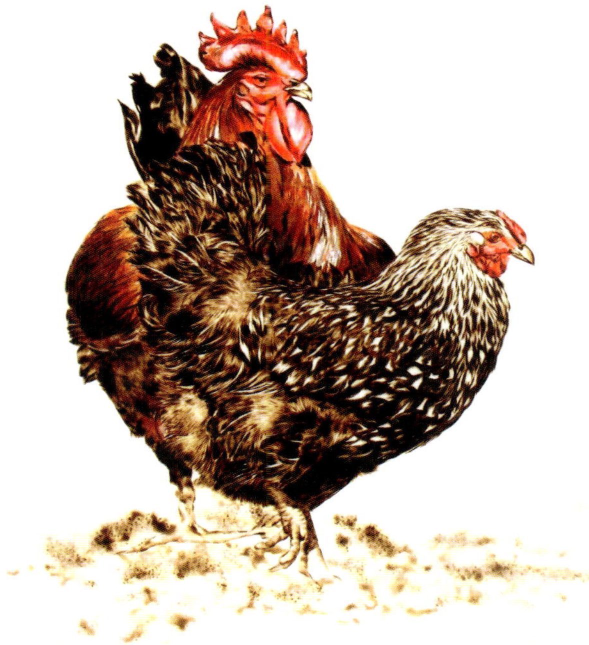

Going My Way?, 2012
Pyrography and India ink on Arches hot press paper
17 x 17

Collection of the artist

Birds in Art: 2010-11

BORN: 1957, United States
RESIDES: Loveland, Colorado
EDUCATION: B.F.A. and B.S., University of Missouri, Columbia
EXHIBITIONS: *A Salute to the World Equestrian Games*, 2010, Lexington History Museum, Lexington, Kentucky; *Art and the Animal*, 2010, San Diego Natural History Museum; *Art for the Sangres*, 2012, Historic Pines Ranch, Westcliffe, Colorado
BIBLIOGRAPHY: "A Letter from Yellowstone, as Interpreted by a Pyrographer," *Wildlife Art Journal*, July 2010 OL; *Strokes of Genius 3: The Best of Drawing, Fresh Perspectives*, North Light Books, 2011; "Art & Etc.," *Sporting Classics Magazine*, January/February 2012; "The Art of the Horse," *Western Art Collector*, May 2012
REPRESENTATIVES: Lovetts Fine Art Gallery, Tulsa, Oklahoma; Expressions Gallery, Scottsdale, Arizona, and Ketchum, Idaho

Inspired by the amazing color and iridescent quality of this handsome rooster, my eyes kept as busily focused on his whereabouts as the eight hens that shadowed his every move. Though his girls held steadfast to their own agenda, my sole business was observing and capturing memorable scenes, patterns, and pigments that I might transform into worthy artwork. I came to realize I would execute this piece on paper so I could experiment with the addition of color. As a result – and after ten years of burning solely on wood – paper now has my full attention as it yields countless possibilities and the promise of an exciting future.

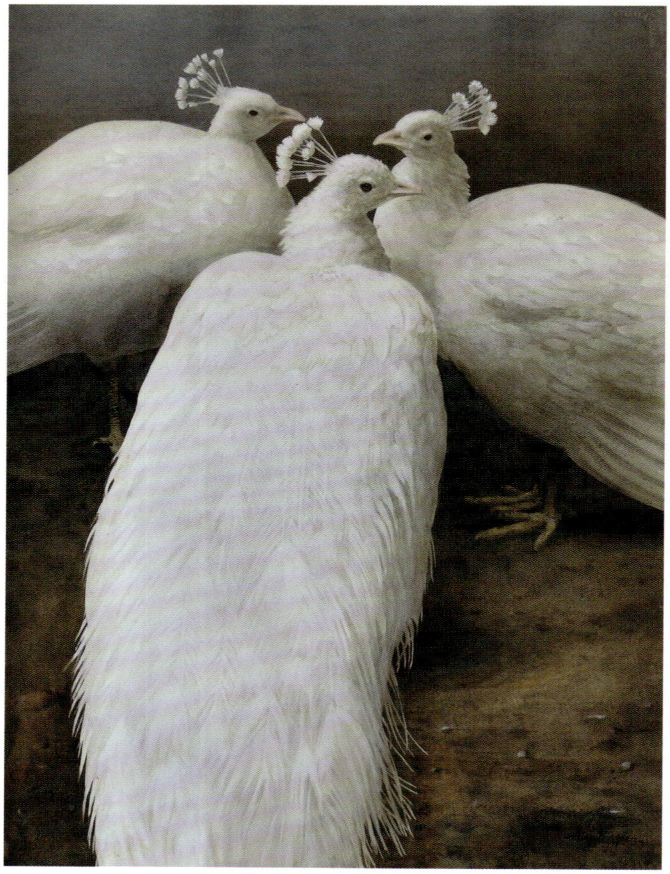

Gossip, 2012
White peacock
Watercolor on Arches paper
30 x 22

Collection of the artist

Birds in Art: 1986-90, 1993, 1997, 2001-03, 2007, 2010

W

BORN: 1938, United States
RESIDES: Salisbury, Connecticut
EDUCATION: B.F.A., Cornell University, Ithaca, New York
EXHIBITIONS: *Art and the Animal,* 2010, San Diego Natural History Museum, 2011, Dennos Museum Center, Northwestern Michigan College, Traverse City, and 2012, Hiram Blauvelt Art Museum, Oradell, New Jersey
COLLECTIONS: Adirondack Museum, Blue Mountain Lake, New York; Albright-Knox Art Gallery, Buffalo, New York; New Britain Museum of American Art, New Britain, Connecticut
REPRESENTATIVES: Artis Group, Palm Beach, Florida

Although I prefer the true blue Indian peacock, I was delighted to come upon these three that look as though they are gossiping about a mutual acquaintance. I tackled the challenges of painting white birds, striving to capture softness and subtle shading in a monochromatic composition.

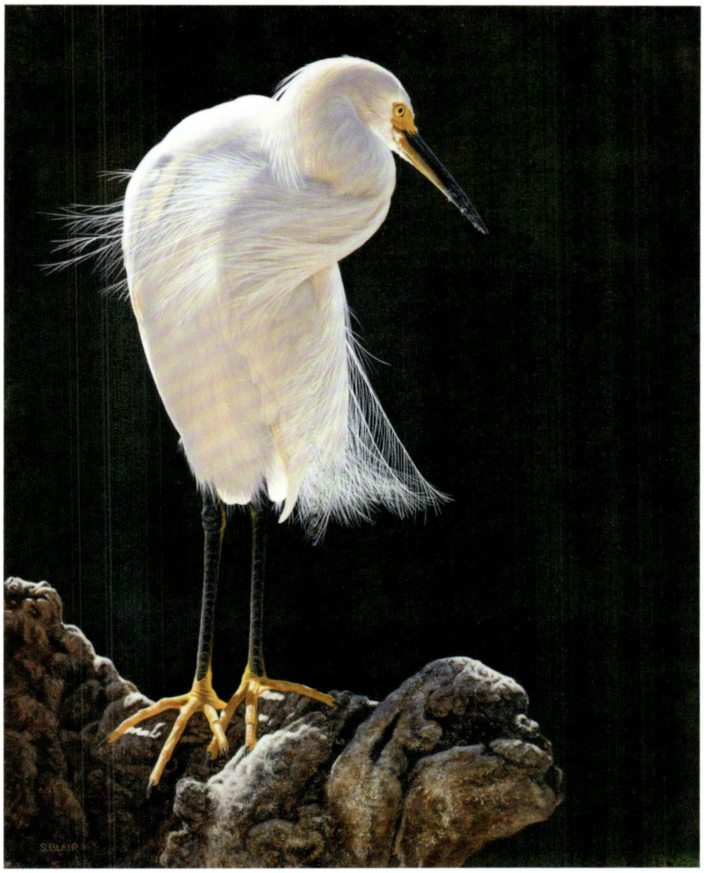

Sun Catcher, 2011
Snowy egret
Acrylic on Ampersand gessobord
18 x 14

Collection of the artist

BORN: 1953, United States
RESIDES: New Oxford, Pennsylvania
EDUCATION: A.D., Art Institute of Pittsburgh
EXHIBITIONS: *Artists for Conservation,* 2011, Spirit Gallery, Grouse Mountain, Vancouver, British Columbia, Canada; *Art and the Animal,* 2012, Hiram Blauvelt Art Museum, Oradell, New Jersey
BIBLIOGRAPHY: *Splash 12: Celebrating Artistic Vision,* North Light Books, 2011; *Best of America Watermedia Artists Volume II,* Kennedy Publications, 2012
REPRESENTATIVES: Village Artisans Gallery, Boiling Springs, Pennsylvania

Some think white has no color; in fact, white is the combination of all the colors of the spectrum. The glow of sunlight surrounding a snowy egret at the San Diego Zoo's Wild Animal Park reminded me of a prismatic sun catcher seen in a window that allows all colors to appear. The light was enhanced by dark green foliage, mirrored in the water behind the egret. I couldn't deny this egret its moment in the spotlight. The blue sky, warm rose-gray tones of the hollowed-out tree stump, and the bird's bright yellow feet are reflected in the feathers, while the shadows take on a lavender cast. I intensified these colors as much as possible, allowing the plumage to emerge as white.

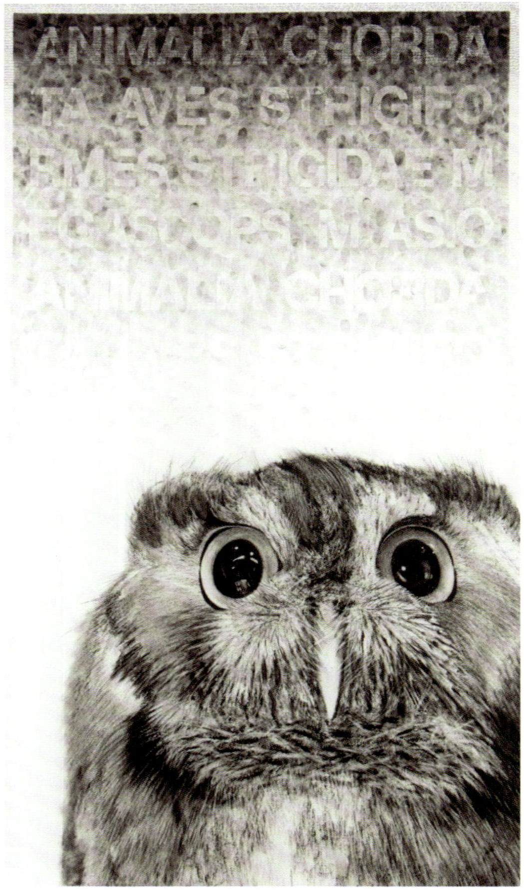

My name is Hubert and I am not an owl, 2011
Screech owl
Charcoal and ink on Hahnemühle paper
54 1/2 x 34

Collection of the artist

Birds in Art: 2008, 2010-11

BORN: 1964, Canada
RESIDES: Kalamazoo, Michigan
EDUCATION: M.F.A., Ohio State University, Columbus; B.F.A., Nova Scotia College of Art and Design University, Halifax
EXHIBITIONS: William and Florence Schmidt Art Center, 2011, Belleville, Illinois; *Lay of the Land,* 2011, Visual Arts Gallery, University of Illinois, Springfield; *Multiple Encounters Second Edition,* 2012, National Academy of Fine Art, New Delhi, India; Flora Kirsch Beck Gallery, Alma College, 2012, Alma, Michigan; Sarratt Gallery, Vanderbilt University, 2012, Nashville; *International Drawing Annual 7,* 2012, Manifest Gallery, Cincinnati
AWARDS: Artists Fellowship, 2011, Virginia Center for the Creative Arts, Amherst; Director's Choice, 2011, *International Juried Works on Paper,* 212 Gallery, Richmond, Virginia
COLLECTIONS: Kalamazoo Institute of Arts
BIBLIOGRAPHY: "Picking Up the Pieces: Roadside Art," *Corvi Chronicle,* July 2011; "Sarratt Gallery Installation Explores 'Pecking Order,'" *The Tennessean,* April 2012; "Karen Bondarchuk Brings a Murder to Vanderbilt's Sarratt Gallery," *ArtNowNashville,* May 2012

Hubert the screech owl is a resident at Barnswallow, an extraordinary bird rehabilitation center in Wauconda, Illinois. Hubert is an imprinted owl; during the critical phase of his early development he came to identify with humans. As a result, Hubert is calm and relaxed around people, but in the presence of fellow owls (or other birds) he becomes agitated and fearful. From a behavioral standpoint he apparently is unaware of his identity as a screech owl. The drawing material and process I used were intended to evoke this sense of identity confusion by interpreting imprinting through a fingerprinted taxonomy of owls and an increase in the owl's scale to suggest species transformation.

Jim Bortz

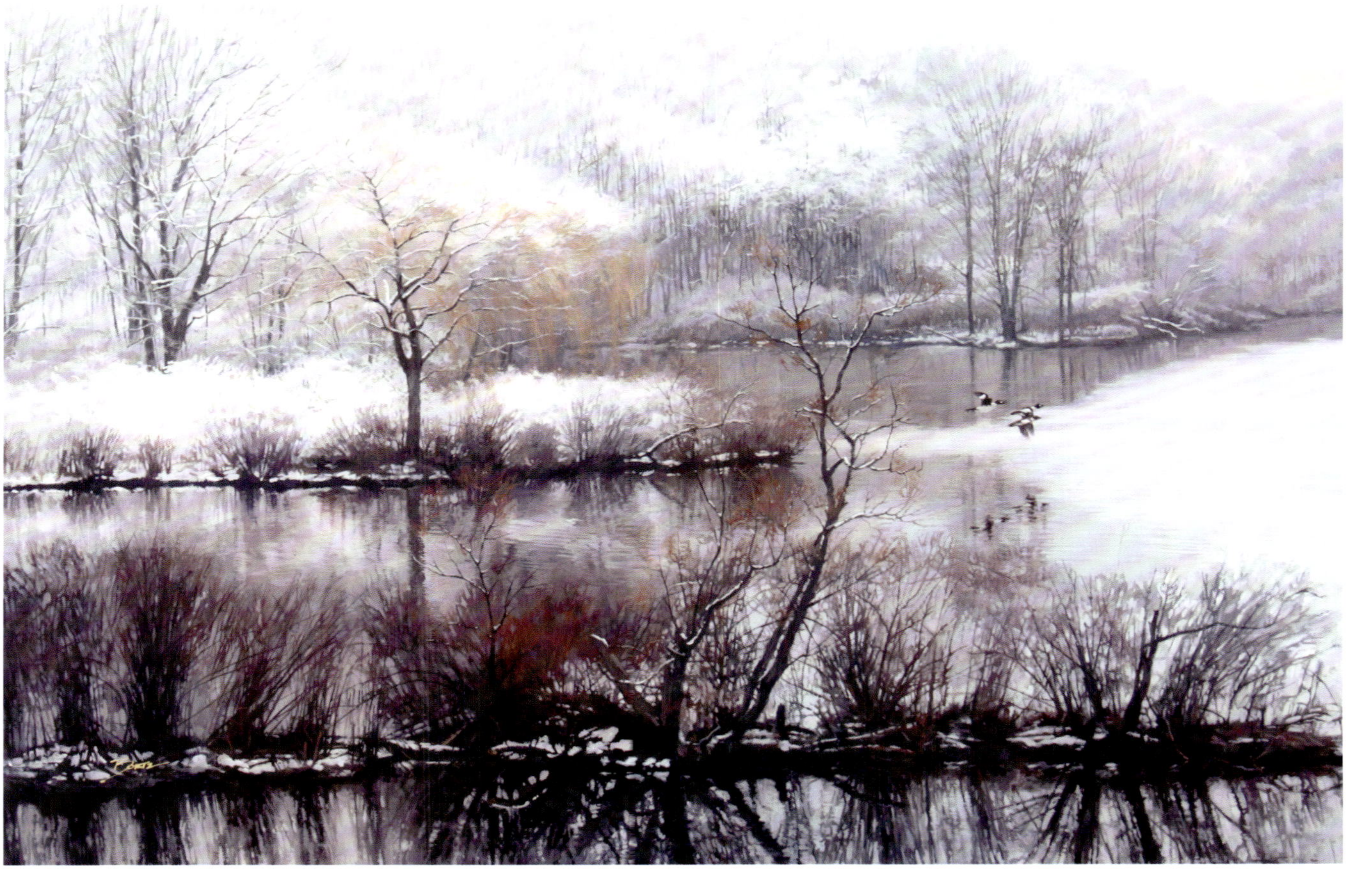

Snow on Willow Bay, 2012
Common goldeneye
Acrylic on hardboard
20 x 30

Collection of John Baron

Birds in Art: 2007-11

W

BORN 1963, United States
RESIDES: Stoneboro, Pennsylvania
EDUCATION: B.S., Slippery Rock University, Slippery Rock, Pennsylvania
EXHIBITIONS: *Small Works,* 2011, Bennington Center for the Arts, Bennington, Vermont
AWARDS: Working Together for Wildlife Conservation Print, 2011, Pennsylvania Game Commission, Harrisburg
COLLECTIONS: C and M Sales Company, Franklin, Pennsylvania
BIBLIOGRAPHY: *The Long Way Home,* 2010 SP
REPRESENTATIVES: Lord Nelson's Gallery, Gettysburg, Pennsylvania

My most memorable days afield are those when the temperatures hover near freezing, marble-sized wet snowflakes blanket the countryside, and the world takes on a storybook appearance. Waterfowl activity reaches a crescendo on days like these. Common goldeneyes, one of my favorite ducks, were an obvious choice as they seem oblivious to winter, thriving in pockets of open water on otherwise frozen lakes and rivers. Stark, contrasting plumage and an unusual shape make the goldeneye a truly handsome bird.

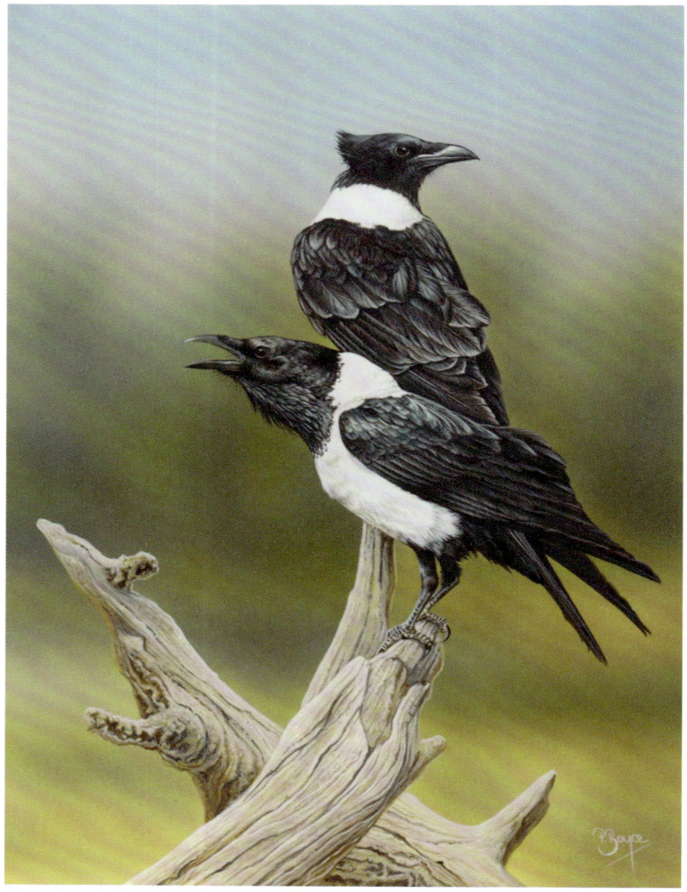

The Pied Spruiker, 2011
Pied crow
Gouache on claybord
16 x 12

Collection of the artist

BORN: 1957, Australia
RESIDES: Mooloolah Valley, Queensland, Australia
EXHIBITIONS: *Artists for Conservation,* 2011, Spirit Gallery, Grouse Mountain, Vancouver, British Columbia, Canada; *Art and the Animal,* 2010, San Diego Natural History Museum, 2011, Dennos Museum Center, Northwestern Michigan College, Traverse City, and 2012, Hiram Blauvelt Art Museum, Oradell, New Jersey
AWARDS: Best in Show and Best Bird, 2012, *International Wildlife in Art,* Logan City, Queensland
REPRESENTATIVES: Gallery Beneath, Mooloolaba, Queensland

A cheeky and particularly handsome African pied crow wandered among parked cars at a waterhole in Namibia. As he walked by, he glanced up at the occupants with that odd sideways look that only a bird can master. Not finding much to eat, he hopped onto an old branch and then let the world know what a clever chap he was. In Australia, 'spruiker' is slang for someone who toots his own horn; that's the bold posture of this bird. I placed the second bird in such a way to suggest that it's thinking, 'Oh no, there he goes again.'

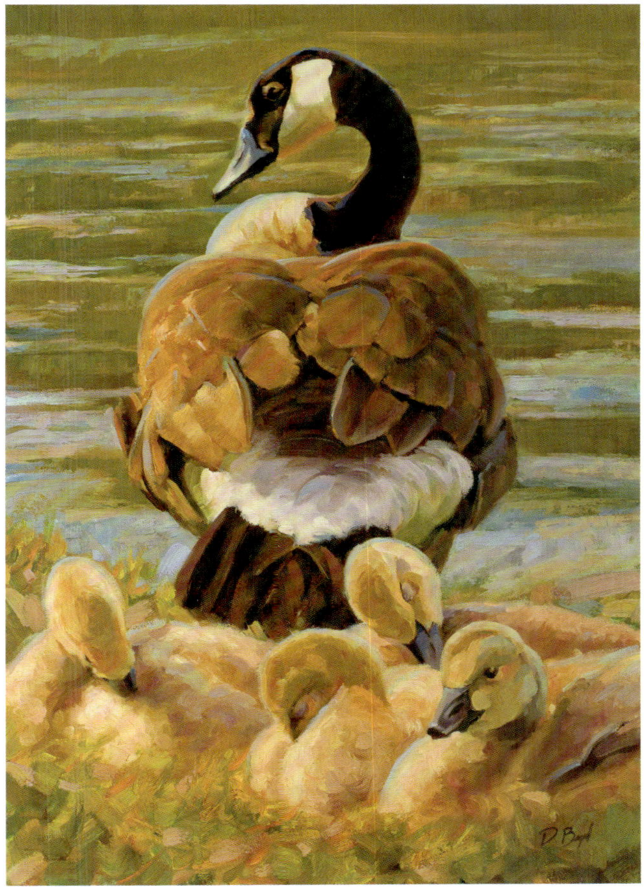

Mother Goose, 2012
Western Canada goose
Oil on panel
20 x 14

Collection of the artist

BORN: 1968, United States
RESIDES: Billings, Montana
EDUCATION: A.D., Art Institute of Colorado, Denver
REPRESENTATIVES: Gallery Interiors, Billings; RiverStone Gallery, Ennis, Montana; Samarah Fine Art, Whitefish, Montana

Living in Montana affords me the luxury to paint many of the subjects I love, including Canada geese. I do not depict every feather; I prefer a more impressionistic approach, applying thick layers of broken color to suggest detail and a sense of motion. My goal is to capture how a scene affects me at the moment I pick up a brush. The whimsical yet heartfelt title, Mother Goose, *is intended to help the viewer relate to the goose guarding her goslings as they rest on the peaceful banks of the Yellowstone River on a late June afternoon.*

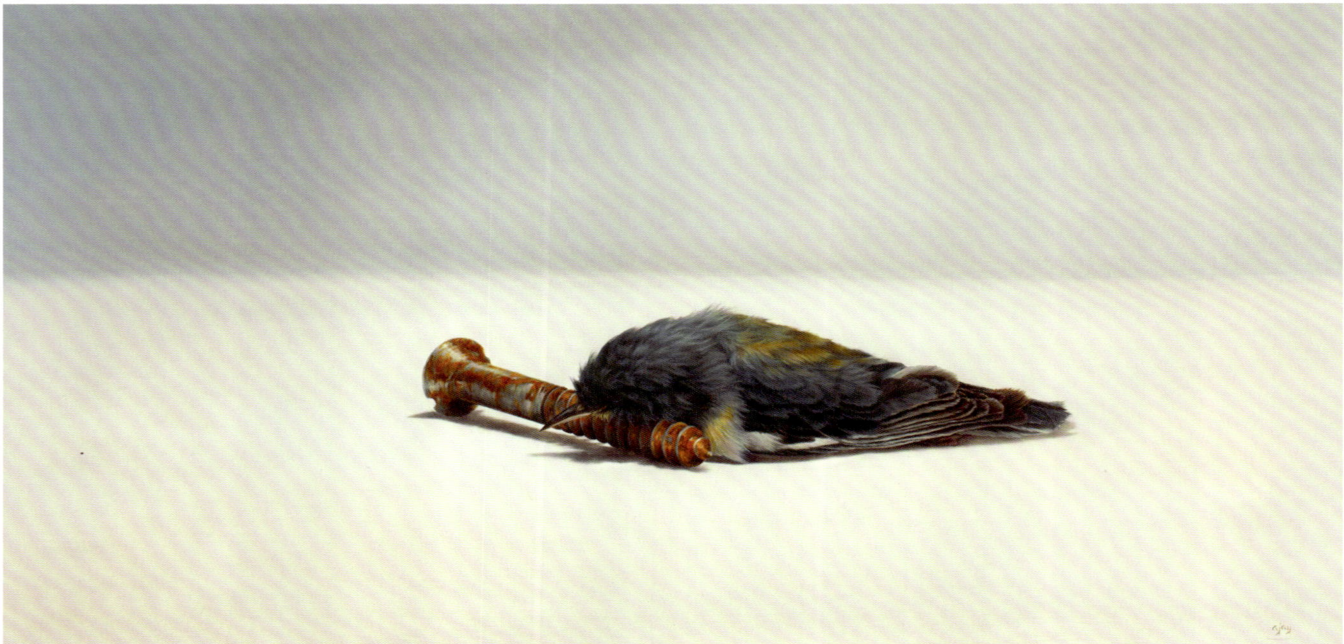

The Final Embrace, 2011
Northern Parula warbler
Oil on hardboard
20 x 40

Collection of the artist

Birds in Art: 2011

BORN: 1971, United States
RESIDES: Naugatuck, Connecticut
EDUCATION: B.F.A., Paier College of Art, Hamden, Connecticut
EXHIBITIONS: *Members Exhibition,* 2010-11, New Britain Museum of American Art, New Britain, Connecticut; Madison Art Cinemas, 2011, Madison, Connecticut; *Small Works,* 2011, Goldsmith's Art & Frame Gallery, Cheshire, Connecticut; *Art Party of the Year,* 2011-12, New Britain Museum of American Art
AWARDS: Herbert J. Gute Memorial Prize, 2011, and Outstanding Achievement in Fine Arts, 2011, Paier College of Art

My primary goals in painting are to convey a mood and to elicit an emotion in the viewer. I encourage observers to have a conversation with the piece and generate their own personal narratives. For me, The Final Embrace *is about showing the beauty that exists in two starkly different objects. The subjects are placed in an empty space to give the painting a dreamlike, ethereal quality. The contrasting hard, precise industrial characteristics of the screw combined with the soft, natural elegance of the warbler serve as metaphors for aspects of life and death. The title suggests that in the end, the two objects have set their obvious differences aside and come together to endure the same fate.*

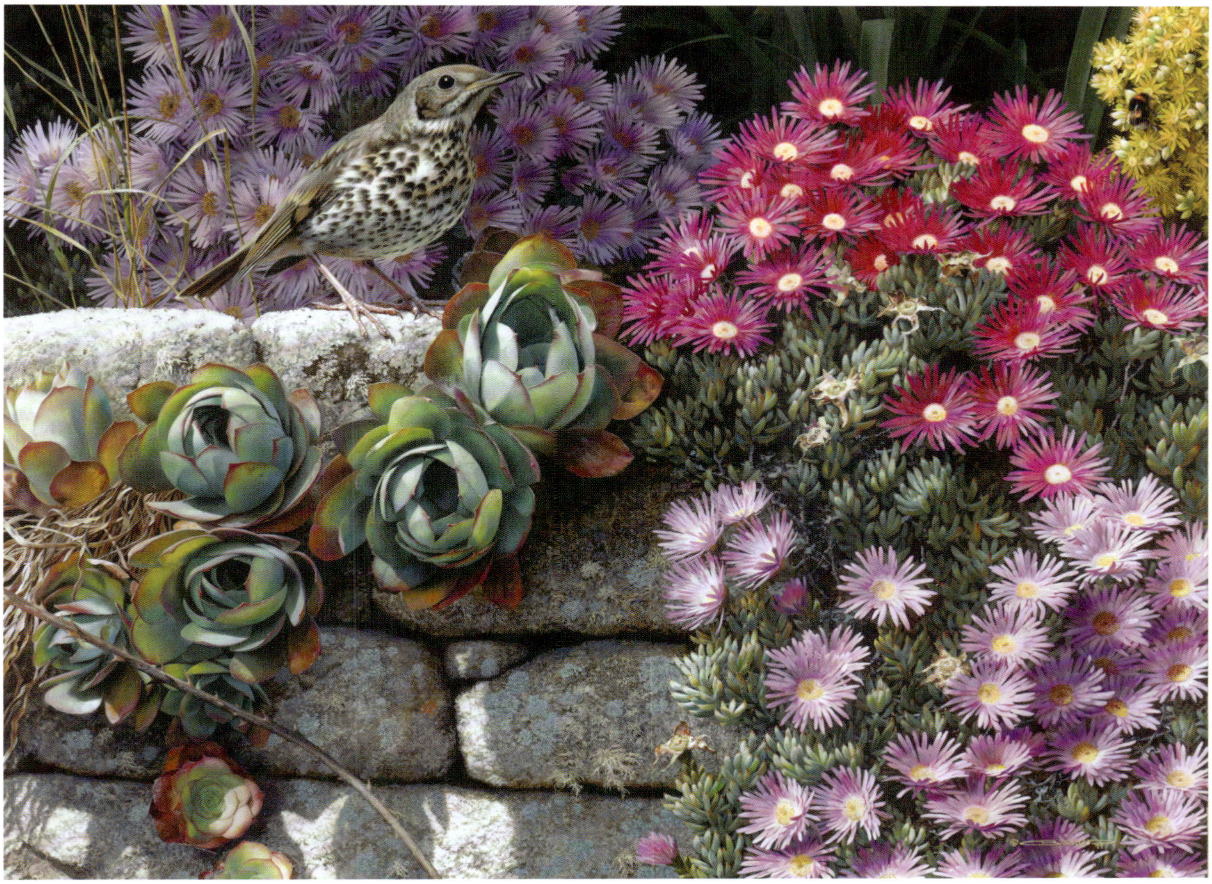

Singer in Paradise, 2011
Wood thrush
Gouache and watercolor on illustration board
20 1/2 x 27

Collection of the artist

Birds in Art: 1985-00, 2002-11
Master Wildlife Artist: 2002

W

BORN: 1937, Belgium
RESIDES: Zoersel, Belgium
EXHIBITIONS: *Change: An Artist's Perspective,* 2010, Algonquin Art Centre, Algonquin Provincial Park, Ontario, Canada; *David Shepherd's 80th Birthday Exhibition,* 2011, Mall Galleries, London; *Alaska 2012: A Celebration of Wildlife Art,* 2012, Kenai Visitors & Cultural Center, Kenai
COLLECTIONS: Bennington Center for the Arts, Bennington, Vermont
REPRESENTATIVES: Christiane Katcham, Gordonsville, Virginia; Mill Pond Press, Venice, Florida

The wood thrush belongs to the American robin family. With its wonderful singing range and large repertoire of songs, it's one of my favorite birds. The thrush keeps singing even after sunset, filling evenings with melodic poetry. Some say birds only sing to tell other birds 'this is my territory.' I prefer the notion that they also sing to express a joie de vivre. *When such a bird lands on a rocky wall covered with colorful flowers and climbing plants, the excitement is complete. As an artist, my mind overflows with ideas. Waiting until I can get to the studio to start painting is frustrating.*

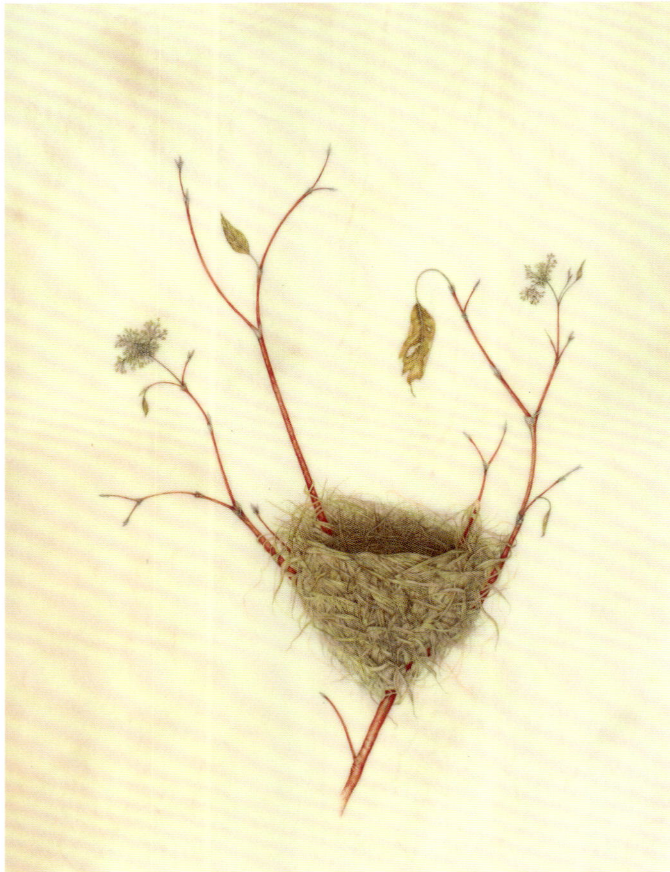

Remembrance, 2012
Watercolor on Cowley's veiny calfskin vellum
15 x 11

Collection of the artist

Birds in Art: 2010-11

W

BORN: 1953, United States
RESIDES: Edina, Minnesota
EXHIBITIONS: *Portraits of a Garden,* 2010, Shirley Sherwood Gallery of Botanical Art, Royal Botanic Gardens, London; Woodson Art Museum, 2012
AWARDS: Best of Show, 2010, *The Bird Show: An Exhibition Celebrating Birds,* Edina Art Center, Edina
COLLECTIONS: Andersen Horticultural Library, University of Minnesota, Chaska; Bell Museum of Natural History, University of Minnesota, Minneapolis; Brooklyn Botanic Garden Florilegium Society, Brooklyn, New York

Every once in a while, I see a nest that feels special and awakens my imagination. I found this tiny nest, woven from weeds and thistledown, on a winter afternoon tucked away in the branches of a red dogwood thicket. A delicate legacy of summer, its unexpected discovery was the starting point for a spare winter composition highlighting the subtle tones of the little nest against the bare, crimson dogwood twigs. I wanted to paint the nest accurately as well as convey a sense of time, place, and season.

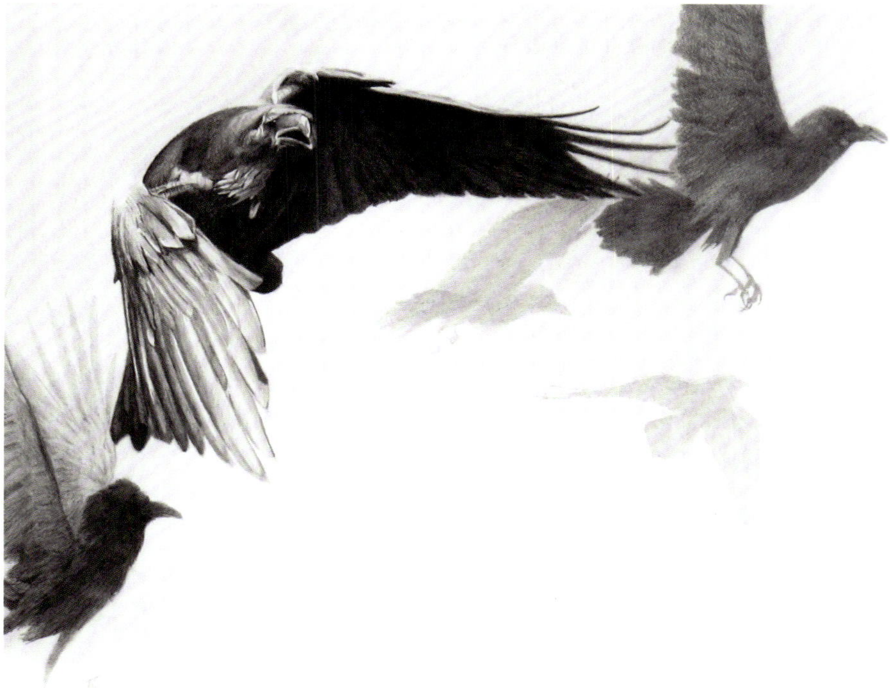

Exodus, 2012
Common raven
Pencil on Strathmore Bristol board
16 x 20

Collection of the artist

Birds in Art: 2010

BORN: 1966, United States
RESIDES: Lake Forest, California
EDUCATION: B.S., Towson State University, Towson, Maryland
BIBLIOGRAPHY: *Strokes of Genius 3: The Best of Drawing, Fresh Perspective,* North Light Books, 2011
REPRESENTATIVES: Cody Fine Art Gallery, Cody, Wyoming; Horizon Fine Art Gallery, Jackson Hole, Wyoming; Main Street Gallery, Annapolis, Maryland

Of all the wildlife I saw during my first trip to Yellowstone National Park many years ago, the ravens stuck in my head. Soaring over the mountains or open plains, dancing in the sky or through the trees, they encompass all that the wilderness embodies: freedom, wisdom, perseverance, and the joy and struggle of life.

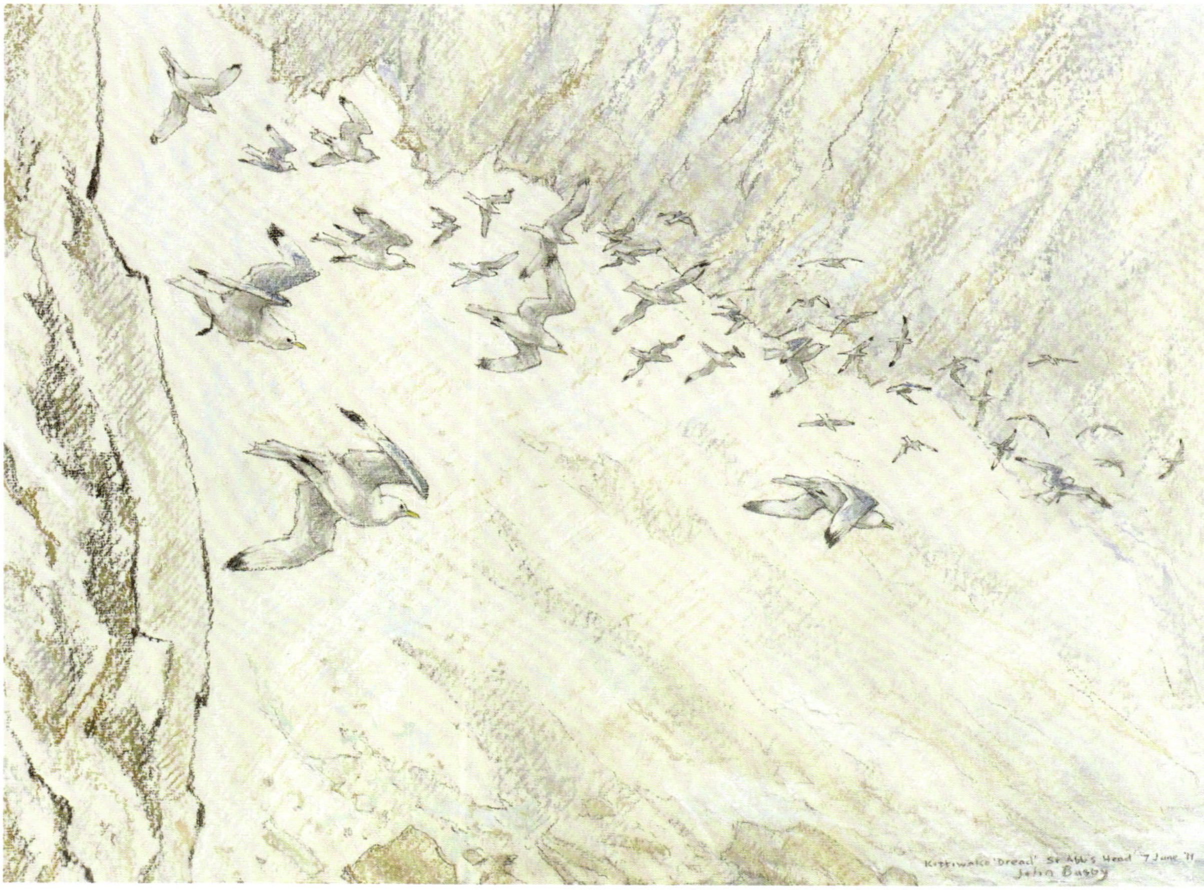

Kittiwake Dread at St. Abbs Head, Scotland, 2012
Black-legged kittiwake
Conté and pastel on handmade paper
14 x 18

Collection of the artist

Birds in Art: 2009-11
Master Wildlife Artist: 2009

W

BORN: 1928, England
RESIDES: Ormiston, East Lothian, Scotland
EDUCATION: Leeds College of Art & Design, Leeds, England; Edinburgh College of Art, Edinburgh
EXHIBITIONS: *Inverarity One to One,* 2010, Inverarity Gallery, Edinburgh; Royal Scottish Academy, 2010-12; Waterston House Gallery, 2011, Aberlady; Rockcliffe Gallery, 2011, Dumfries; *Drawing Inspiration from the Hula Valley,* 2011, Agamon Park Gallery, Upper Galilee, Israel; *Artists for Nature Jubilee,* 2012, Orangerie Landgoed Vollenhoven, De Bilt, Netherlands
COLLECTIONS: City of Edinburgh; Scottish Arts Council, Edinburgh; Mass Audubon Visual Arts Center, Canton, Massachusetts; University of Oxford, Oxford, England
BIBLIOGRAPHY: "The Master of Visual Poetry," *Bird Art & Photography,* Spring 2010; *Landscapes at the Edge of the Sea,* 2010 SP; *Drawing Inspiration from the Hula Valley,* Society for the Protection of Nature in Israel, 2011
REPRESENTATIVES: Wildlife Art Gallery, Lavenham, Suffolk, England

Kittiwakes are true sea gulls, only coming ashore to nest on the ledges of sea cliffs. They are named after their call – kittywaaak, kittywaaak – and several hundred nesting birds make quite a noise. Sometimes, without an apparent reason, the whole colony takes off and flies out to sea in complete silence, circles for a few minutes, then returns to the nest site, and the noise resumes. This phenomenon is known as a 'dread.' It's an uncanny experience! The challenge for an artist is to convey both the tension and the silence of the event.

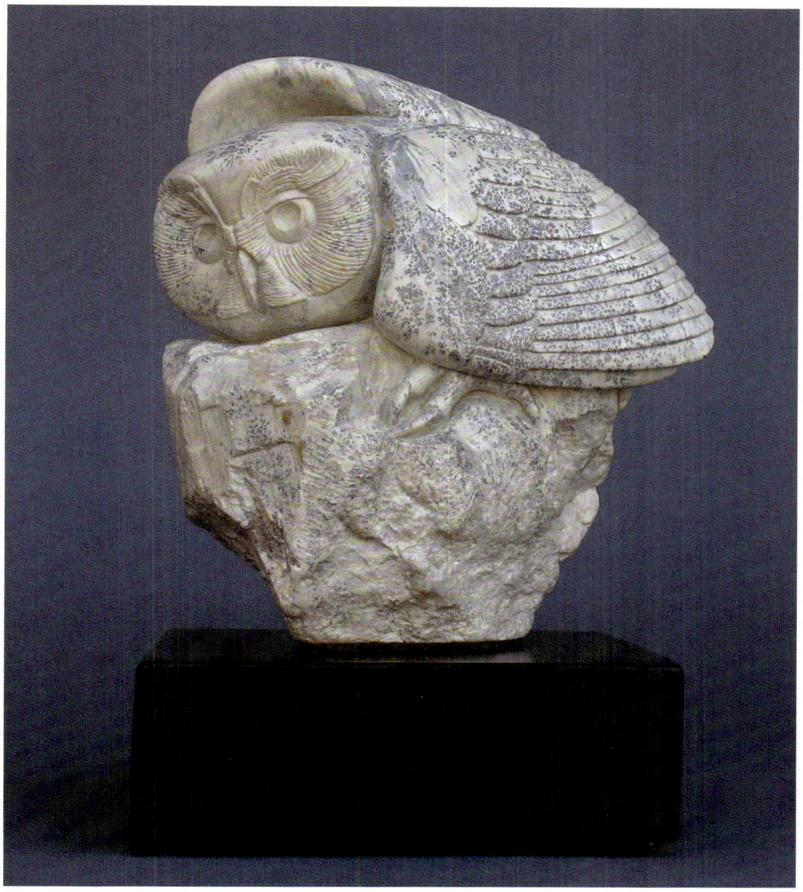

In the Moment, 2012
Northern saw-whet owl
Montana dendritic soapstone
7 1/2 x 7 x 5 1/2

Collection of the artist

Birds in Art: 1989, 1993, 1995, 1997, 2000, 2003, 2005, 2007, 2011

W

BORN: 1941, United States
RESIDES: Madison, Wisconsin
EXHIBITIONS: *Wisconsin Visual Artists,* 2010, Wisconsin Arts Board Gallery, Madison; *Mixed Greens,* 2010, Promega Gallery, Fitchburg, Wisconsin; *Artists for Conservation,* 2011, Spirit Gallery, Grouse Mountain, Vancouver, British Columbia, Canada
COLLECTIONS: ARCOM Corporation, Salt Lake City; Bradshaw-Knight Foundation, Madison; Retirement Research Foundation, Chicago
BIBLIOGRAPHY: "The Owlman Swoops in for Art Fair," *Wisconsingazette.com,* July 2011 OL; "Area Artists Flock Together," *Wisconsin State Journal,* September 11, 2011

The first live owl I held is named 'Boopie.' Although she was quite old when a car hit her in 2000 and lost most of her left wing, she has the good fortune to live at a wonderful raptor rehabilitation center in Illinois. Now, Boopie is almost blind, but she still maintains the essence of her kind. Creatures survive by living in the moment. Occasionally, we still are able to find ourselves in that special place.

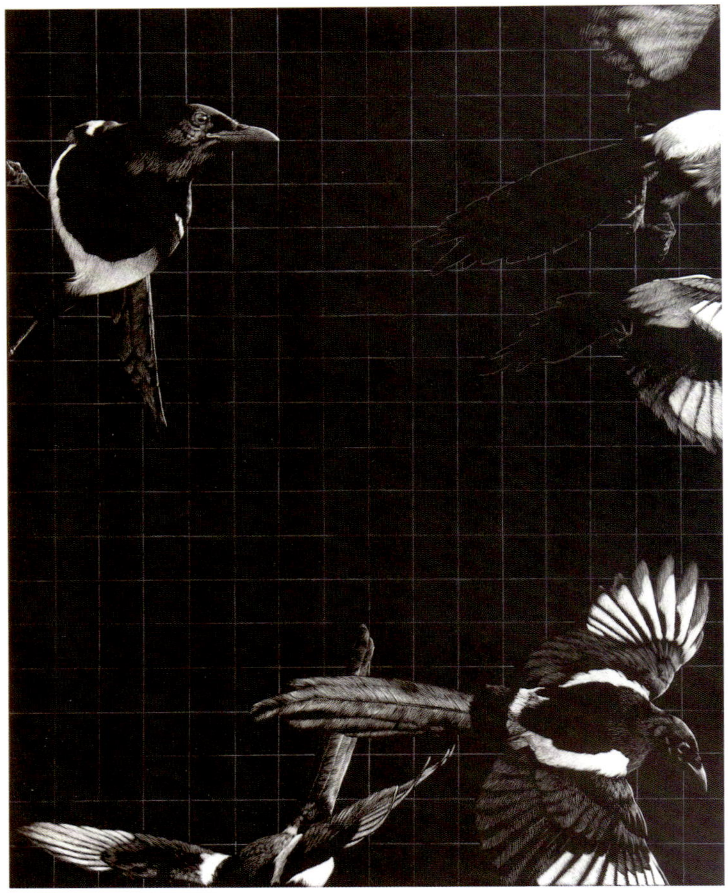

Scatter, 2012
Black-billed magpie
Ink on claybord
20 x 16

Collection of the artist

Birds in Art: 2003, 2006

W

BORN: 1963, United States
RESIDES: Missoula, Montana
EDUCATION: B.S., Case Western Reserve University, Cleveland
EXHIBITIONS: *Wild West: Beauty of the Beast,* 2011, Rockwell Museum of Western Art, Corning, New York
AWARDS: Best of Show, 2011, *Calgary Stampede Western Showcase,* Stampede Park, Calgary, Alberta, Canada; Honorable Mention, Artistic Excellence, 2011, *Southwest Art Magazine*
BIBLIOGRAPHY: "Artists of the Horse: Julie T. Chapman," *Wildlife Art Journal,* October 2011 OL; "Artistic Excellence: Julie T. Chapman," *Southwest Art Magazine,* December 2011
REPRESENTATIVES: Ann Korologos Gallery, Basalt, Colorado; Mountain Trails Gallery, Jackson, Wyoming; Pitzer's Fine Art, Wimberley, Texas

The initial idea for Scatter *stemmed from a handful of magpies that spent a week working their tailfeathers off trying to get to suet we'd set out in a cage for woodpeckers. Magpies lack the adaptations necessary to cling to the cage and get to the food but persisted in their efforts (fairly successfully, I might add!). Their comings and goings and gyrations on the suet cage, along with their general chutzpah, provided inspiration. It was more than a year before the material coalesced in my mind as a composition. I'd been experimenting with scratchboard, and the boldly monochromatic birds seemed a perfect fit for the medium.*

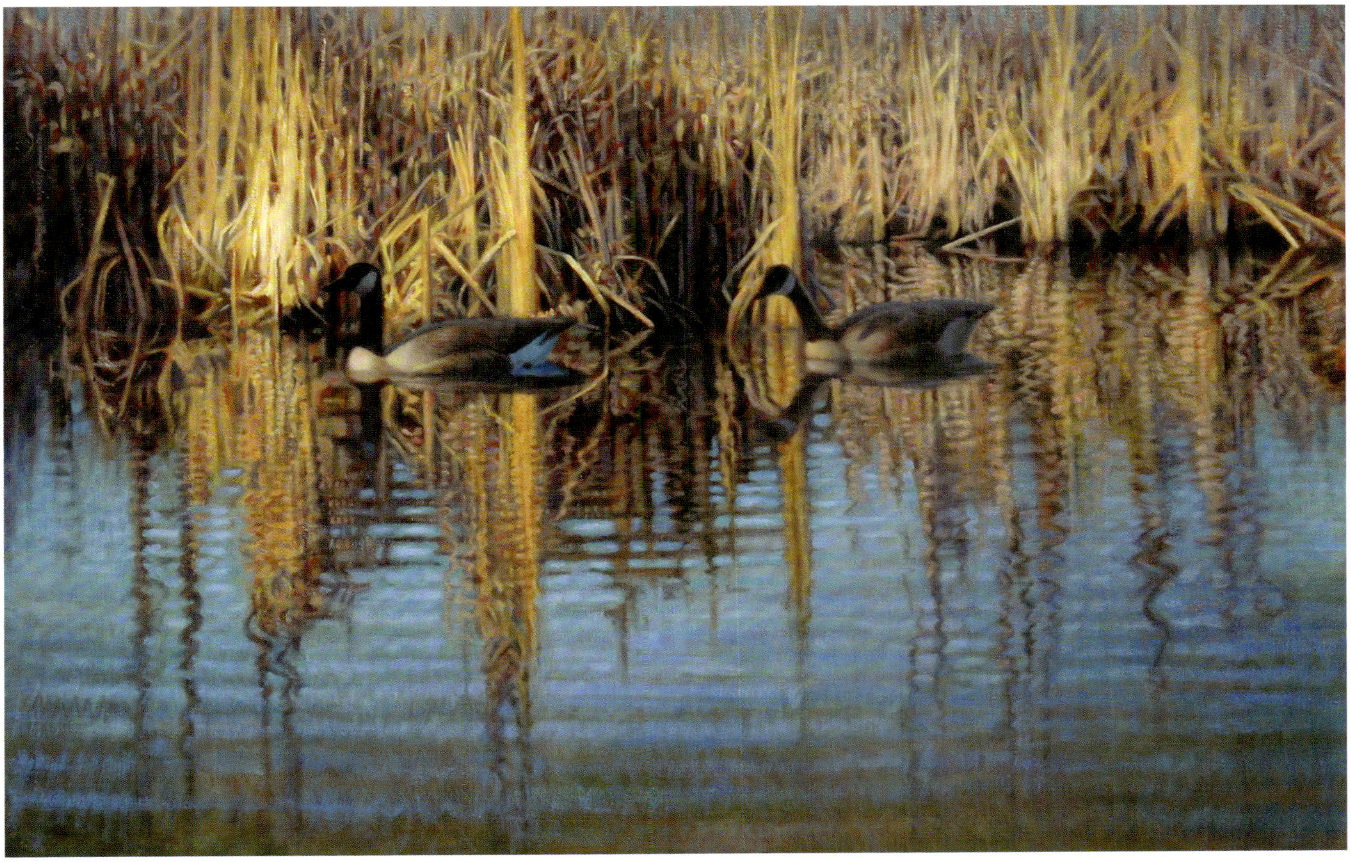

Gentle Reflection, 2012
Canada goose
Oil on canvas
24 x 36

Collection of the artist

Birds in Art: 2000, 2008

BORN: 1971, United States
RESIDES: Vancouver, British Columbia, Canada
EDUCATION: B.F.A., University of Michigan, Ann Arbor
COMMISSIONS: Studeo55, Vancouver; Twenty One Inc., Vancouver
REPRESENTATIVES: Harrison Galleries, Vancouver

I'm drawn to the alluring sounds of water and the cooling presence of a stream along a favorite hike. Discovering a hidden pool deep in the woods is a magical experience, and studying the interplay of reflections in a pond was my earliest form of meditation. In Gentle Reflection, *I explore the intricate patterns created on the calm water's surface. The harmonious quality is enhanced by the calligraphic nature of the intertwining winter reeds along the marsh border.*

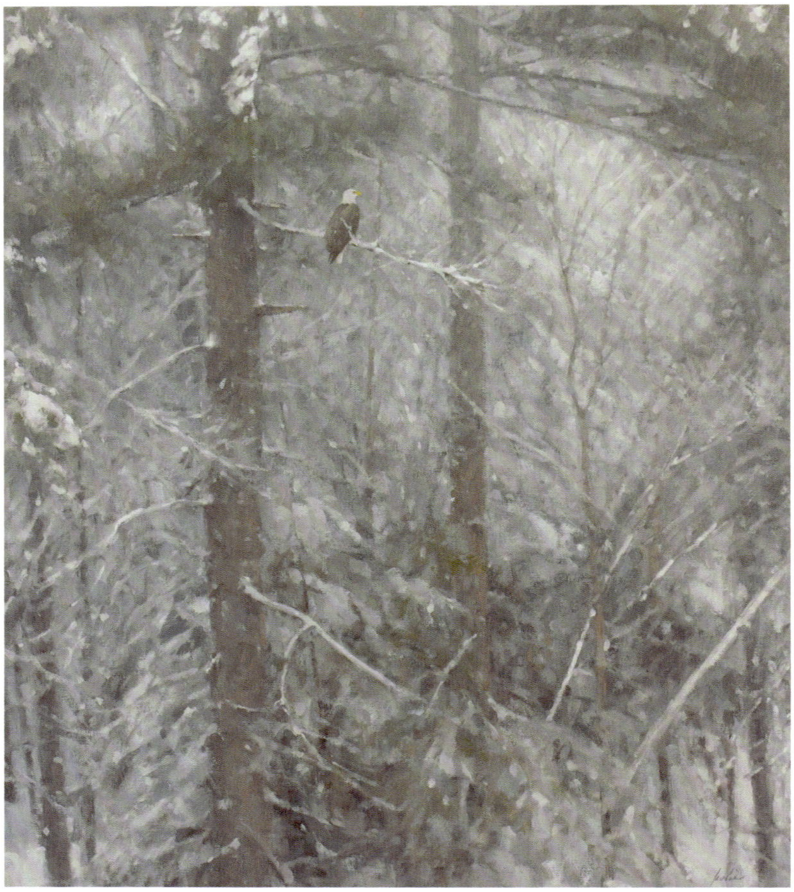

Winter Tapestry, 2011
Bald eagle
Oil on Belgian linen
30 x 26

Collection of the artist

Birds in Art: 1980, 1982, 1984, 1986, 2003, 2005-09, 2011
Master Wildlife Artist: 2011

W

BORN: 1957, United States
RESIDES: Hannacroix, New York
EDUCATION: M.F.A., Parsons The New School for Design, New York City; A.B., Harvard University, Cambridge, Massachusetts
EXHIBITIONS: *Creative Convergence: Cape Cod,* 2011, Cape Cod Museum of Art, Dennis, Massachusetts; *Award-Winning Artists, Three Distinct Views,* 2011, Addison Gallery, Orleans, Massachusetts; Addison Gallery, 2012; *Artists' Favorite Places,* 2012, McBride Gallery, Annapolis, Maryland
AWARDS: Award of Excellence, 2011, *Art and the Animal,* Dennos Museum Center, Northwestern Michigan College, Traverse City; Alden Bryan Medal, 2012, *Land and Light and Water and Air,* Bryan Memorial Gallery, Jeffersonville, Vermont
COLLECTIONS: Mass Audubon Visual Arts Center, Canton, Massachusetts; New York State Museum, Albany
BIBLIOGRAPHY: "Wildlife in the Landscape," *PleinAir Magazine,* Fall 2011; "Finding Sanctuary," *American Art Collector,* May 2012
REPRESENTATIVES: Banks Gallery, Portsmouth, New Hampshire; Gregory James Gallery, New Milford, Connecticut; Walt Horton Fine Art, Beaver Creek, Colorado

Winter Tapestry *challenged me to take a conventional subject – a bald eagle perched in a pine tree – and 'reframe' it as a statement that is original and entirely personal. I did everything possible to soften the visual impact of the eagle and subdue the color palette of the pine grove. By doing so, I was able to create a painting that suggests a tapestry of subtle grays and in which there is a tension between surface pattern and pictorial space. These conceptual matters were more important to me than the subject matter.*

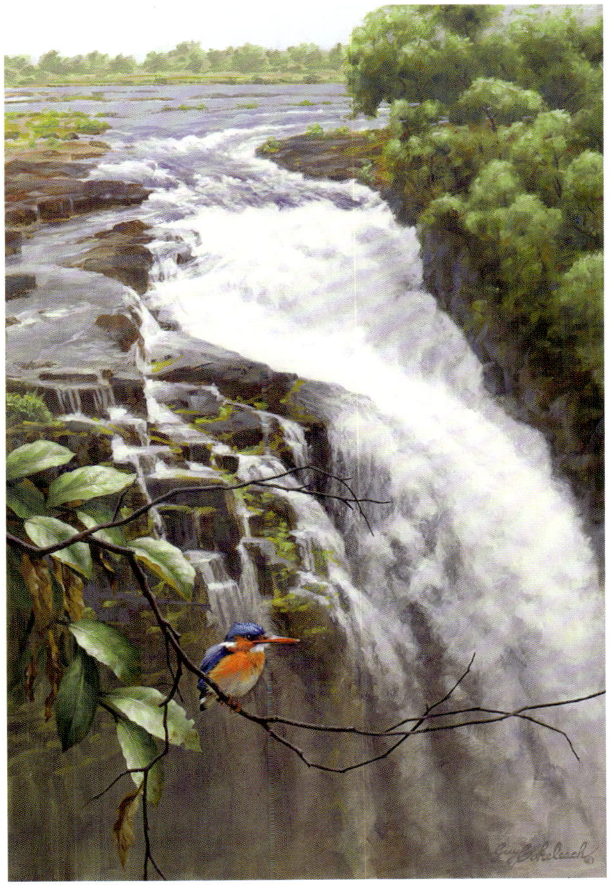

Devil's Cataract, Victoria Falls, 2012
Malachite kingfisher
Oil on linen
36 x 24

Collection of the artist

Birds in Art: 1976-11
Master Wildlife Artist: 1983

W

BORN: 1933, United States
RESIDES: Stuart, Florida
EDUCATION: B.A., Cooper Union Art School, New York City
EXHIBITIONS: *Art and the Animal,* 2010, San Diego Natural History Museum, 2011, Dennos Museum Center, Northwestern Michigan College, Traverse City, and 2012, Hiram Blauvelt Art Museum, Oradell, New Jersey; *Artists for Conservation,* 2011, Spirit Gallery, Grouse Mountain, Vancouver, British Columbia, Canada
AWARDS: Medal of Excellence, 2010, *Artists for Conservation*
REPRESENTATIVES: K&K Wildlife Art Prints, Alpharetta, Georgia

I learned from Bruno Liljefors, Louis Fuertes, and Don Eckelberry to paint what I see, not what I think I know. I love Victoria Falls and will never tire of painting them, especially the fascinating Devil's Cataract. The malachite kingfisher adds just the right flash of color.

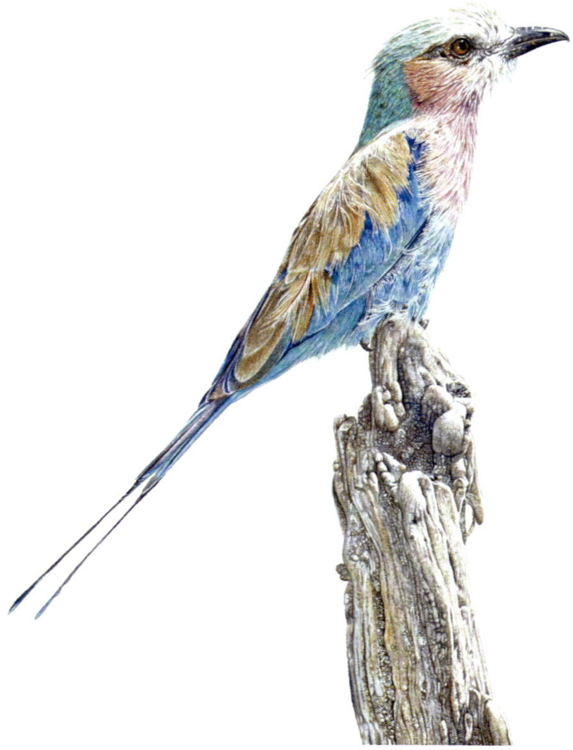

Pride of Kenya, 2011
Lilac-breasted roller
Watercolor on Lanaquarelle hot press paper
13 1/2 x 11 1/2

Collection of Joseph B. Orlick and Robert K. Powell

BORN: 1964, United States
RESIDES: Charlottesville, Virginia
EDUCATION: B.S., University of Virginia, Charlottesville

Without question I was captivated by the brightly colored lilac-breasted roller on my first trip to Africa. This particular bird struck many engaging poses, quite content to perch for artist-friendly periods of time. My hesitation to paint this bird stemmed from the desire to do justice to the radiant colors and varied textures using only transparent watercolor . . . no opaque or semi-opaque pigments. In the end, all the white you see is paper, carefully preserved from the start. I put the size zero brush to the test in my push to capture the varied lengths and intricacies of the feathers. My excitement for the complexity of the process equals my delight for the subject.

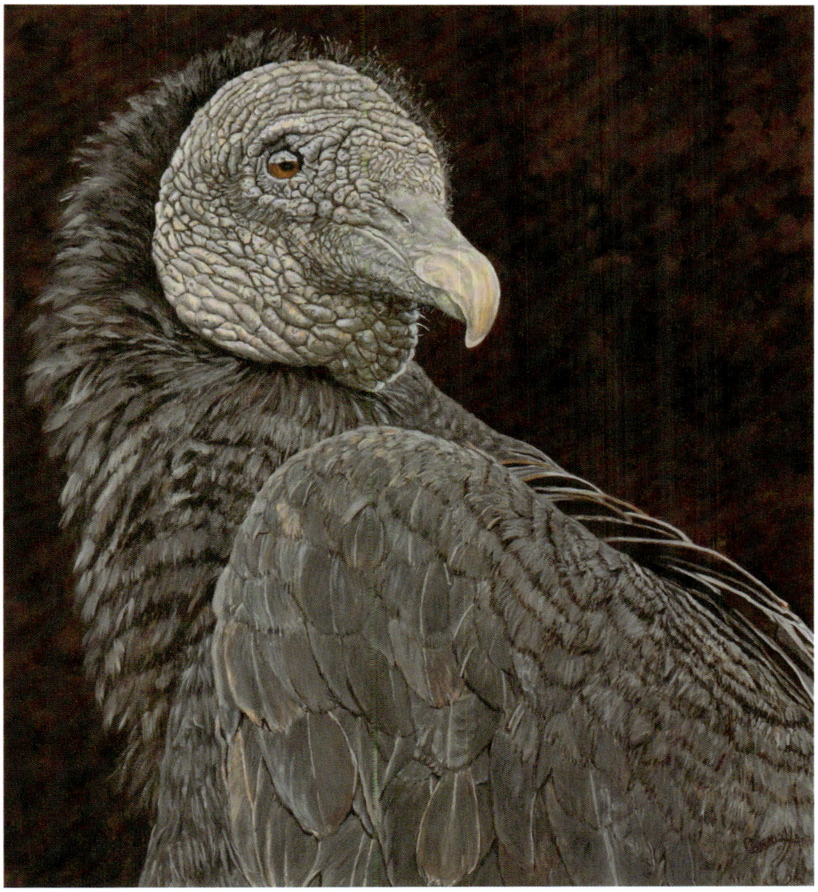

The Barrister, 2012
American black vulture
Casein on acrylic gessoed panel
16 1/2 x 14 3/4

Collection of the artist

Birds in Art: 2007-11

W

BORN: 1950, United States
RESIDES: Warrenton, Virginia
EDUCATION: A.O.S., Northwest College of Art, Poulsbo, Washington
EXHIBITIONS: *Schuler School of Fine Arts Animal Exhibition,* 2010, Schuler School of Fine Arts, Baltimore; *Art and the Animal,* 2011, Dennos Museum Center, Northwestern Michigan College, Traverse City
COLLECTIONS: Alexander Properties, Wausau; Washington State Arts Commission, Olympia
BIBLIOGRAPHY: "Miniatures," *The Piedmont Virginian,* Winter 2010; *Strokes of Genius 3: The Best of Drawing, Fresh Perspectives,* North Light Books, 2011
REPRESENTATIVES: Berkley Gallery, Warrenton

Birds not considered beautiful by most people are the ones that pique my interest. The American black vulture seemed an ideal candidate; its facial details were both fascinating and challenging to paint. My goal was to portray the bird's true beauty despite the visual repulsion associated with the vulture. This particular bird reminded me of the barristers of old, dressed in long black robes and court wigs.

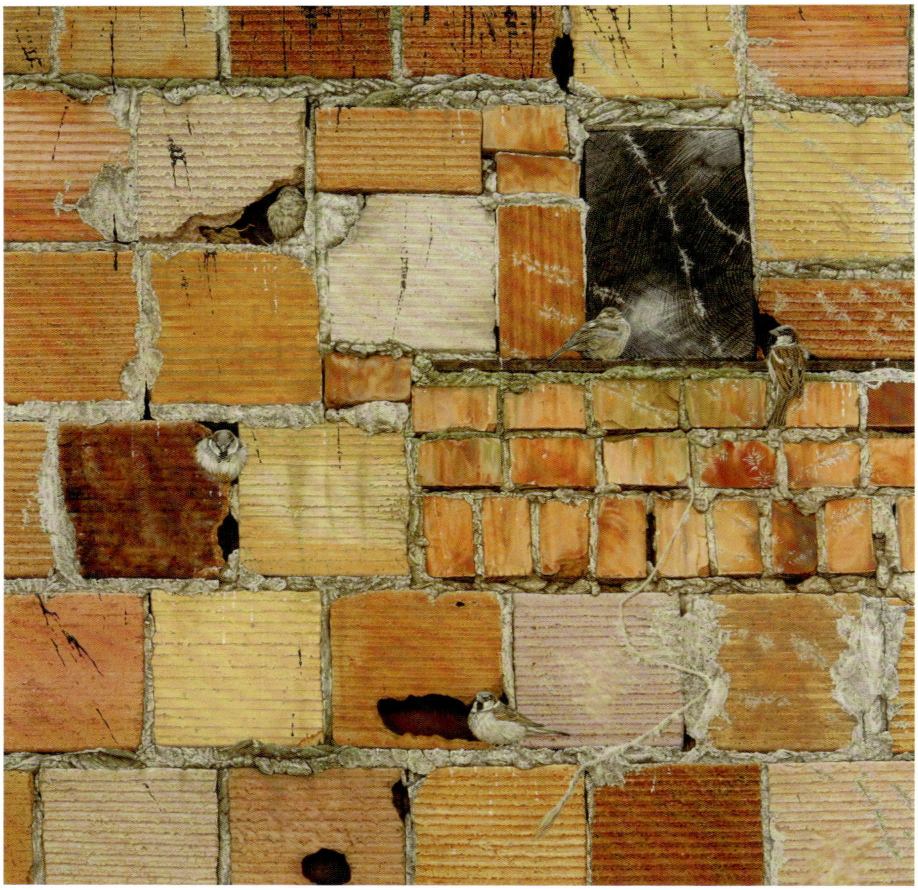

Chinatown, 2010
House sparrow
Oil on hardboard
32 x 32

Collection of the artist

Birds in Art: 1993, 1995, 2003, 2005, 2007

W

BORN: 1955, United States
RESIDES: Milton, Washington
EDUCATION: A.A., West Valley College, Saratoga, California
EXHIBITIONS: *Art and the Animal,* 2010, San Diego Natural History Museum; *Artists for Conservation,* 2011, Spirit Gallery, Grouse Mountain, Vancouver, British Columbia, Canada

As if I had been dreaming of Mondrian, the idea for Chinatown *presented itself unexpectedly. After a day of photographing birds with friends, I was window-shopping in Gig Harbor when I spotted sparrow activity on a wall. The variety of shapes and patterns immediately sparked my imagination. As a realist, I find surfaces, textures, and the unusual presentation of things fascinating, yet the artistic side of me is equally excited by abstraction and strong design elements. In this wall I found everything – textures, soft feathers, brick, moss, and old wood – happily laid out before me! All I had to do was execute. In the end – as with Mondrian's work – no single element is any more or less important; all elements engage equally to yield a strong composition.*

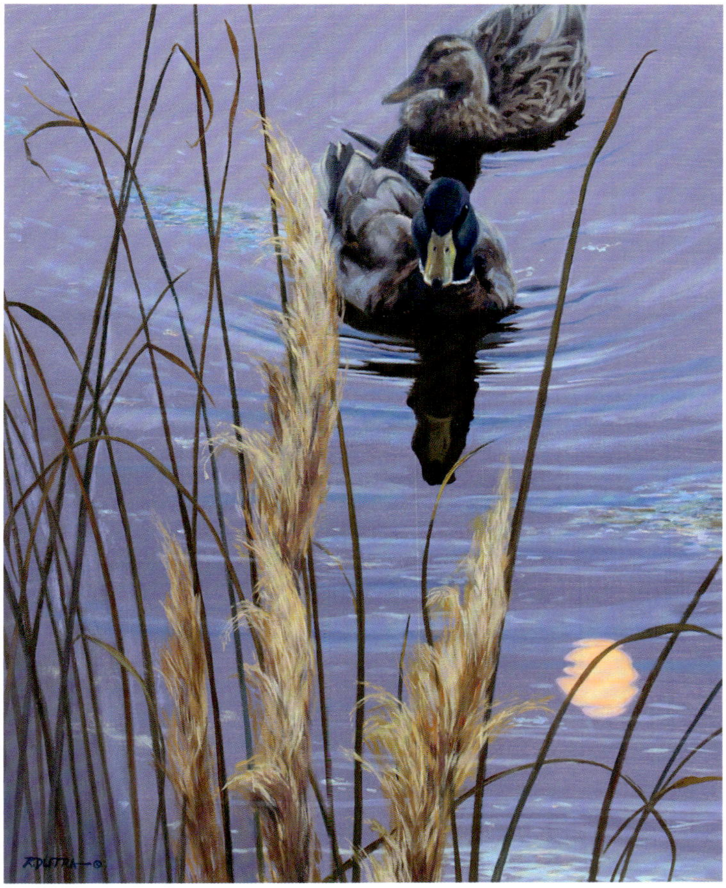

Mallard Moon, 2011
Oil on Belgian linen
30 x 24

Collection of the artist

Birds in Art: 1991, 1993-94, 1996, 1999-00, 2004, 2006-08

W

BORN: 1958, United States
RESIDES: Castro Valley, California
EXHIBITIONS: *Prix de West Invitational,* 2012, National Cowboy & Western Heritage Museum, Oklahoma City
COLLECTIONS: National Museum of Wildlife Art, Jackson, Wyoming
BIBLIOGRAPHY: "A Personal Destination," *Art of the West,* May/June 2010; *Strokes of Genius 4: The Best of Drawing,* North Light Books, 2012; "On Leaving Hollywood Behind: An Interview with Randal M. Dutra," *Wildlife Art Journal,* May 2012 OL
REPRESENTATIVES: InSight Gallery, Fredericksburg, Texas

Mallard Moon *draws on influences from both the West and the East. Realistic, carefully modeled passages are combined with a larger, subtly graded color field. I walked a challenging tightrope to integrate the two aesthetics, but that was the very reason for doing so.*

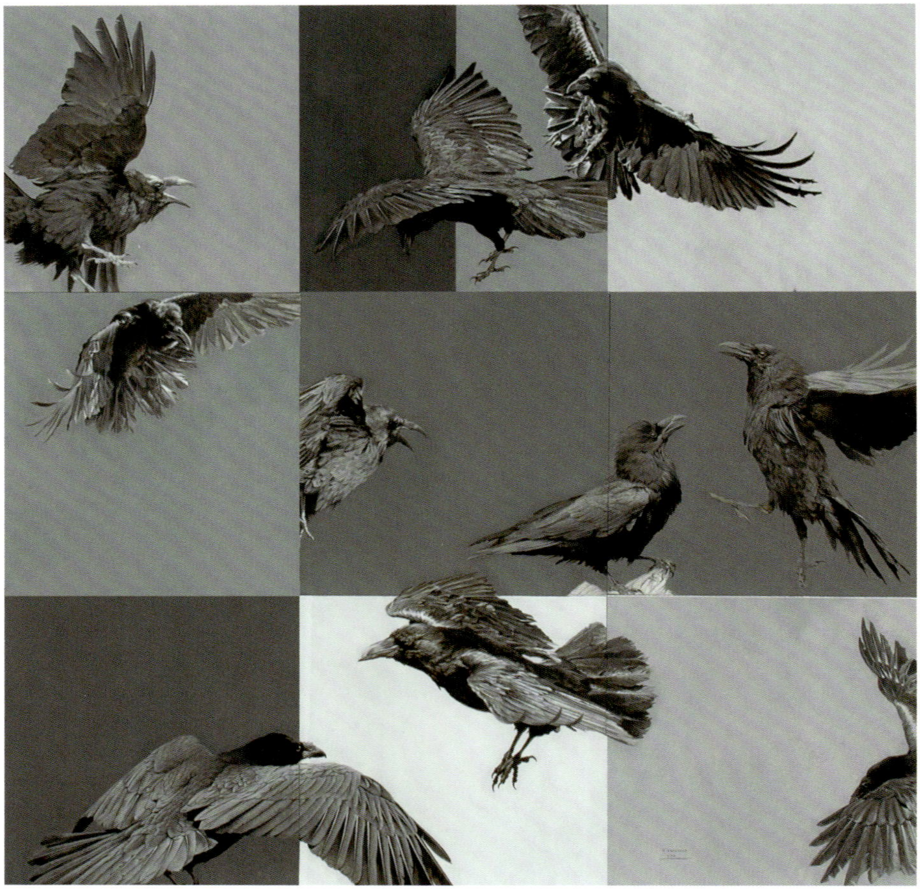

Square Dance, 2010
Common raven
Oil on hardboard
33 x 33

Collection of the artist

*Birds in Art:*1997-02, 2004-09, 2011

W

BORN: 1949, United States
RESIDES: Terrace Park, Ohio
EDUCATION: M.F.A., Yale University, New Haven, Connecticut; B.S., University of Cincinnati
EXHIBITIONS: Astoria Fine Art Gallery, 2011, Jackson, Wyoming; National Museum of Wildlife Art, 2011, Jackson; Row House Gallery, 2011, Milford, Ohio
AWARDS: Trustee's Purchase Award, 2011, *Western Visions,* National Museum of Wildlife Art
COLLECTIONS: Frisch's Restaurants, Cincinnati; Uline, Waukegan, Illinois
BIBLIOGRAPHY: "On the Edge," *Western Art Collector,* October 2011
REPRESENTATIVES: Astoria Fine Art Gallery; Huey's Fine Art, Santa Fe, New Mexico; Row House Gallery

The raven is a big, glossy, purplish-black bird. It's been the subject of superstitions, myths, and folklore from Noah and the Ark to present-day Britain, where ravens with clipped wings are kept in the Tower of London to keep England safe from invasion. In many cultures throughout the world, the raven has been considered a trickster; it plays a prominent role in many Native American creation tales. After much observation, I think aerial acrobat and dancer can be added to its list of attributes.

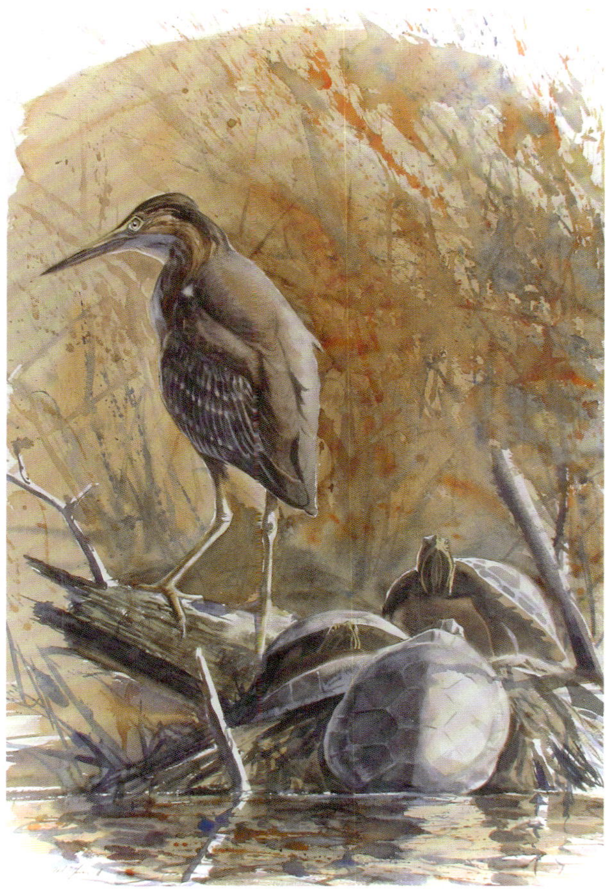

Watching the River Flow,
2011
Green heron
Watercolor on Arches paper
23 x 15

Private collection

Birds in Art: 1998, 2001, 2004, 2006, 2009, 2011

BORN: 1966, Sweden
RESIDES: Eslov, Sweden
BIBLIOGRAPHY: "I Sverige har naturkonst haft svart att sla igenom," *Var Fagelvärld,* January 2012

Following the opening of Birds in Art *last fall, I visited some of Wisconsin's major wildlife areas. At Horicon Marsh, I saw this young green heron and painted turtles, which I sketched and photographed. During the flight back home, I began some composition sketches of the scene that later became this finished painting. Both herons and amphibians have a prehistoric look and can sit motionless for hours. For me they are perfect models.*

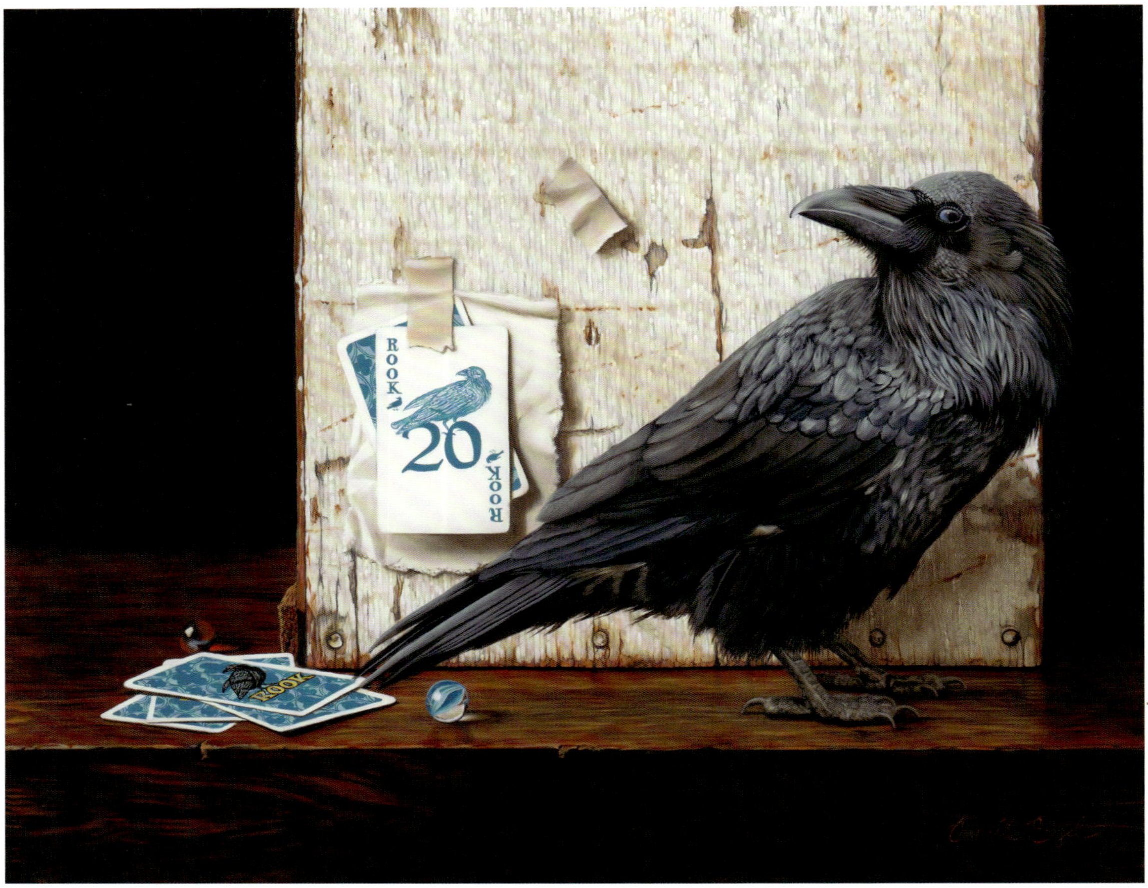

Strike a Pose, 2011
Common raven
Oil on cradled Ampersand gessobord
16 x 20

Collection of
Tennessee State Museum, Nashville

BORN: 1955, United States
RESIDES: Nashville
EXHIBITIONS: *New Reality: Frontier of Realism in the 21st Century,* 2010, Appleton Museum of Art, Ocala, Florida; *International Guild of Realism,* 2011, Sage Creek Gallery, Santa Fe, New Mexico; Customs House Museum, 2012, Clarksville, Tennessee
AWARDS: People's Choice, 2010, *Central South National Exhibition,* Tennessee Art League, Nashville; Best Wildlife, 2010, *International Guild of Realism*, J. Willot Gallery, Palm Desert, California
COLLECTIONS: Chattanoogan Hotel, Chattanooga, Tennessee; Metropolitan Nashville Government; Vanderbilt Law School, Nashville
COMMISSIONS: Middle Tennessee Medical Center, Murfreesboro; Northeast Georgia Medical Center, Gainesville; Vanderbilt Children's Hospital
BIBLIOGRAPHY: "Three to Watch," *Fine Art Connoisseur,* July/August 2010; "Miniatures and Small Works," *American Art Collector,* November 2010
REPRESENTATIVES: Dean Day Gallery, Houston; Giacobbe-Fritz Fine Art, Santa Fe; Lovetts Fine Art Gallery, Tulsa, Oklahoma

'Strike a pose' is a familiar phrase, generally used by photographers with their models. Strike a Pose *is a light-hearted and witty endeavor to glamorize this 'bad boy,' as its pose mimics that of the raven on the Rook playing cards. Creating the rough texture of the weathered wood juxtaposed with the raven's feathers and the smooth marbles was challenging. However, I find rewards in the extraordinary details in ordinary things such as the miniature reflections in the marbles.*

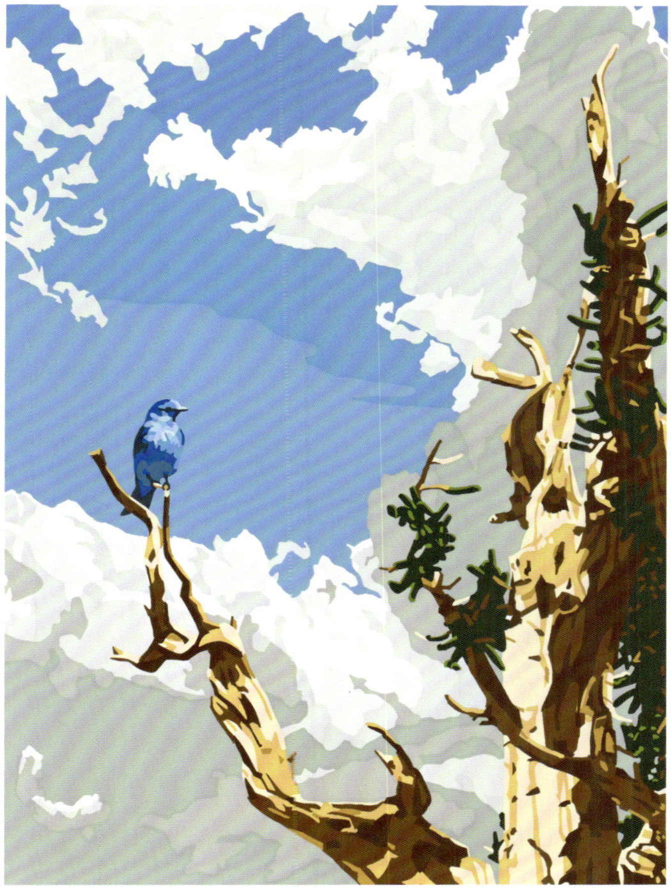

Touch the Sky (1/14), 2012
Mountain bluebird
Serigraph on Strathmore paper
22 x 16

Collection of the artist

Birds in Art: 1981-82, 1984-91, 1993-11
Master Wildlife Artist: 1999

W

BORN: 1936, United States
RESIDES: Baton Rouge, Louisiana
EDUCATION: M.A.Ed., University of Hartford, West Hartford, Connecticut; B.F.A., Boston University
EXHIBITIONS: *Kentucky National Wildlife Art Exhibition,* 2010, Henderson Fine Arts Center, Henderson; *Art of the Animal Kingdom,* 2010-12, Bennington Center for the Arts, Bennington, Vermont; *Art and the Animal,* 2010, San Diego Natural History Museum, 2011, Dennos Museum Center, Northwestern Michigan College, Traverse City, and 2012, Hiram Blauvelt Art Museum, Oradell, New Jersey; *Judith Ryan Williams Nature & Wildlife Art,* 2011, Saint Augustine Art Association, Saint Augustine, Florida
COLLECTIONS: Bennington Center for the Arts; DeCordova Museum and Sculpture Garden, Lincoln, Massachusetts; Mass Audubon Visual Arts Center, Canton, Massachusetts; New Britain Museum of American Art, New Britain, Connecticut

In the mountains high
Reaching up to touch the sky
A little blue bird

I first saw a mountain bluebird high in the Rockies twenty-five years ago. The idea for a print percolated a long time and came together this year when I wrote the somewhat ambiguous Haiku. Are the mountains reaching up to touch the sky, or is it the bird? No matter. I wanted to suggest a feeling of rising, of uplift, of reaching skyward. To do so, the viewer needed to be below the bird, looking up. An ancient, storm-wracked conifer in which to place the bird was essential; I used a small section of a giant tree, lit from the same side as the bird. The final element to reinforce upward movement was a semi-frame of clouds.

Joe Garcia

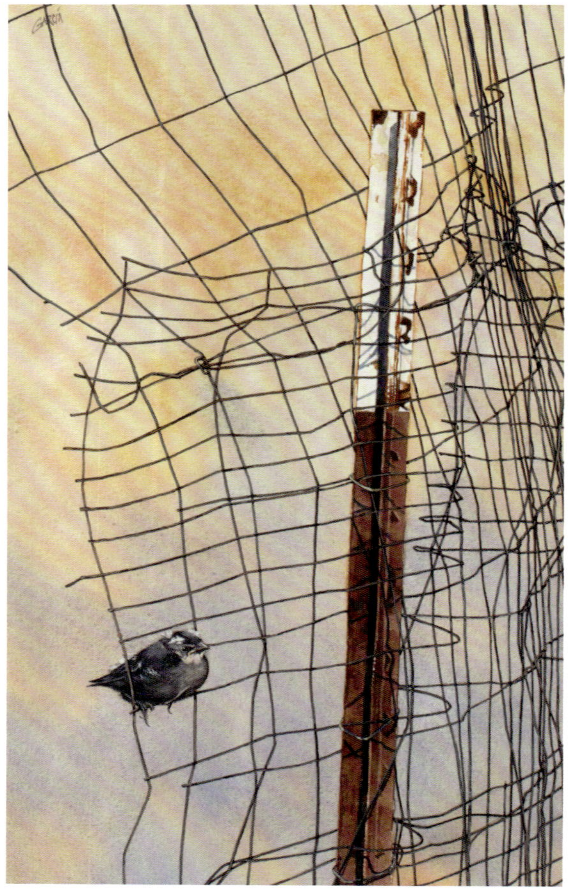

Hold On and Hang Tight,
2012
Red-winged blackbird
Watercolor on Arches cold press paper
21 1/2 x 13 1/2

Collection of the artist

Birds in Art: 1993, 1995-96, 1998-00, 2002-07, 2009-10

W

BORN: 1944, United States
RESIDES: Julian, California
EDUCATION: B.F.A., Art Center College of Design, Pasadena, California
EXHIBITIONS: Santa Ysabel Gallery, 2011, Santa Ysabel, California
COLLECTIONS: Arizona-Sonora Desert Museum, Tucson; Bennington Center for the Arts, Bennington, Vermont

Red-winged blackbirds and old fences are common features of the landscape where I live. I was drawn to the complexity of the wire and texture of the fence post and wanted to use these elements to move away from a traditional landscape but still suggest the surroundings. Depicting an adult bird was my first thought; however, a fledgling was visually unexpected, suggesting that this might be the young bird's first flight and perch. Playing with the composition and getting all the elements to work together were a joy.

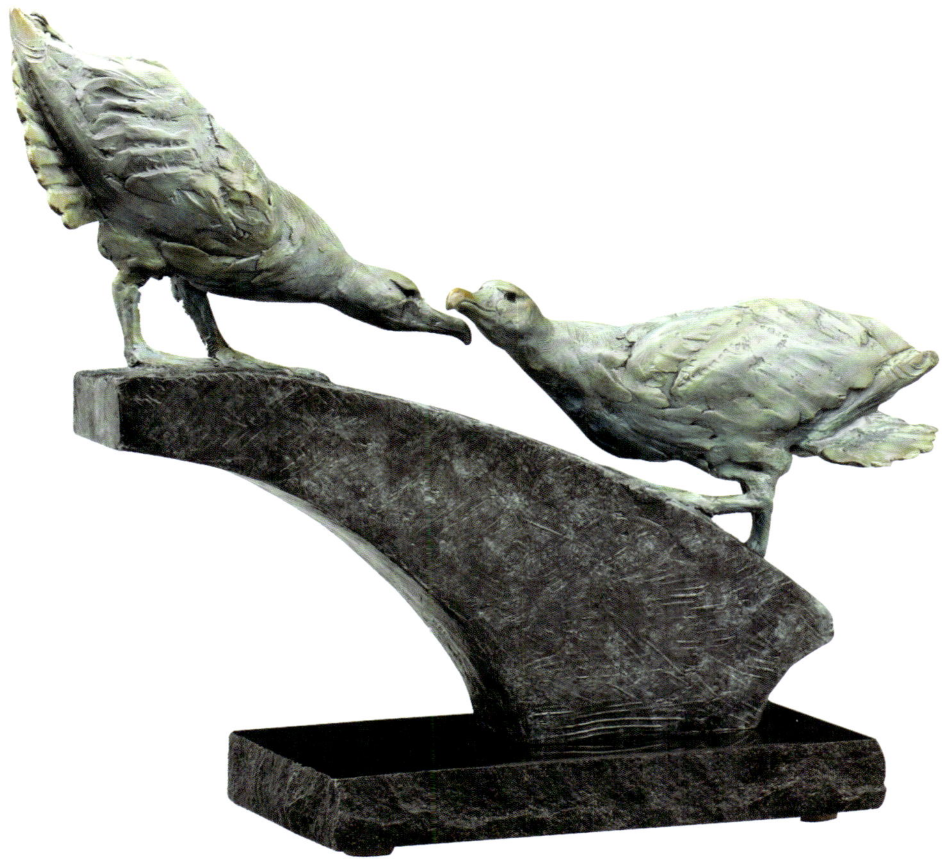

Courtship (ed. 30), 2011
Black-browed albatross
Bronze
14 x 15 x 5

Collection of the artist

Birds in Art: 2006, 2011

BORN: 1956, United States
RESIDES: Masonville, Colorado
EXHIBITIONS: *Art and the Animal,* 2010, San Diego Natural History Museum, 2011, Dennos Museum Center, Northwestern Michigan College, Traverse City, and 2012, Hiram Blauvelt Art Museum, Oradell, New Jersey; *Impressions of Spring* and *American Art Invitational,* 2011, Saks Galleries, Denver
AWARDS: Best in Show, Sculpture, 2010, *Representing the West,* Sangre de Cristo Arts Center, Pueblo, Colorado; Best German Shorthaired Pointer, 2010, and Second Place, Sculpture, 2012, *Art Show at the Dog Show,* Kansas Coliseum, Wichita
COLLECTIONS: Benson Sculpture Garden, Loveland, Colorado; Liberty National Bank, Dakota Dunes, South Dakota; The Wildlife Experience, Parker, Colorado; Witt Stevens Central Arkansas Nature Center, Little Rock
COMMISSIONS: City of Little Rock, Arkansas; Longmont Humane Society, Longmont, Colorado
REPRESENTATIVES: Cogswell Gallery, Vail, Colorado; RS Hanna Gallery, Fredericksburg, Texas; Saks Galleries

Courtship *is an earthbound display of one of the world's great aerial wanderers. I've had the good fortune of seeing albatross soar in the southern latitudes and visiting their terra firma nesting sites. It's difficult to imagine what their communications might entail as they cruise the ocean swells. Once on land, it seems their vocalizations are nonstop. And most surprising and unexpected were the black-browed albatross's antics and apparent curiosity toward me. The result was this small window into their lives.*

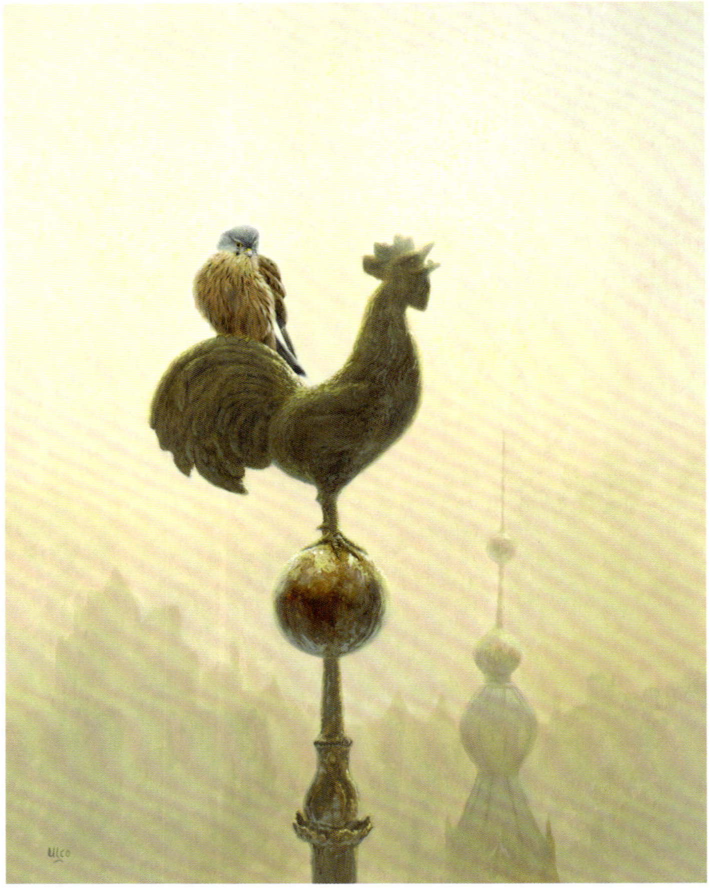

Medieval Kestrel, 2012
European kestrel
Oil on hardboard
33 x 25

Collection of the artist

Birds in Art: 1992, 1994-95, 1997-98, 2000, 2002-09

W

BORN: 1958, Netherlands
RESIDES: Dwingeloo, Netherlands
EDUCATION: Ph.D., Universiteit Utrecht, Utrecht
EXHIBITIONS: *Octopussen, Stieren en Andere Dieren,* 2012, Museum Elburg, Elburg
COMMISSIONS: City of Zevenaar
BIBLIOGRAPHY: *Verleden van een bewogen landschap,* Matrijs, 2011; *Historische Atlas van Zutphen,* Vantilt, 2011; *Vikingen,* WBooks, 2012

The kestrel's Dutch name is Torenvalk *or Tower Falcon for a reason. My work on a large mural of a medieval Dutch town – a reconstruction of what it might have looked like around 1700 – sparked the idea for this interesting combination of birds: a kestrel perching calmly on a bronze weathervane, a very active cock. I added soft, early morning light to keep the scene as tranquil as it may have been in those days.*

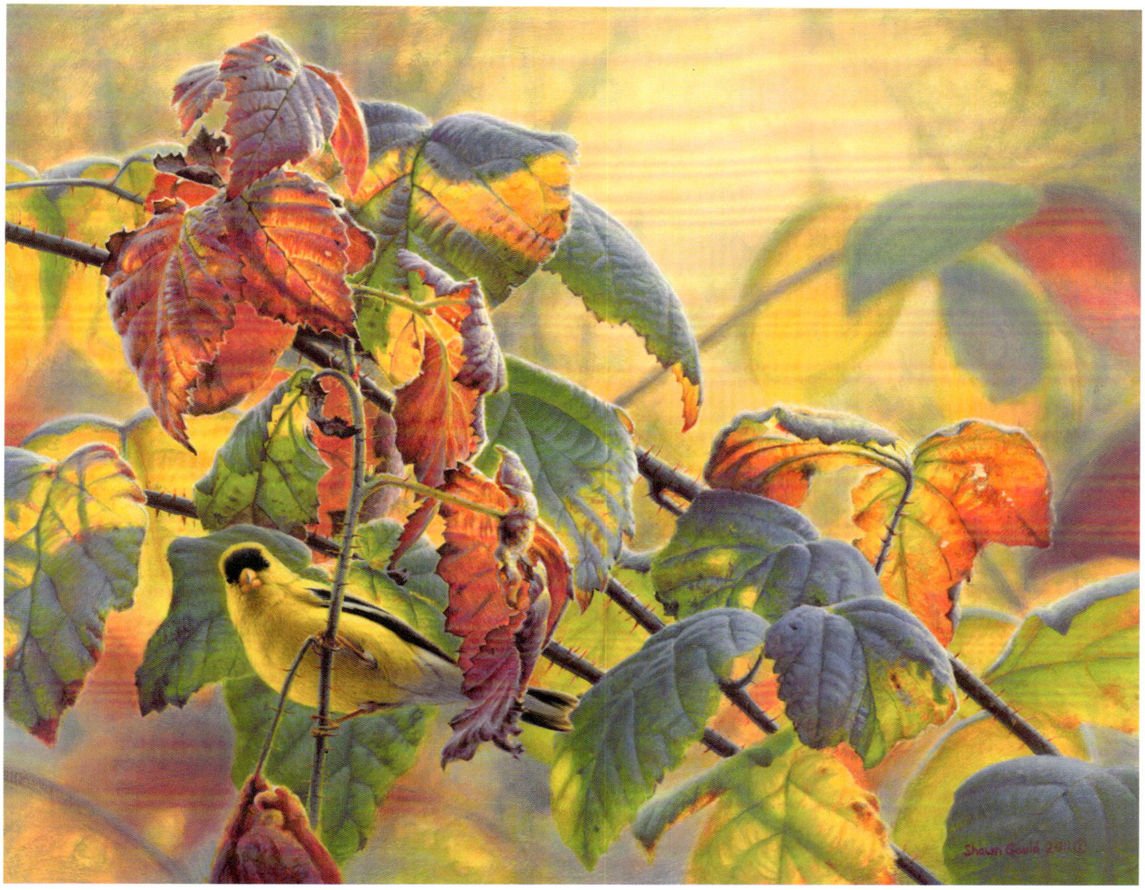

Chihuly's Garden, 2011
American goldfinch
Acrylic on hardboard
16 x 20

Collection of the artist

Birds in Art: 2007-08

BORN: 1974, United States
RESIDES: Eureka, California
EDUCATION: B.A., Iowa State University, Ames
EXHIBITIONS: Journeys West Gallery, 2010, San Diego; Piante Gallery, 2010, Eureka; *Art and the Animal,* 2010, San Diego Natural History Museum, and 2011, Dennos Museum Center, Northwestern Michigan College, Traverse City; *Art of the Animal Kingdom,* 2010-11, Bennington Center for the Arts, Bennington, Vermont; Morris Graves Museum of Art, 2012, Eureka
AWARDS: Best of Painting, 2010, *Redwood Art Association Spring Exhibition,* and Honorable Mention, 2010, *Humboldt Arts Council Members Exhibition,* Morris Graves Museum of Art
COLLECTIONS: Evergreen Federal Bank, Grants Pass, Oregon
BIBLIOGRAPHY: "Untamed Art," *Western Art Collector,* February 2010
REPRESENTATIVES: Big Horn Galleries, Cody, Wyoming; Sewell Gallery, Eureka

A few years ago I saw a large Dale Chihuly glass installation and was mesmerized by the play of light as it passed over and through the various highly colored forms. The experience changed both the way I look at nature and how I think about color and light in my own work. I now seek out situations where sunlight creates a kaleidoscope of color as, in this case, it passes through a bramble of old blackberry leaves.

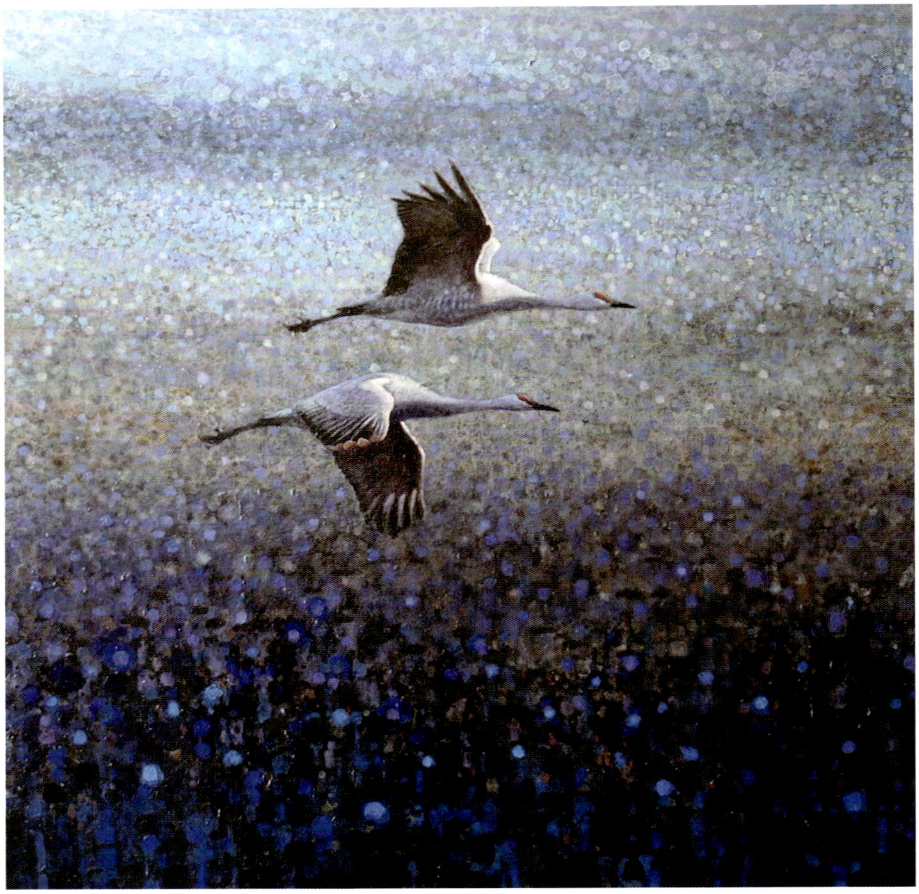

Two Sandhills, 2012
Sandhill crane
Oil on linen
43 x 43

Collection of the artist

Birds in Art: 2002-03, 2005-09, 2011

W

BORN: 1969, Netherlands
RESIDES: Egmond aan Zee, Netherlands
EDUCATION: B.F.A., Academie Minerva, Groningen
EXHIBITIONS: *Contemporary Naturalism,* 2010, and *Reflective Nature,* 2012, Gerald Peters Gallery, Santa Fe, New Mexico
COLLECTIONS: International Council for the Exploration of the Sea, Copenhagen; Rijkswaterstaat, The Hague
BIBLIOGRAPHY: "Contemporary Naturalism," July 2010, and "Flight Patterns," September 2010, *Western Art Collector;* "Ewoud de Groot Paints Alla Prima!," *Western Art and Architecture,* June/July 2012
REPRESENTATIVES: Astoria Fine Art, Jackson, Wyoming; Gerald Peters Gallery; Visions West Gallery, Bozeman, Montana, and Denver

Fishing on the Shields River near Livingston, Montana, I saw several pairs of magnificent sandhill cranes flying from one meadow to another. While I've portrayed many sandhills, they have always been standing, not flying. In an earlier spoonbill painting, I presented a 'layered' landscape, actually quite abstract, with two birds flying in the center. I used the same concept here, stacking layers of landscape and painting in an impressionistic, minimal style using complementary colors. The realistic birds are a contrast to the landscape as well as an enhancement.

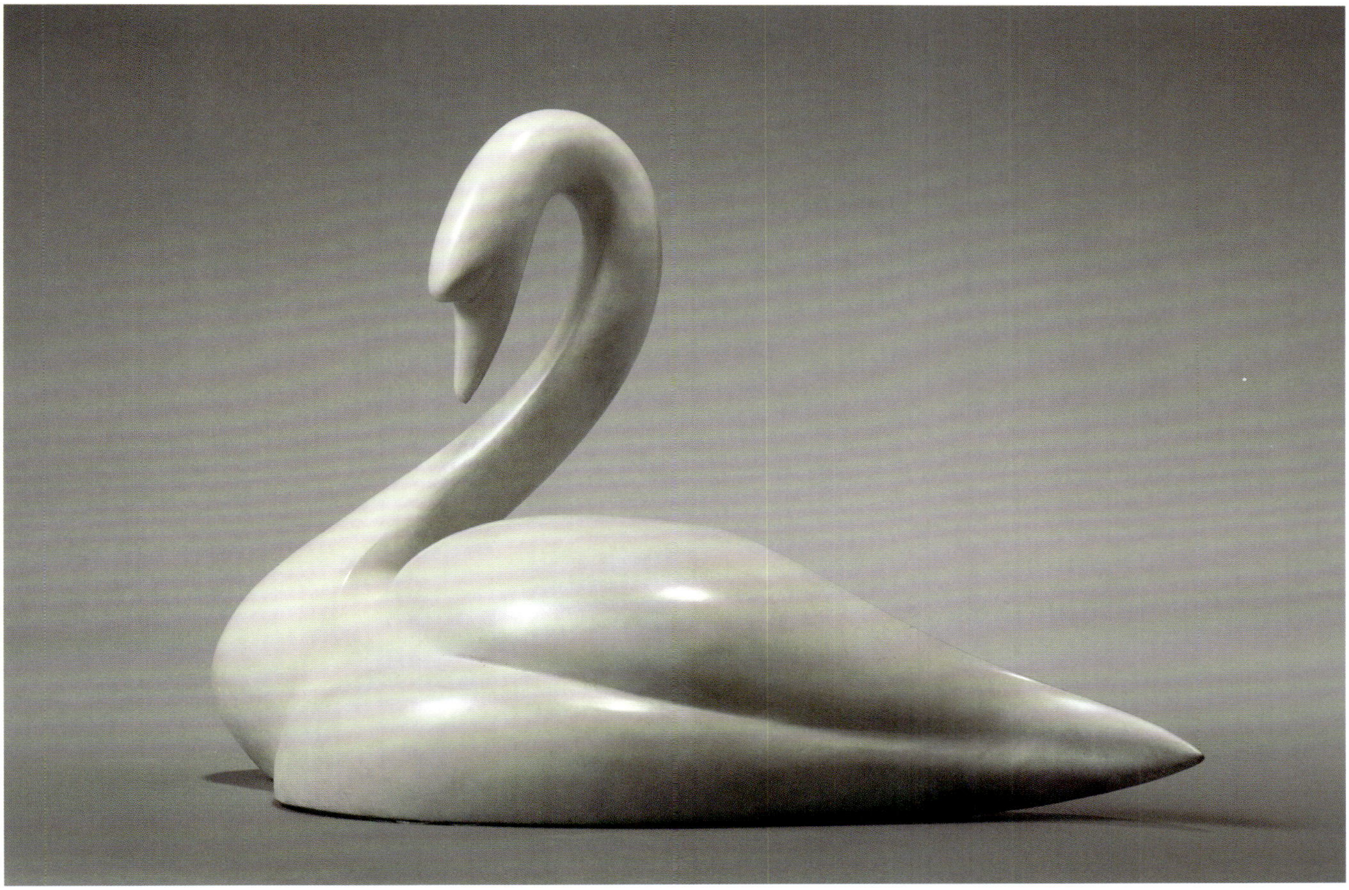

Swan (ed. 9), 2012
Bronze
10 1/2 x 18 x 7

Collection of the artist

Birds in Art: 2005-07, 2009-11

W

BORN: 1958, England
RESIDES: Pallington, Dorset, England
EXHIBITIONS: Halcyon Gallery, 2010-12, London; *Art and the Animal,* 2010, San Diego Natural History Museum, and 2012, Hiram Blauvelt Art Museum, Oradell, New Jersey; *Art and the Landscape,* 2011, Halcyon Gallery; Sculpture by the Lake, 2011, Pallington
COLLECTIONS: Duke of Bedford, Woburn Abbey, Bedfordshire; Duke of Northumberland; HRH The Duke of Edinburgh
COMMISSIONS: National Museum of Wildlife Art, Jackson, Wyoming; Royal Parks Foundation, London
BIBLIOGRAPHY: "Catching Up with the Past: Simon Gudgeon," *Wildscape,* March 2010; "An Interview with Simon Gudgeon," and "A Meditation on Wildlife Art," October 2010 and "An Interview with UK Sculptor Simon Gudgeon," May 2012, *Wildlife Art Journal* OL; *Sculpture by the Lakes,* Halcyon Gallery, 2011; "Inside-Out," *Western Art Collector,* July 2012
REPRESENTATIVES: Halcyon Gallery

My home is a regular haunt for many birds, including the graceful swan, which seemed a natural choice to complement the increasing tendency toward abstraction emerging in my work. I wanted to explore a variety of elements that suited the swan: flow, sensuous vitality, and visual movement. Henry Moore's reclining figures exemplify the movement I was seeking, especially the relationship between figure and landscape. The swan shares many similarities with the female form as demonstrated by the flowing lines and surfaces I achieved.

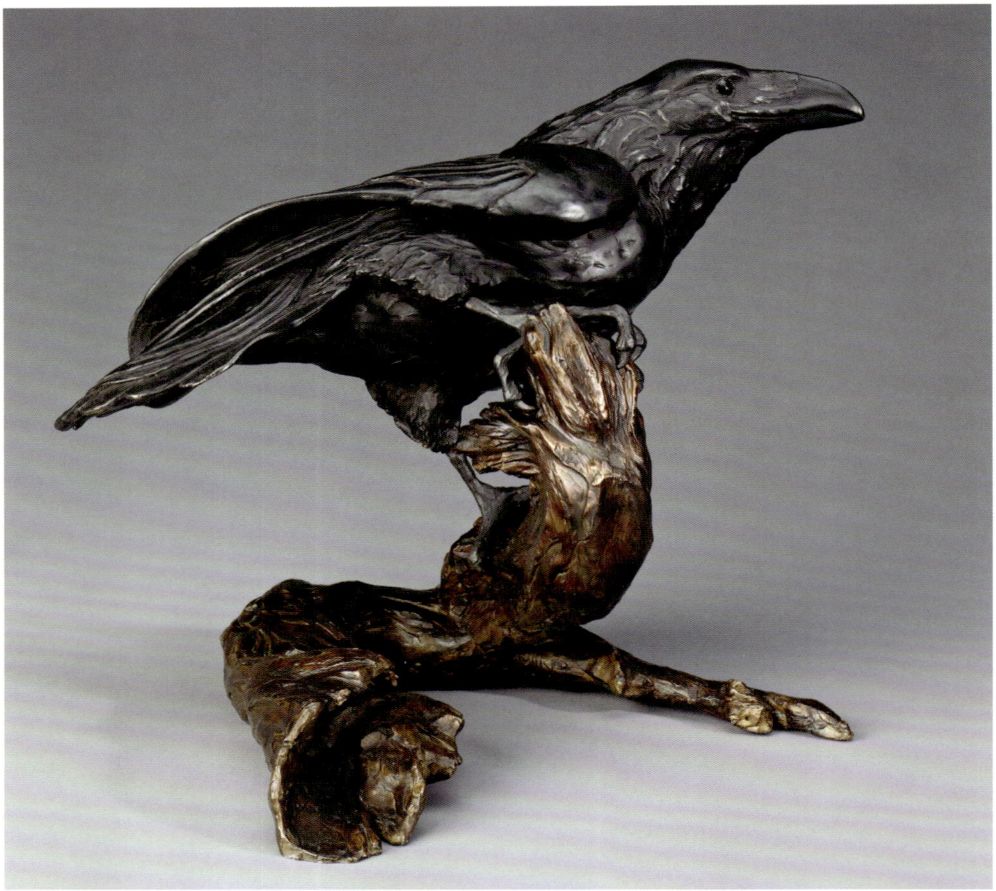

Guinevere (ed. 8), 2011
Common raven
Bronze
12 x 17 x 11

Collection of the artist

BORN: 1967, United States
RESIDES: Durango, Colorado
EDUCATION: B.A., Fort Lewis College, Durango
COLLECTIONS: Durango Discovery Museum
REPRESENTATIVES: Karyn Gabaldon Fine Art, Durango; Studio 150, Salida, Colorado

Guinevere *started out as* Trouble, *and her first perch, a real rock. My reference was a raven about to take flight from a rock in the Utah desert. As I watched, the bird started to spread its wings and slipped, regaining composure with such panache it was as if the raven had intended the display. After many engineering standoffs with the armature and stance, I gave her a stable branch to perch on. While* Trouble *seemed appropriate, a strong-willed, feminine name – Guinevere – won out.*

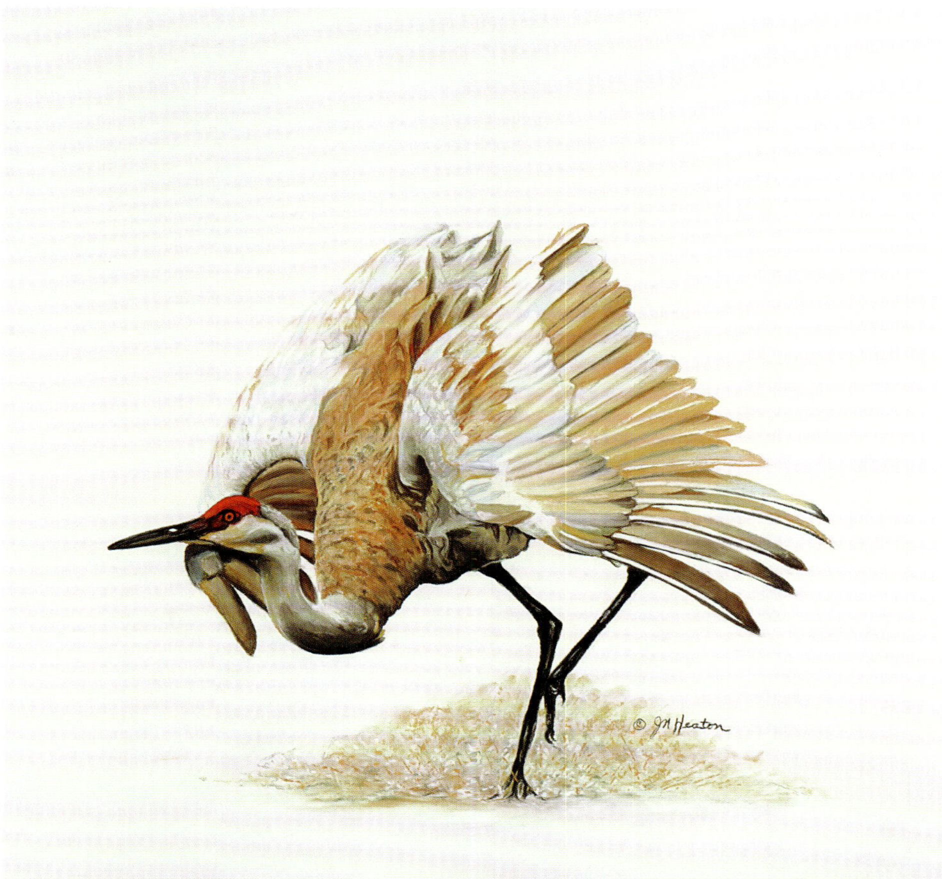

An Elegant Display, 2012
Sandhill crane
Chalk pastel on
Schoellershammer rag board
29 x 28

Collection of
Mr. and Mrs. John O'Rourke

Birds in Art: 1988, 1990-93, 1995-97, 1999-02, 2006-09

W

BORN: 1936, United States
RESIDES: West Palm Beach, Florida
EXHIBITIONS: *Survey of Transportation in Art,* 2010, Midtown Payson Gallery, Hobe Sound, Florida; *Art and the Animal,* 2011, Dennos Museum Center, Northwestern Michigan College, Traverse City
BIBLIOGRAPHY: *Vanishing Circles: Portraits of Disappearing Wildlife of the Sonoran Desert Region,* Arizona-Sonora Desert Museum Press, 2011

The dancing ritual of mating sandhill cranes is a spectacular sight that allows me to see magnificent feathers not visible at other times of the year. Underneath the wings are hundreds of small feathers that are essential for flight and protection for the underbody of the bird. During the courtship display, the top feathers rise and become enormous, appearing distorted in comparison to the bird's normally smooth, lustrous frame. It's a sight to behold.

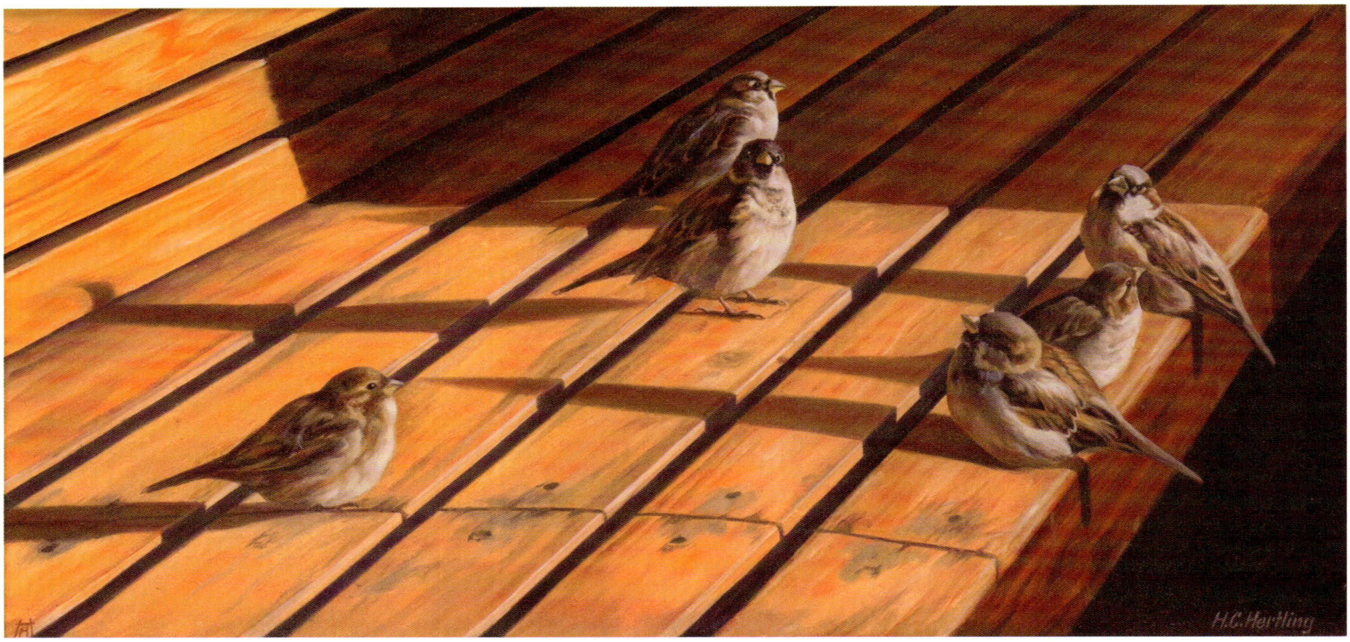

Benched, 2011
House sparrow
Oil on canvas
15 x 30

Private collection

Birds in Art: 1983, 1985-86, 2003

BORN: 1940, Germany
RESIDES: Milford, Michigan

I often find unexpected encounters with birds to be the most rewarding; Benched *is a successful example. Strolling through Boise, Idaho, while visiting my daughter, I saw these opportunistic house sparrows hanging around an outdoor restaurant. With forty years of experience as an illustrator, the graphic elements of the boards and the shadows appealed to me. I especially liked the contrast between the hard surfaces and the fluffy house sparrows – the worker bees of the bird world.*

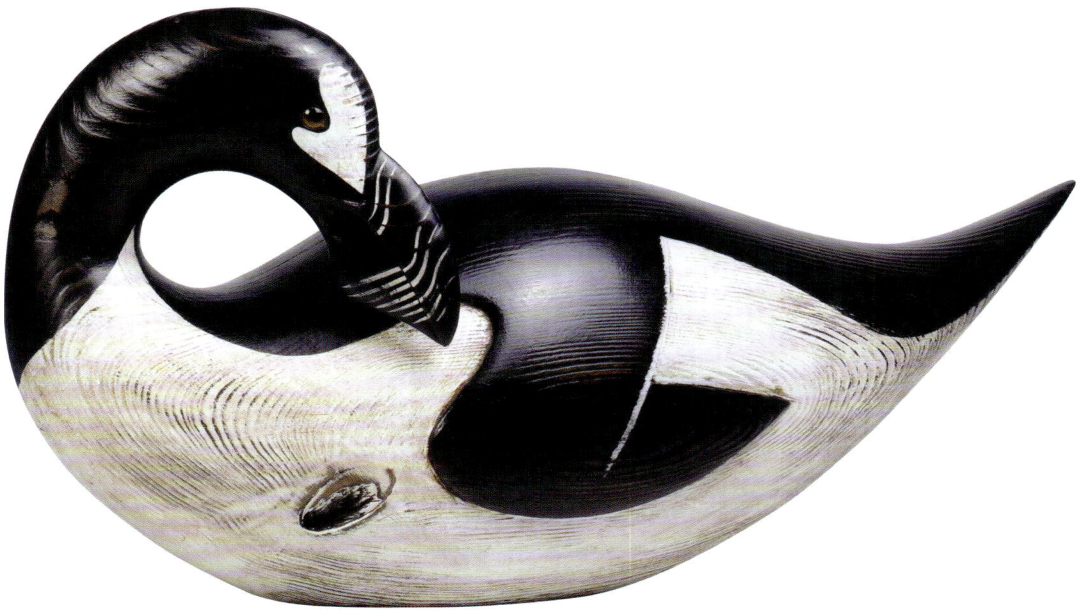

Great Auk, 2011
Painted pine
10 x 21 x 8

Collection of the artist

BORN: 1958, England
RESIDES: Oakmere, Cheshire, England
EXHIBITIONS: *National Exhibition of Wildlife Art,* 2011, Gordale Garden Centre, Burton, South Wirral; *Society of Wildlife Artists,* 2011 and *Wildlife Artist of the Year,* 2012, Mall Galleries, London
AWARDS: Best Interpretive, 2010, *British Decoy and Wildfowl Carving,* Bakewell Centre, Bakewell, Derbyshire Gold Citation, Best Sculpture, 2010, *Wildlife Art Society International,* Nature in Art, Twigworth, Gloucester; Highly Commenced, 2011, *Wildlife Artist of the Year*
BIBLIOGRAPHY: "Carve a Goldeneye Decoy," May 2011, and "Carve a Passenger Pigeon," July 2011, *GMC/Woodcarving Magazine*

With a keen awareness of Earth's plight and a need for the conservation of both habitats and species, it's obvious to me that to plan for the future we need to learn lessons from the past. The great auk is a symbol of extinction – a beautiful creature which, like many of today's endangered birds and other animals, was abused by humans and whose demise was a direct result of our interference. In keeping with my environmental beliefs, I carve birds from reclaimed pine sourced from demolition yards. Knots and grain patterns add character to the finished piece, which I design and carve to be both contemporary in content and reflective of a time gone by.

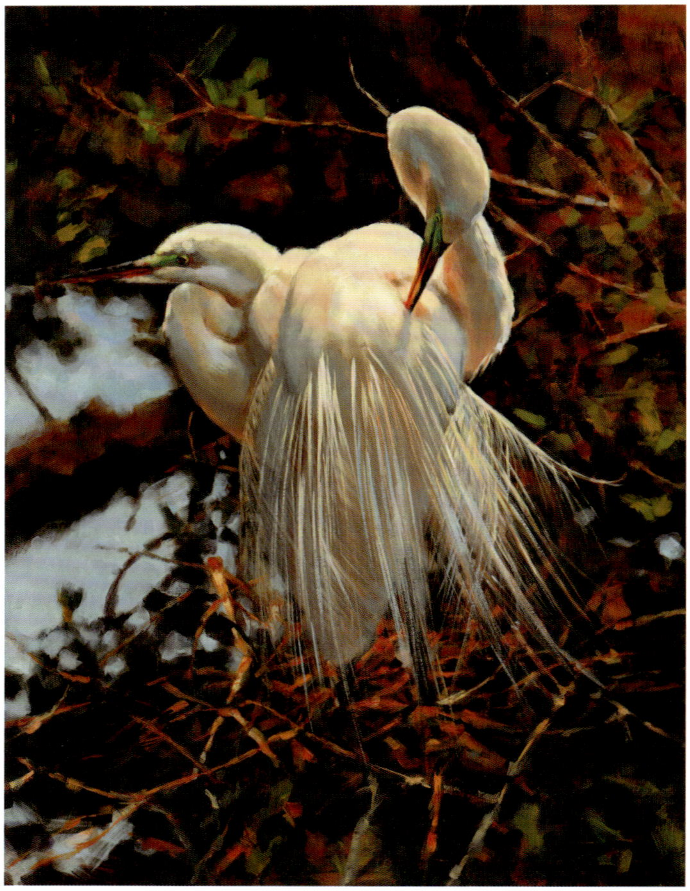

Two of a Kind, 2011
Great egret
Acrylic on canvas
40 x 30

Collection of the artist

BORN: 1954, United States
RESIDES: Mishawaka, Indiana
EXHIBITIONS: *U.S. Coast Guard Art Program Exhibition,* 2011, Salmagundi Club, New York City; *The Art of Trees,* 2012, Corse Gallery & Atelier, Jacksonville, Florida; *Lake, Legends, and Landscapes,* 2012, 3 Pillars Gallery, Benton Harbor, Michigan
AWARDS: First Place, 2011, *Portrait and Figure Show,* Best in Show, 2011, *Fantastic Florida,* and First Place, 2011, *Spring Members Show,* Saint Augustine Art Association, Saint Augustine, Florida; U.S. Public Service Award, 2011, U.S. Coast Guard, Washington
COLLECTIONS: NTE Energy, Saint Augustine
COMMISSIONS: Memorial Hospital of South Bend, South Bend, Indiana
REPRESENTATIVES: Corse Gallery & Atelier

I watched this breeding pair of great egrets in a rookery near Saint Augustine. To me they seemed like graceful dancers, with their arched necks and sense of satisfied, quiet composure as they groomed and posed. I worked the color to evoke the warm, brilliant light of the Florida sun, and used deliberate, clean brush strokes to achieve a fresh, painterly result.

Cindy House

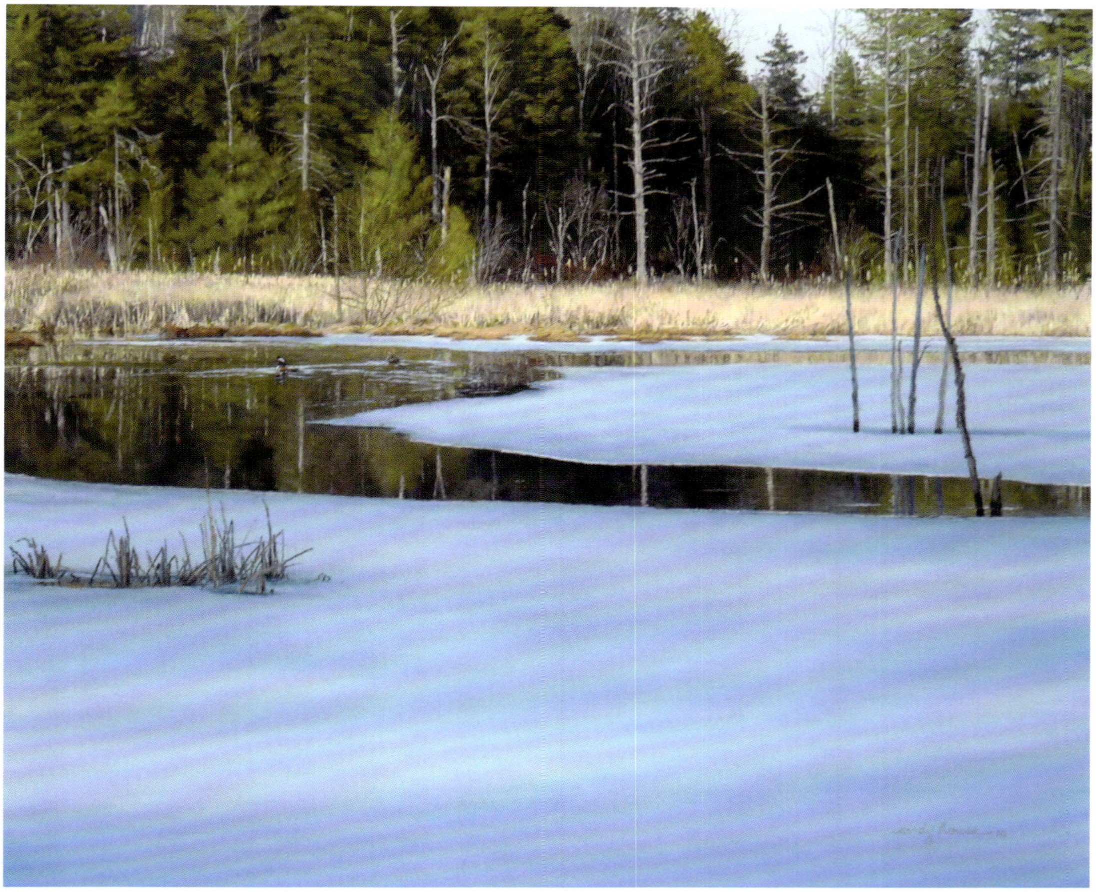

Spring Thaw, 2010
Hooded merganser
Pastel on Wallis sanded paper
9 x 12

Collection of the artist

Birds in Art: 1981, 1984-85, 1987, 1989, 1996-07, 2009-11

W

BORN: 1952, United States
RESIDES: Warner, New Hampshire
EDUCATION: B.S., University of Maine, Orono
EXHIBITIONS: *Each One Invites One,* 2011, McBride Gallery, Annapolis, Maryland; *Today's Legacy,* 2011 and *The Pastelists,* 2012, Bryan Memorial Gallery, Jeffersonville, Vermont; *Landscapes for Landsake,* 2012, Aubson Sargent Land Trust, New London, New Hampshire; *Enduring Brilliance: The Pastel Society of America at 40,* 2012, Noyes Museum of Art, Oceanville, New Jersey
AWARDS: Bronze Medal, 2010, *Annual Regional Juried Exhibition,* Guild of Boston Artists; Director's Choice/First Place, 2010, *Almost Miniatures,* Francesca Anderson Fine Art, Lexington, Massachusetts; First Place and Honorable Mention, Landscapes and Interiors, 2012, *The Pastel Journal*
COLLECTIONS: Mass Audubon Visual Arts Center, Canton, Massachusetts
BIBLIOGRAPHY: "Outdoor Palette," *Northern Woodlands,* Summer 2011; *Art Journey America, Landscapes,* North Light Books, 2011
REPRESENTATIVES: Cooley Gallery, Old Lyme, Connecticut; Haley & Steele Gallery, Boston; Haynes Galleries, Nashville

After a long New Hampshire winter, it's always a delight to wake up to a day I would refer to as 'downright balmy' – in the mid-fifties. While I consider myself a studio artist, on this particular day, a friend and I couldn't resist going outdoors to paint. At Chadwick Meadows Wildlife Area, ice was beginning to melt and the open water allowed waterfowl to gather. Ribbons of water enhanced by the shadows across the ice created interesting compositions. We saw several species of waterfowl; I chose to depict one of my favorites, hooded mergansers.

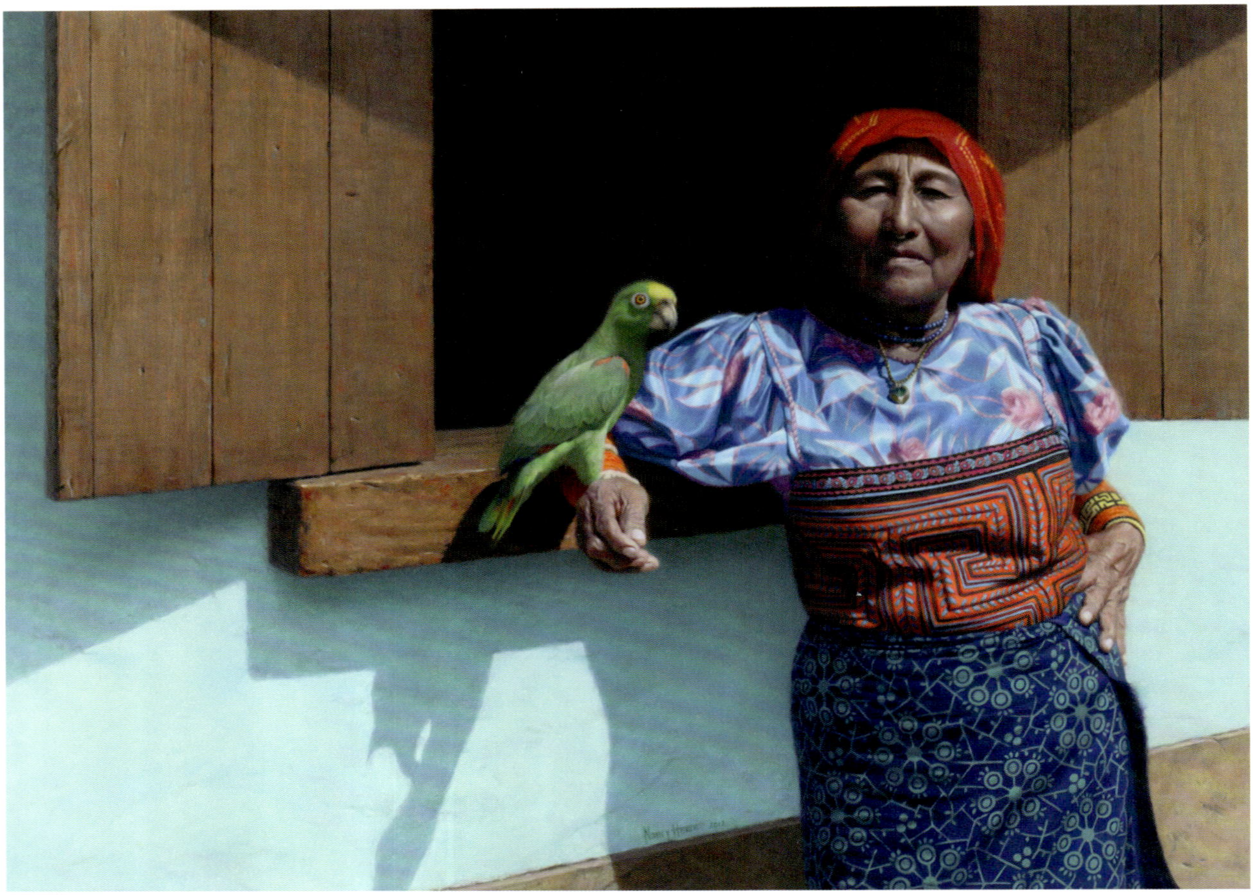

Unruffled, 2012
Yellow-crowned Amazon parrot
Oil on Belgian linen
22 x 30

Collection of the artist

Birds in Art: 1991, 1993-96, 1998-11
Master Wildlife Artist: 2005

W

BORN: 1950, United States
RESIDES: East Dorset, Vermont
EDUCATION: A.B., Middlebury College, Middlebury, Vermont
EXHIBITIONS: *International Masters of Fine Art,* 2010-11, Greenhouse Gallery of Fine Art, San Antonio; *Art and the Animal,* 2010, San Diego Natural History Museum, and 2011, Dennos Museum Center, Northwestern Michigan College, Traverse City; *Oil Painters of America,* 2010, Legacy Gallery, Scottsdale, Arizona, and 2011, Devin Galleries, Coeur d'Alene, Idaho; *Art of the Animal Kingdom,* 2010 and 2012, Bennington Center for the Arts, Bennington, Vermont; *Scottsdale Salon of Fine Art,* 2011, Legacy Gallery
AWARDS: Award of Recognition, 2010, *American Women Artists Master Signature Exhibition,* Southwest Gallery, Dallas; Award of Excellence, 2011, *Oil Painters of America Eastern Regional Exhibition,* Addison Galleries, Orleans, Massachusetts
COLLECTIONS: Bennington Center for the Arts; National Museum of Wildlife Art, Jackson, Wyoming

Unruffled *references the posture and attitude of both the Kuna Indian woman of Panama and her Amazon parrot. This portrait speaks to the self-confidence and character strength of these semi-autonomous indigenous people, for which family structure is matrilineal. Girls are the center of attention in households and considered gifts from Father God and Mother Earth. This status helps women develop a positive and powerful self-image clearly visible in their conduct and demeanor.* Unruffled *is part of my cultural project, 'Painting a Brighter Future for Women,' which has benefited women around the globe since 2007.*

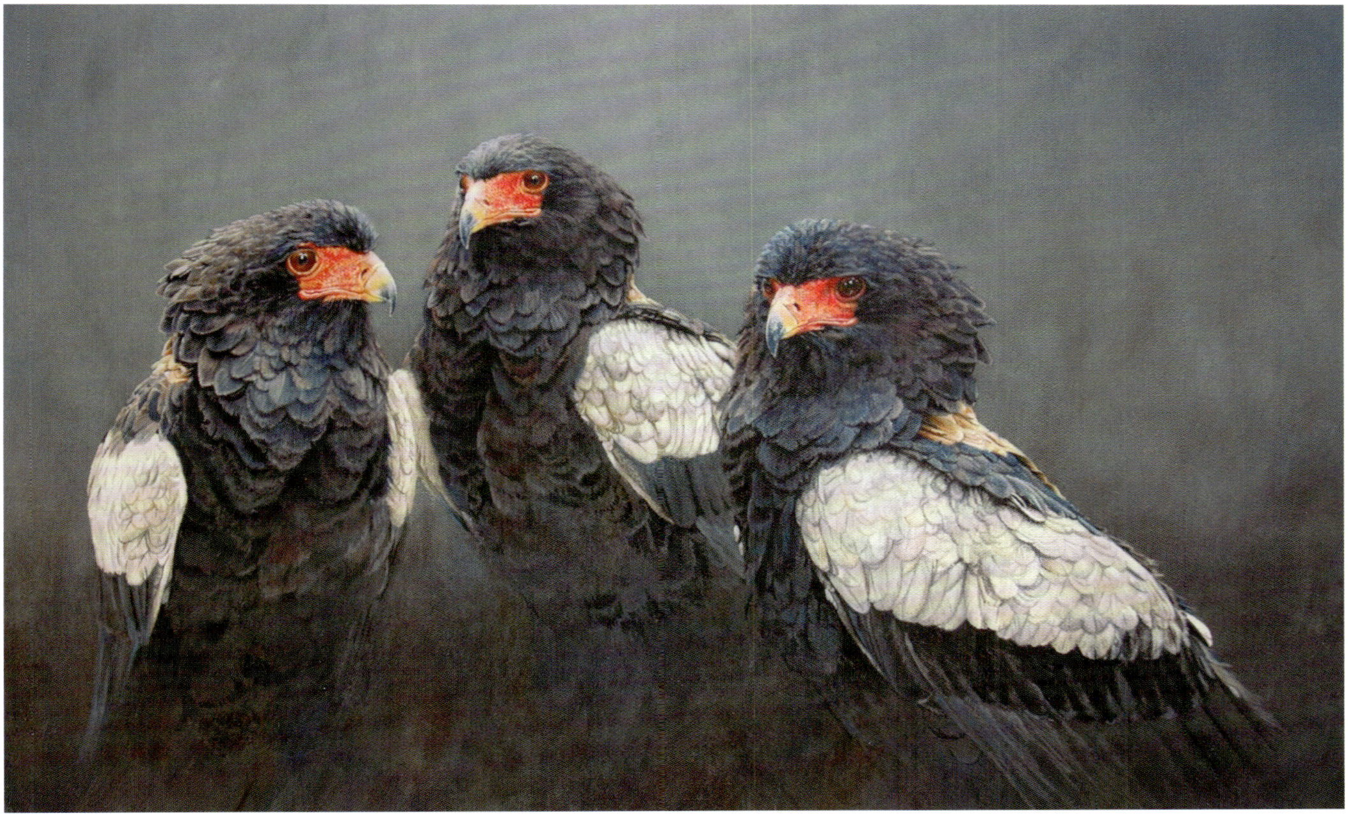

Bateleurs of Maun, 2010
Bateleur eagle
Acrylic on canvas
14 3/4 x 22

Collection of the artist

Birds in Art: 2008-11

W

BORN: 1955, South Africa
RESIDES: Magaliesburg, Gauteng, South Africa
EDUCATION: Graphic Design Diploma, Johannesburg College of Art, Johannesburg
EXHIBITIONS: *Wild in de Natuur,* 2010, Kunsthuis van het Oosten, Enschede, Netherlands; *Art for Survival,* 2010-11, and *Wildlife Artist of the Year,* 2011, Mall Galleries, London
AWARDS: High Commended, 2010, *Wildlife Artist of the Year*
COLLECTIONS: South African National Biodiversity Institute, Pretoria
BIBLIOGRAPHY: *Flowering Plants of Africa,* South African National Biodiversity Institute, 2011; *Penroc Seeds and Plants,* November 2011 – February 2012 OL
REPRESENTATIVES: Cape Gallery, Cape Town; Everard Read Gallery, Johannesburg

On a trip to Maun, Botswana, we visited friends who had a magnificent male bateleur eagle in a large cage. I went inside the cage with the owner and crept closer and closer to photograph the bird. Whenever I got too close, the bird raised all his feathers to enhance his size and stature. This made him look so beautiful that I couldn't wait to get home and into the studio. I didn't want to paint just one image, as I had fallen in love with the bird's many moods. Eventually, three images made for the best composition. Bateleurs are stately looking creatures; with three birds together, they took on the appearance of rather distinguished-looking gentlemen, squires of their estates. This, in turn, prompted my mother to give the painting its title, Bateleurs of Maun.

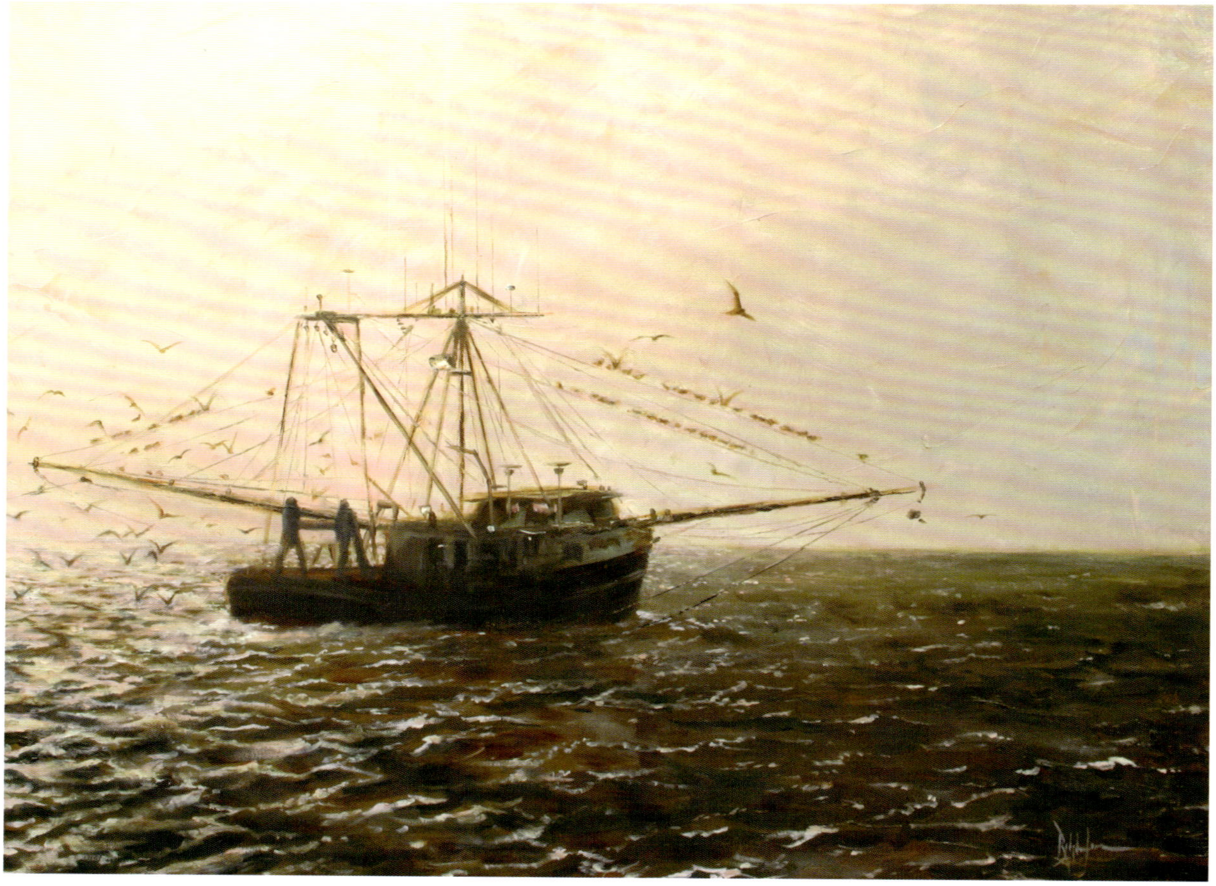

Trawling with the Gulls,
2012
Oil on linen
18 x 24

Collection of the artist

Birds in Art: 2009, 2011

W

BORN: 1957, United States
RESIDES: Mocksville, North Carolina
EXHIBITIONS: *Paint the Parks 100,* 2010, Jefferson National Expansion Memorial, Saint Louis; *American Impressionist Society,* 2010, Richland Fine Art, Nashville; *Salon International,* 2010-11, Greenhouse Gallery of Fine Art, San Antonio; North Carolina Museum of Natural Sciences, 2011, Raleigh; Edward Dare Gallery, 2011, Charleston, South Carolina
AWARDS: Honorable Mention, 2011, *Laumesiter Fine Art Competition,* Bennington Center for the Arts, Bennington, Vermont
COLLECTIONS: North Carolina Museum of Natural Sciences
BIBLIOGRAPHY: "An Artistic Journey," *Winston-Salem Monthly,* July 2011; "22nd Anniversary Show: Howard/Mandville Gallery," *Southwest Art,* June 2012
REPRESENTATIVES: Edward Dare Gallery; Germanton Gallery, Germanton, North Carolina; Howard/Mandville Gallery, Kirkland, Washington

On North Carolina's Outer Banks lies Ocracoke Island, a birding paradise. The ferry from Swan Quarter to Ocracoke takes more than two hours to cross Pamlico Sound. On the last trip of the day, a passing shrimp trawler is transformed by light and salt spray. Gulls following the shrimp boats are as much a part of the trawler as the nets on the boat. Relentless beggars, they look for bits of food as they play out their daily survival game. Today, America's shrimp trawlers face difficult times. Some have not withstood the pressure of increasing overseas competition. Sadly, we'll likely see fewer of these grand old boats and the gulls that accompany them.

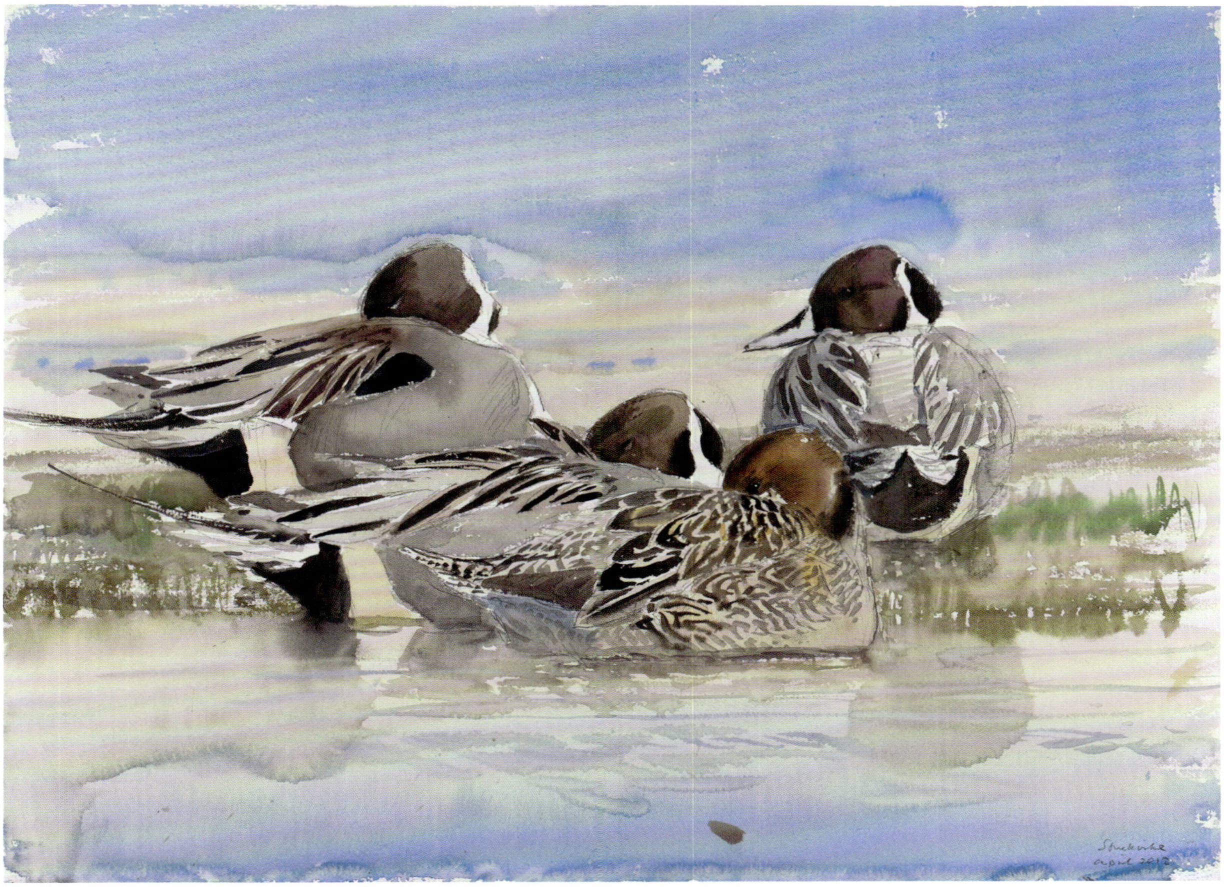

Spring Pintails, 2012
Northern pintail
Watercolor on Arches paper
23 x 30 1/2

Collection of the artist

Birds in Art: 1982-11
Master Wildlife Artist: 1988

W

BORN: 1952, Sweden
RESIDES: Burgsvik, Gotland, Sweden
EXHIBITIONS: Kulturhuset, 2010, Stockholm; Skövde Art Museum, 2010, Skövde; *Brutus Östling och Lars Jonsson: Ringmärkt,* 2010, Kulturhuset; Galleri 316, 2011, Hudiksvalls Konstgille; Sundre Arts, 2011, Gotland; *Works on Paper,* 2012, Gerald Peters Gallery, Santa Fe, New Mexico; *Artists for Nature Jubilee,* 2012, Orangerie Landgoed Vollenhoven, De Bilt, Netherlands
AWARDS: Award of Excellence, 2010, *Art and the Animal,* San Diego Natural History Museum
COLLECTIONS: Gotland Museum of Art, Visby; Mass Audubon Visual Arts Center, Canton, Massachusetts; National Museum of Wildlife Art, Jackson, Wyoming; Skövde Art Museum; Swedish Museum of Natural History, Stockholm
REPRESENTATIVES: Gerald Peters Gallery

My local birding area has a freshwater lake that sometimes gets flooded by the sea. In spring, ducks on their way north stop in this brackish water for a few weeks. Small gatherings of pintails are common in April, especially with so many clear, sunny days and frostbitten nights. Early one morning, I watched as the ducks rested, waiting for the thin layer of overnight ice to disappear. It was as if the pintails were sitting still just for me to paint.

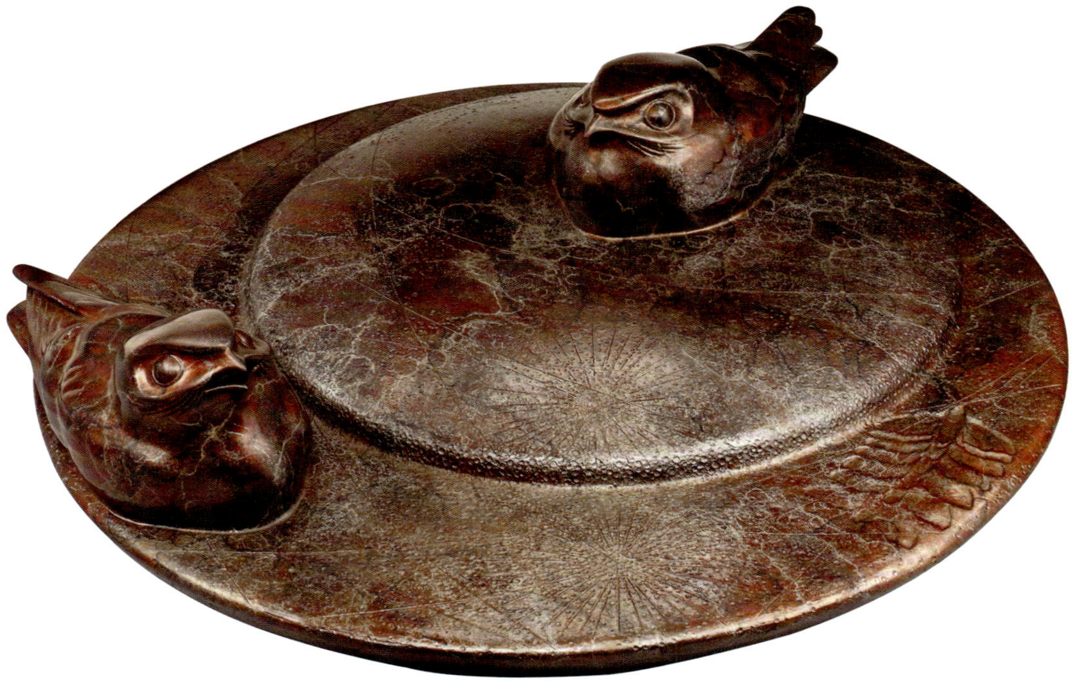

A Map of the Nightjar's Heart (ed. 36), 2011
Common poorwill
Bronze
6 x 18 x 18

Collection of Cindi Kestrel

Birds in Art: 1985, 1988, 1990, 1993, 2000, 2003, 2007, 2011

W

BORN: 1947, United States
RESIDES: Loveland, Colorado
EXHIBITIONS: *Prix de West Invitational,* 2010-12, National Cowboy & Western Heritage Museum, Oklahoma City; *Cold-Blooded Art: Reptiles, Amphibians, Fish, and Insects,* 2011, and *Out of the Wild: Animals in Sculpture,* 2011, Brookgreen Gardens, Murrells Inlet, South Carolina; *Romantic Contours, Modern Terrain,* 2011, Gerald Peters Gallery, Santa Fe, New Mexico; *Wild West: Beauty of the Beast,* 2011, Rockwell Museum of Western Art, Corning, New York; *Rendezvous Reunion,* 2012, Gilcrease Museum, Tulsa, Oklahoma
AWARDS: Gold Medal, Sculpture, 2011, *West Select,* Phoenix Art Museum; Featured Artist, 2011, *Coors Western Art Exhibition,* Denver
COLLECTIONS: Denver Art Museum; National Museum of Wildlife Art, Jackson, Wyoming
BIBLIOGRAPHY: "Steve Kestrel, Letting Nature Lead," *Southwest Art,* January 2011
REPRESENTATIVES: Gerald Peters Gallery; James Graham & Sons, New York City; Simpson Gallagher Gallery, Cody, Wyoming

Little is known about the biology, habitat use, and population status of nightjars – a group of birds that includes the nighthawks and whippoorwills – due to their cryptic and nocturnal lifestyle. Most members of this family are on the decline, especially east of the Mississippi. I used the poorwill as a model for this piece; it's the smallest member of its family in North America and the genus name, Phalaenoptilus, *is a compound of the Greek,* phalaina, *moth, and* ptilon, *feather. I used starbursts to represent the unique genetic makeup of the family, and arcs to symbolize migration routes and the success or failure of an individual to complete the circle of life. The flying moth's short arc is in negative relief, suggesting questions about the disappearance of habitat and food sources.*

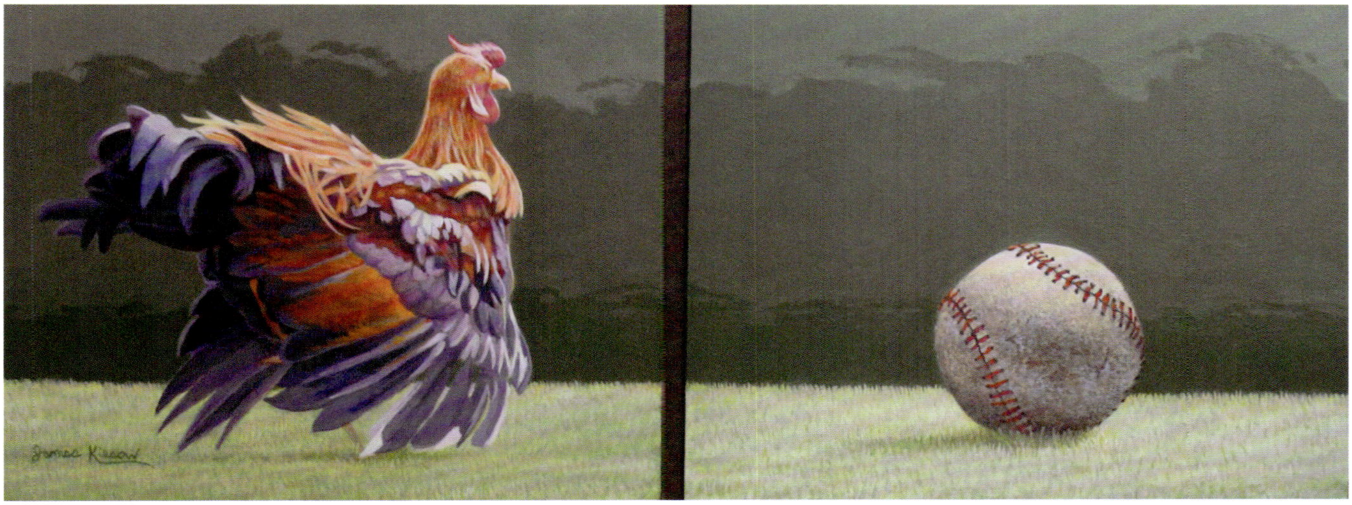

Fowl Ball, 2012
Acrylic on hardboard
8 x 10 (each)

Collection of the artist

Birds in Art: 2004

BORN: 1947, United States
RESIDES: Port Washington, Wisconsin
EXHIBITIONS: *Art and the Animal,* 2010, San Diego Natural History Museum, and 2011, Dennos Museum Center, Northwestern Michigan College, Traverse City

Fowl Ball *is a play on words. I painted the rooster first, drawn to his bright colors and his 'I am beautiful' attitude. Originally I was going to leave it at that, but as I thought about titling the painting, the word 'fowl' came to mind. As a baseball fan, 'ball' came to mind next. Painting a diptych with a baseball featured in the second painting seemed clever. Using the same background gave* Fowl Ball *a surreal feel.*

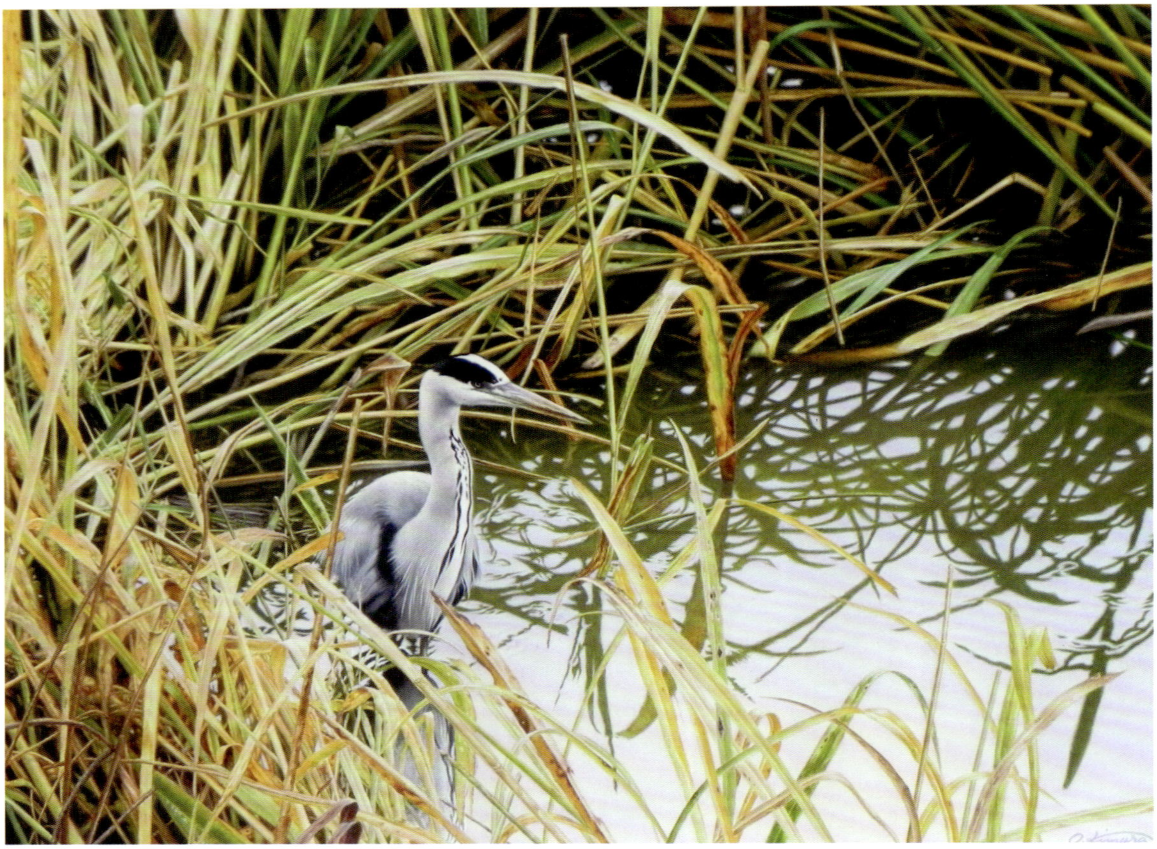

Did You Get Breakfast?, 2011
Gray heron
Acrylic on BB Kent board
11 x 15 1/2

Collection of the artist

Birds in Art: 2007-08, 2010

BORN: 1953, Japan
RESIDES: Minamitsuru-gun, Yamanashi, Japan
EDUCATION: Nippon Design College, Tokyo
EXHIBITIONS: Prince Chichibu Memorial Park Information Center, 2010-11, Gotenba City, Shizuoka; *Wildlife Art,* Yamawaki Art Gallery, 2010-11, Tokyo

I went to the Fukushima Lagoon to observe bean geese and heard their strong 'swish, swish, swish' as they took off from the water. As the sun began to rise and I reached the birdwatching hut, I saw a stately gray heron. It stood still, like a bronze statue, for more than an hour, studying the water's surface. Was the heron looking for breakfast? As I watched this bird, I grew hungry and left for my breakfast. When I returned to the hut, the heron was gone.

Eugen Kisselmann

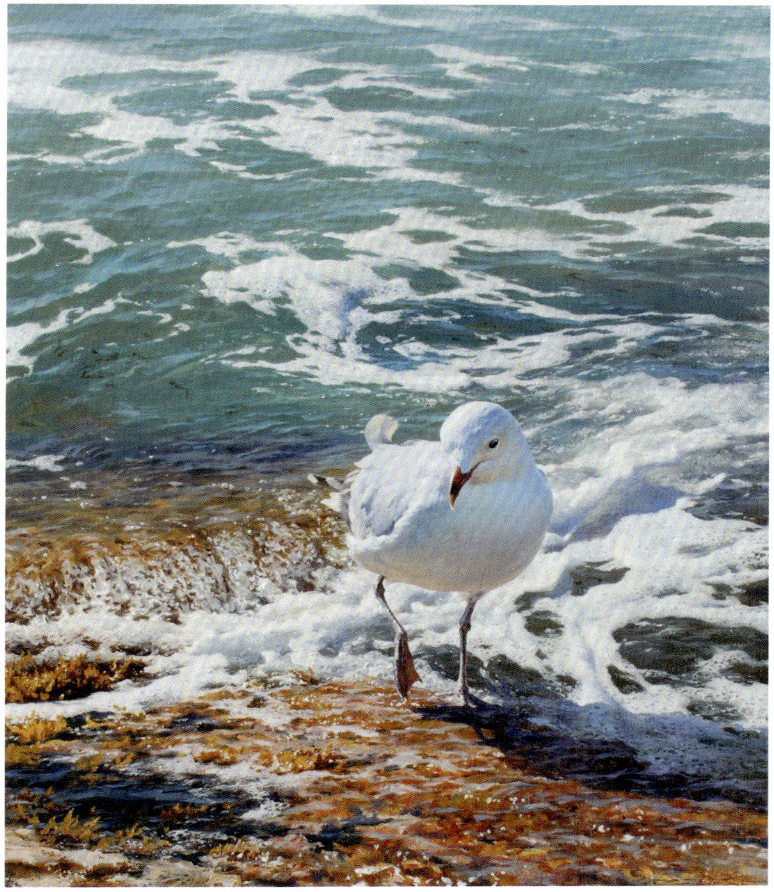

Audouin's Gull, 2012
Oil on canvas
23 1/2 x 19 3/4

Collection of the artist

Birds in Art: 2002, 2005-08

W

BORN: 1964, Russia
RESIDES: Bad Wünnenberg-Fürstenberg, Germany
EDUCATION: Novoaltaisk Art College, Barnaul, Russia
EXHIBITIONS: *Wild in de Natuur,* 2010-12, Kunsthuis van het Oosten, Enschede, Netherlands; *Silberner Uhu,* 2011, Museum Heineanum, Halberstadt
AWARDS: Audience Award, 2010, *ART & Vielfalt: Impressionen aus der Tierwelt,* Museum für Naturkunde, Magdeburg
COLLECTIONS: Kunsthuis van het Oosten

Audouin's gulls are typically shy. However, walking along the coast of Spain's Balearic Islands I observed them at close range. Each wave brings food, and during the retreating intervals the gulls quickly search for crustaceans and mussels. It's this feeding moment that I captured.

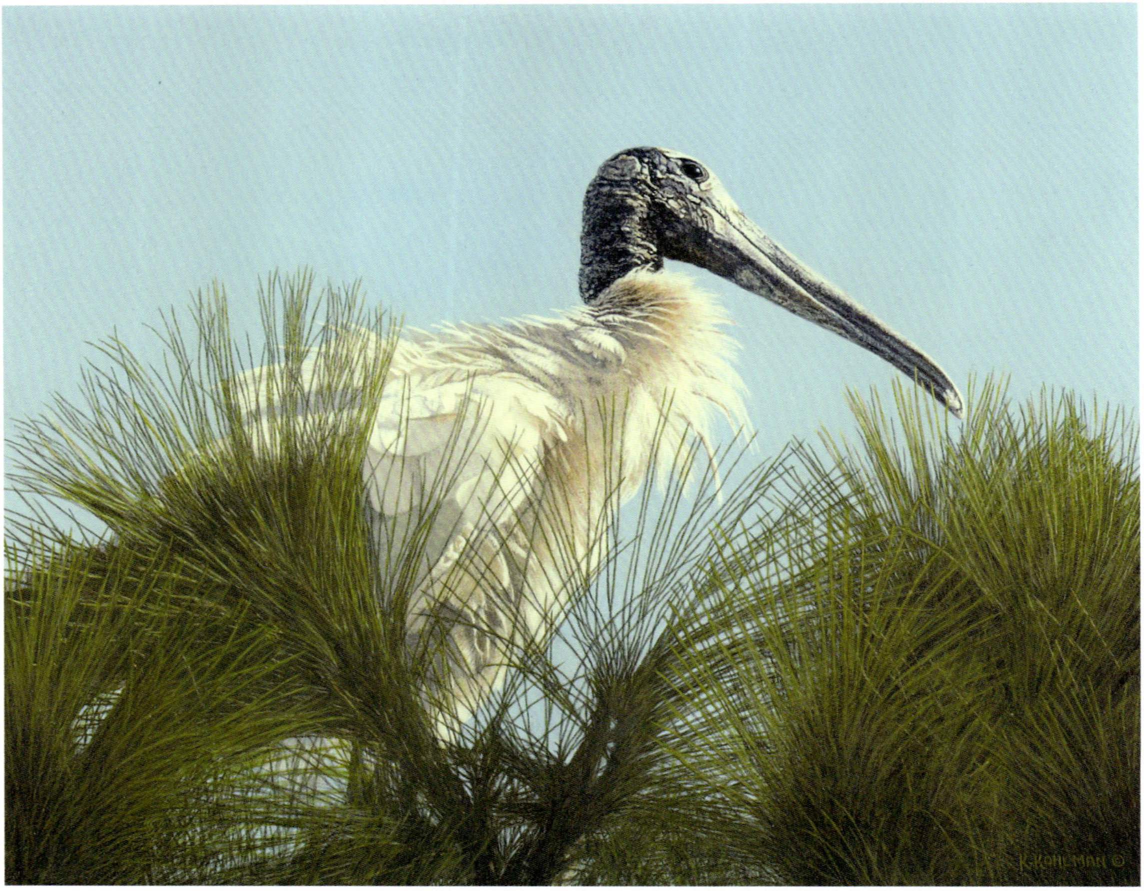

The Sun Catcher, 2011
Wood stork
Acrylic on hardboard
12 x 15

Collection of the artist

BORN: 1954, United States
RESIDES: La Crosse, Wisconsin
EDUCATION: M.M.E., University of North Texas, Denton; B.S., Minot State University, Minot, North Dakota
AWARDS: Naturalist's Favorite, 2010, Myrick Hixon EcoPark, La Crosse
REPRESENTATIVES: Gallery La Crosse

At first glance, a wood stork's beauty isn't apparent, especially because of its almost prehistoric-looking, featherless head and predominantly white feathers. However, as this unusual bird 'catches' the sunlight, a surprising array of subtle colors and contrasting textures is revealed, and its hidden beauty can be seen.

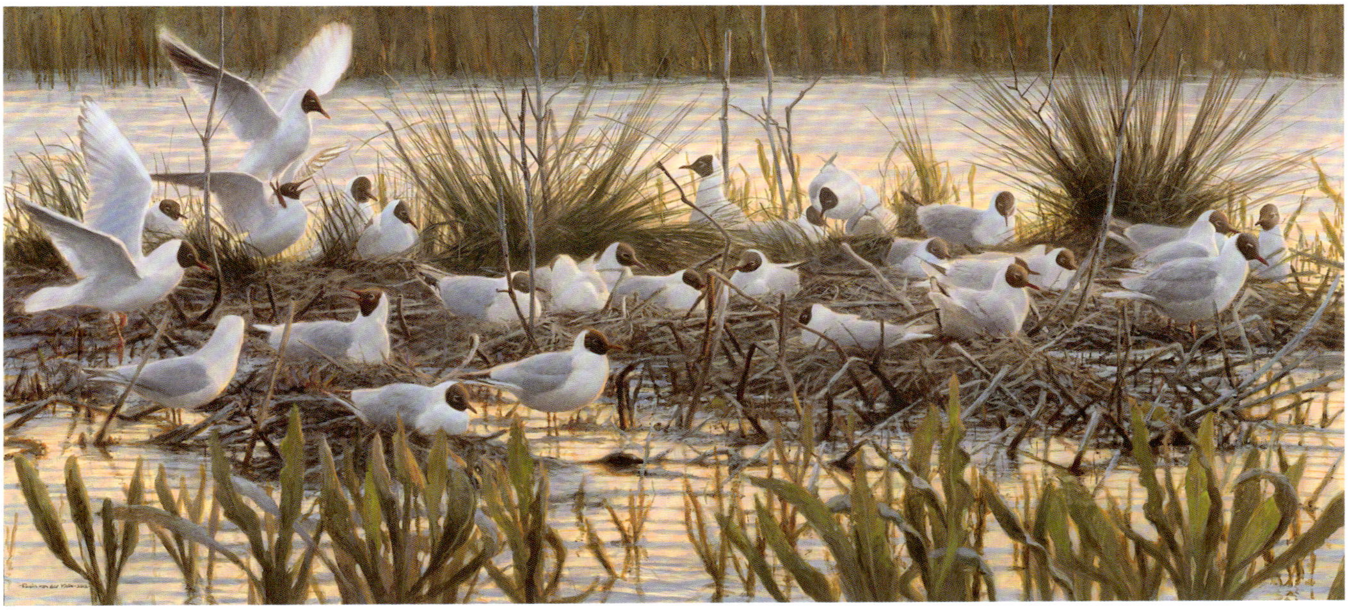

Evening Light, 2012
Black-headed gull
Acrylic on hardboard
16 1/2 x 35 1/2

Collection of the artist

Birds in Art: 2009-11

BORN: 1972, Netherlands
RESIDES: Bennekom, Netherlands
EDUCATION: B.S., Wageningen Agricultural University, Wageningen
EXHIBITIONS: *Winterlandschappen,* 2010, De Beeldenstorm, Bosschenhoofd; *Oog voor Toptalent,* 2010, Kunstgalerie Oog voor Natuur, Opheusden; *Vogels,* 2010, Galerie Het Raadhuis, Eenrum; *Wild in de Natuur,* 2010-12, Kunsthuis van het Oosten, Enschede; *Naturrlijk natuur III,* 2012, Kunstgalerie Staphorsius, Westzaan
COMMISSIONS: KNNV Uitgeverij, Zeist; SOVON Vogelonderzoek Nederland, Beek-Ubbergen; Vogelbescherming Nederland, Zeist
BIBLIOGRAPHY: *Vogelvrij,* het Vogeljaar, 2010; *Herkennings-kaart Vogels van Nederland,* Vogelbescherming/Sovon/KNNV Uitgeverij, 2012; *Kromme snavels en scherpe klauwen,* Uitgeverij Ploegsma, 2012

The black-headed gull is the most widespread species of gull in the Netherlands. You can find these birds at the shore as well as inland. I saw this breeding colony during the last minutes of daylight. The low sun turned the white and gray birds to beautiful blues, violets, and reds. In Evening Light *I tried to create unity in a busy composition by making an abstract overall pattern of dark and light horizontal bands.*

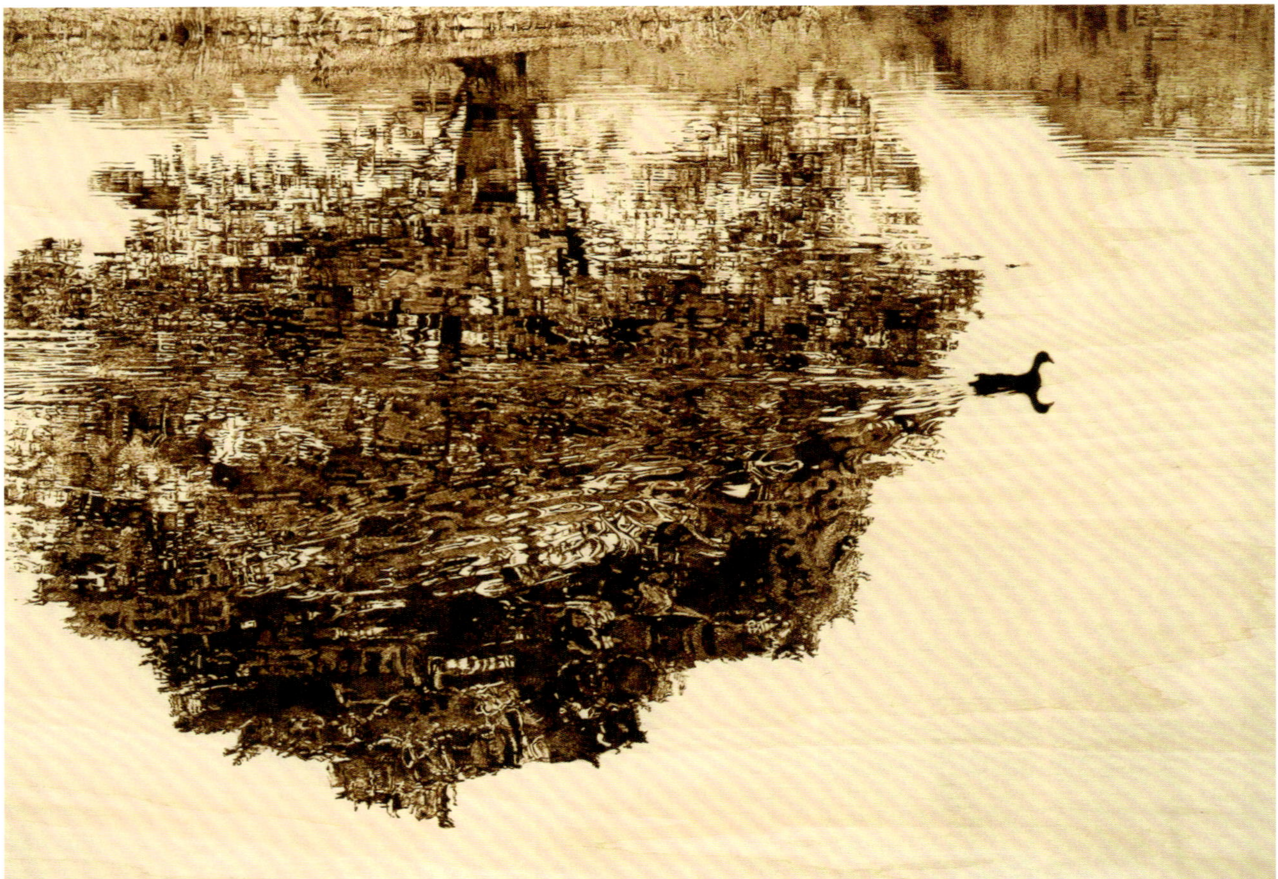

Early Summer, 2011
Coot
Pyrography on basswood
15 x 21

Collection of the artist

Birds in Art: 2007-09, 2011

W

BORN: 1949, Japan
RESIDES: Kawasaki, Kanagawa, Japan
EDUCATION: A.A., Joshibi University of Art and Design, Tokyo
EXHIBITIONS: *Three Wildlife Artists,* 2010, Ryokuinkan Gallery, Tokyo; *Carvings of the Wildbirds,* 2010, Shinjuku Gyoen Park Art Gallery, Tokyo; *Woodburning Art,* 2010, Showa Kinen Park Gallery, Tokyo; *Six Wildlife Artists,* 2012, Pearl Gallery, Tokyo; Ryokuinkan Gallery, 2012; *Birdcarvings and Woodburning Arts,* 2012, Shinjuku Gyoen Park Art Gallery

While coots are common in Japan, especially in the Tokyo suburbs, it is not easy to see these birds because they seek quiet surroundings and shy away from any sign of mankind. Early last summer, on a quiet morning walk around a small pond near my house, I noticed subtle ripples among the reflections on the water's surface. At first I did not know what caused them, but seconds later I understood. A coot swam through the backlight. The shadow of the big tree, the reflections, and the wake created a scene that conveyed a profound peace. Time slipped by casually and gently. This is what I attempted to preserve.

Zev Labinger

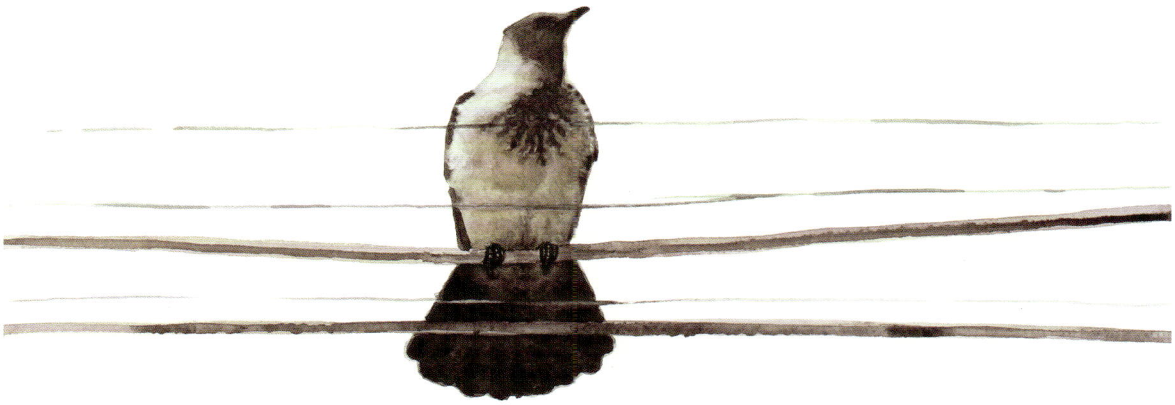

Urban Hood, 2012
Hooded crow
Watercolor on Arches paper
12 x 16

Collection of the artist

Birds in Art: 2010-11

W

BORN: 1962, United States
RESIDES: Tivon, Israel
EDUCATION: M.S., Tel Aviv University, Tel Aviv; B.S., University of California, Davis
EXHIBITIONS: *Drawing Inspiration from the Hula Valley,* 2011, Agamon Park Gallery, Upper Galilee; *Birds,* 2011, Rosh Pina Old City Museum, Rosh Pina
COLLECTIONS: Hotel Spa Mizpe Hayamim, Rosh Pina; San Marcos Foothills Coalition, Santa Barbara, California
BIBLIOGRAPHY: *Drawing Inspiration from the Hula Valley,* Society for the Protection of Nature in Israel, 2011
REPRESENTATIVES: The Well Gallery of Arts and Flavours, Rosh Pina

For many bird lovers and especially wildlife conservationists, crows are considered pests. They eat eggs of other birds, damage agricultural crops, and are particularly abundant around human population centers. I see these traits as successful adaptations of an intelligent, flexible, and opportunistic fellow creature. Crows are usually all black; however, throughout Eastern Europe and the Middle East, the predominant species is the hooded crow – a subspecies of the all-black carrion crow. Since the name hooded crow is a bit menacing, I couldn't resist the title for this watercolor. I emphasized the bird's beauty through a minimalist approach, depicting the urban landscape via a few electric lines.

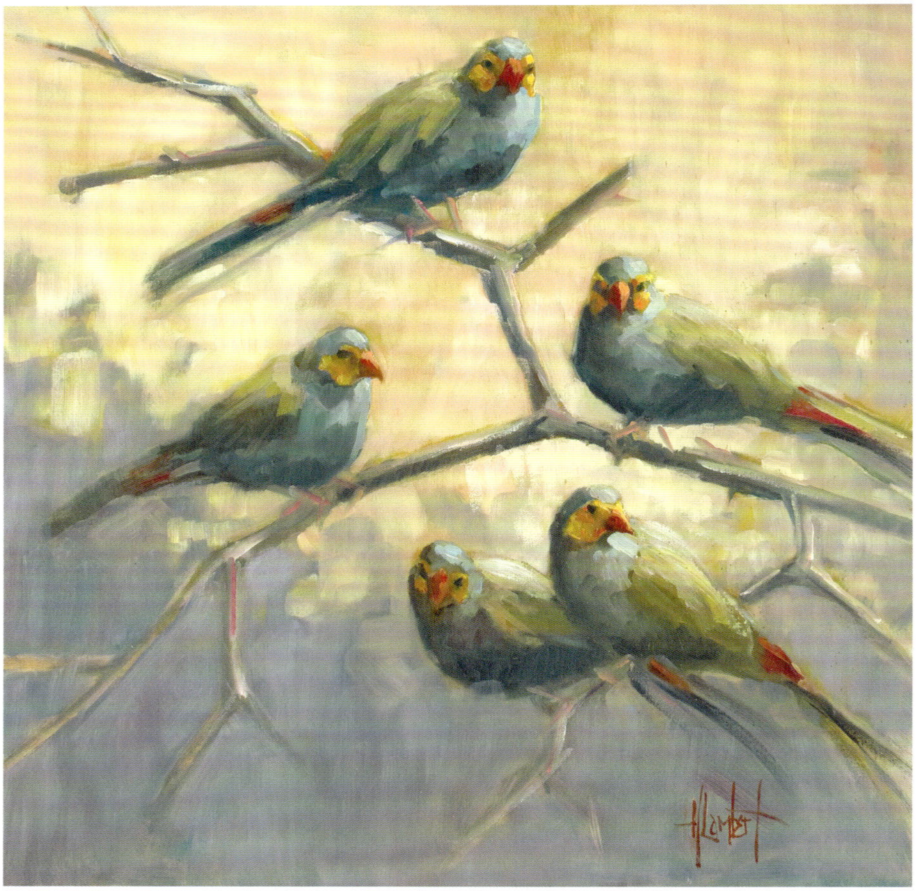

Settled In, 2012
Orange-cheeked waxbill finch
Oil on canvas
24 x 24

Collection of
Jean Elizabeth Aycock

Birds in Art: 2011

BORN: 1952, United States
RESIDES: Charleston, South Carolina
EDUCATION: A.S., Finger Lakes Community College, Canandaigua, New York
EXHIBITIONS: *Southern Traditions,* 2010, Ella Walton Richardson Gallery, Charleston; *Travels in France,* 2010, *European Landscapes,* 2011, and *Under the Sun,* 2012, City Art Gallery, Greenville, North Carolina
AWARDS: Judges Award, 2010, and Third Place, 2011, *Piccolo Spoleto Outdoor Art Exhibition,* Marion Square, Charleston
COLLECTIONS: First Federal, Charleston; Paychex, Rochester, New York
BIBLIOGRAPHY: "Top Emerging Artists 21 Over 31," *Southwest Art,* November 2010; *Best of Artists,* Kennedy Publishing, 2010
REPRESENTATIVES: City Art Gallery; I. Pinckney Simons Gallery, Beaufort, South Carolina

I'm attracted to images with a strong sense of design and composition. Settled In *came about following a visit to a pet store to buy treats for our Quaker parrot. These orange-cheeked waxbill finches were perched on a branch together. I loved their colors and composition and shot dozens of photos, as they're flighty little birds that don't stay long in one place. I really wanted to push the design and the brush strokes and used a palette knife on the wings to emphasize the feathers and layers of color. I wanted the top strokes to be pure color and texture. A new selection of warm and cool colors on my palette turned out to be perfect.*

Stephen Left

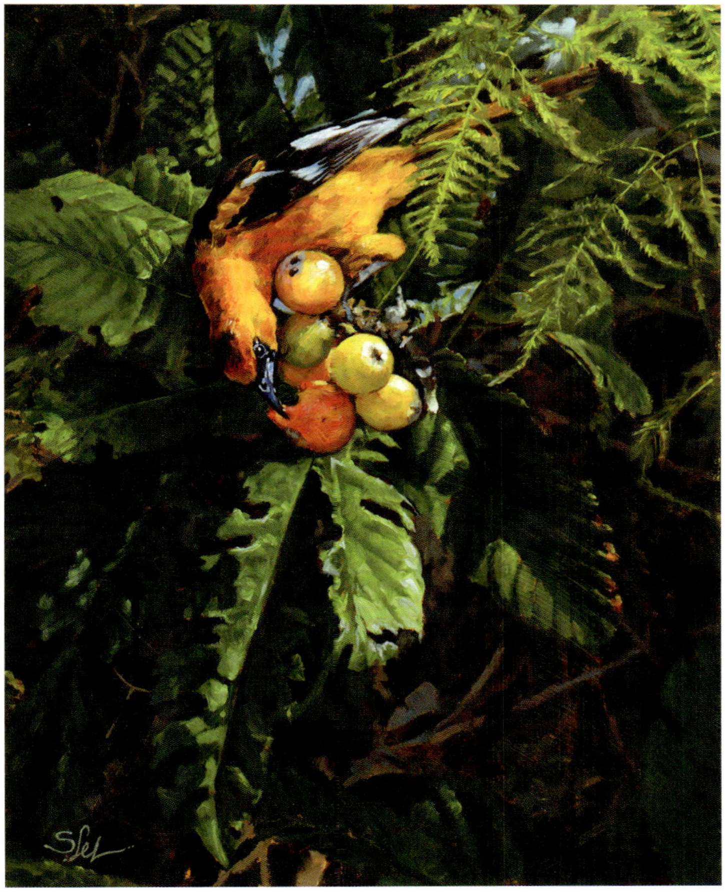

Loquat Twister, 2012
Spot-breasted oriole
Oil on hardboard
14 x 11

Collection of the artist

Birds in Art: 2002, 2005-06, 2010

W

BORN: 1957, United States
RESIDES: Pompano Beach, Florida
EDUCATION: A.A., Art Institute of Atlanta
EXHIBITIONS: *Salon International,* 2010, Greenhouse Gallery of Fine Art, San Antonio; *NOAPS Best of America Exhibition,* 2011, Ella Carouthers Dunnegan Gallery of Art, Bolivar, Missouri
AWARDS: First Place and People's Choice, 2010, *Impressions of South Florida,* Bonnet House Museum and Gardens, Fort Lauderdale
REPRESENTATIVES: Redbone Gallery, Islamorada, Florida

The spot-breasted oriole, one of my favorite birds, is an avian acrobat. Its piercing, crisp call never ceases to make me smile. As soon as I hear its song, I search out the trees to spot its golden feathers. More often than not, I find these orioles dangling upside down on palm fronds eating small bugs.

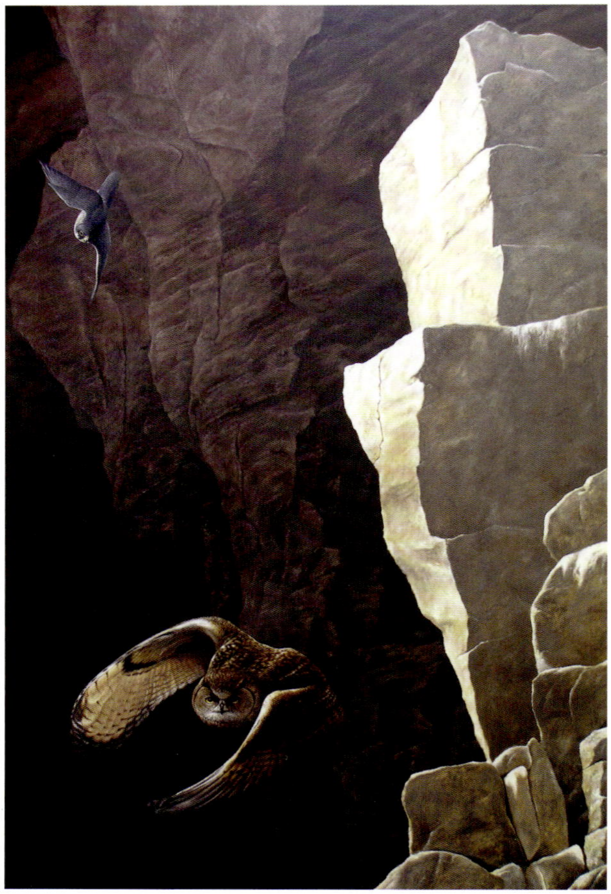

The Intruder, 2012
European eagle owl and peregrine falcon
Oil on Belgian linen
48 x 32

Collection of the artist

Birds in Art: 1990, 1992-93, 2009

W

BORN: 1953, Netherlands
RESIDES: Amerongen, Netherlands
EXHIBITIONS: *Natuurlijk Natuur,* 2010-11, Art Galerie Staphorsius, Westzaan; *Wild in de Natuur,* 2010-11, Kunsthuis van het Oosten, Enschede

The Intruder *was inspired by a movie made in Spain more than thirty years ago by Félix Rodríguez de la Fuente. A scene in which a European eagle owl is attacked by a pair of Bonelli's eagles was etched in my memory. I knew one day I would make a painting with similar scenery. It took years to think it through, as my fantasy changed often. After a few trips to a mountain region in Spain, I was ready. I used a peregrine instead of a Bonelli's eagle, trying to visualize the difference between the huge owl with its slow and weightless way of flying and the falcon that is trying to intimidate the larger bird. The high mountain setting emphasizes the dramatic moment.*

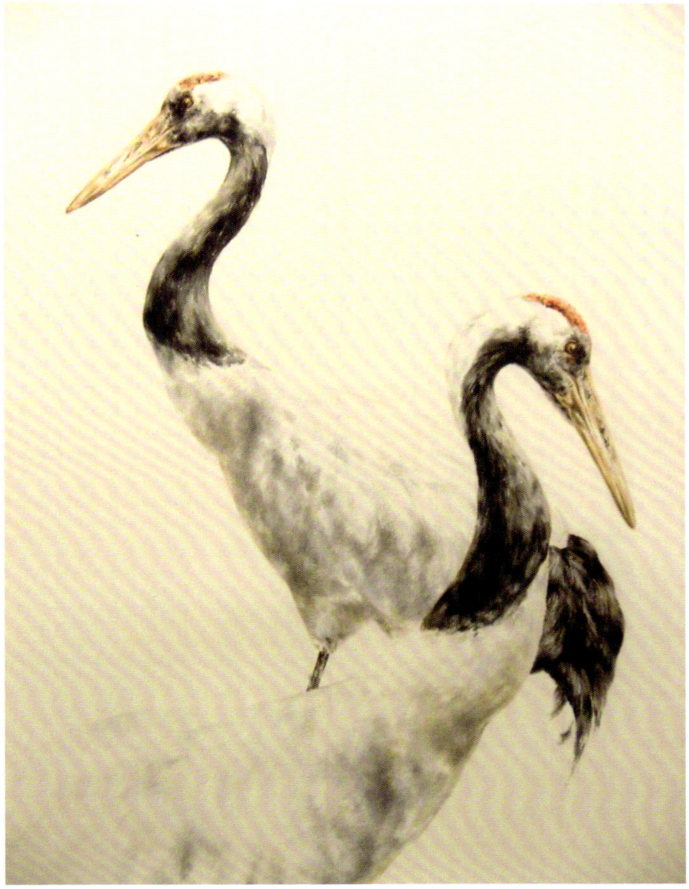

Tancho, 2011
Red-crowned crane
Pastel on Arches paper
30 x 22

Collection of the artist

Birds in Art: 2010

BORN: 1987, England
RESIDES: Newcastle-upon-Tyne, Tyne and Wear, England
EDUCATION: B.A., Newcastle University, Newcastle-upon-Tyne
EXHIBITIONS: *National Exhibition of Wildlife Art,* 2010, Gordale Garden Centre, Burton, South Wirral; *The Natural Eye: Society of Wildlife Artists,* 2011, Mall Galleries, London
AWARDS: Young Artist Bursary, 2010, Society of Wildlife Artists, London
REPRESENTATIVES: Wildlife Art Company, Bristol

This red-crowned crane pastel developed from two sweeping lines on the page, a quick sketch intended to capture the birds as they strutted past each other during my March 2011 artist residency at the International Crane Foundation in Baraboo, Wisconsin. The pair was the first of the species I had seen. I stood in the snow and biting frost and watched them. The male glared balefully back at me with dark eyes flecked with orange and ochre. Eventually I turned and walked away. The birds called a triumphant clangor. Only later did I realize that, oblivious, my face had blistered from the cold.

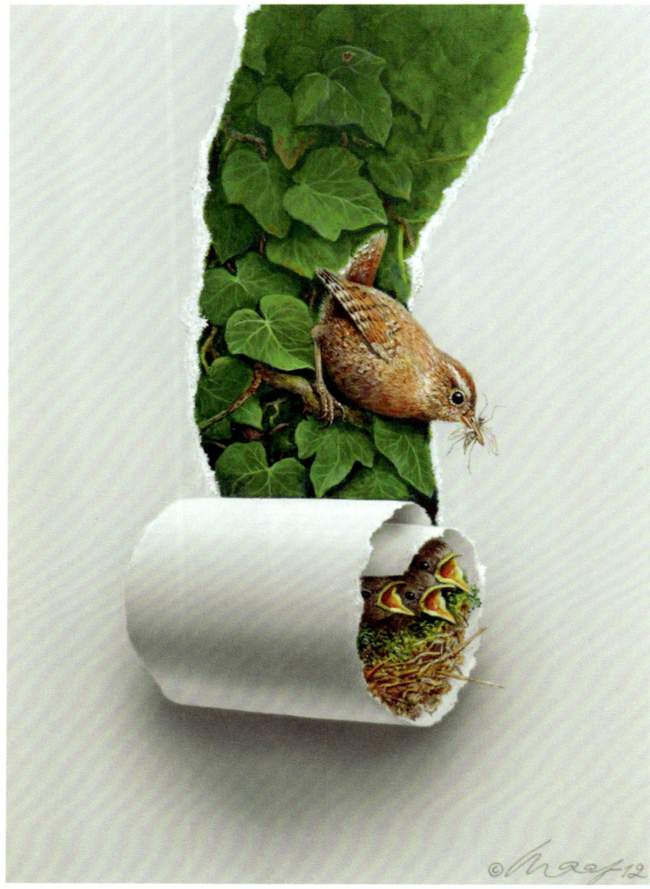

Wren's Nest, 2012
Winter wren
Acrylic on panel
14 x 10

Collection of the artist

Birds in Art: 1994, 1996-97, 2002-03, 2008-09

W

BORN: 1939, Germany
RESIDES: Ratingen, North Rhine-Westphalia, Germany
EDUCATION: B.A., Werkkunstschule, Krefeld
EXHIBITIONS: Senckenberg Museum für Naturkunde, 2010, Görlitz; Kleiner Kursaal Wangerooge, 2011, Wangerooge
AWARDS: Silberner Uhu and People's Choice, 2011, *Moderne Vogelbilder,* Museum Heineanum, Halberstadt; Environmental Statement Award, 2011, *Artists for Conservation,* Spirit Gallery, Grouse Mountain, Vancouver, British Columbia, Canada

Four years ago, I started a series of paintings focused on surfaces. Here, the wren appears to come out of the ivy to feed its chicks. I take great pleasure in developing concepts that give viewers visual surprises, which in this case, could be a problem for the wren. The need for a home, though, often demands creative solutions!

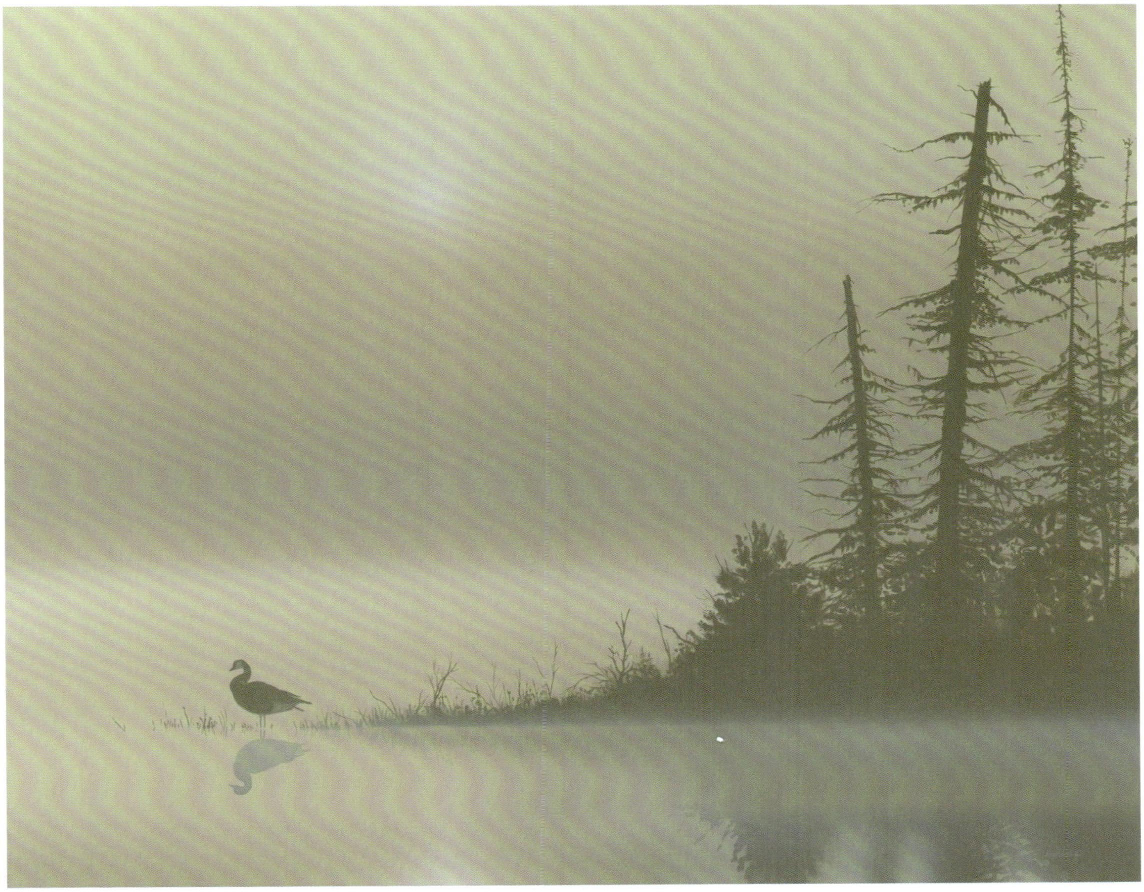

Silence, 2011
Canada goose
Acrylic on hardboard
16 x 20

Collection of the artist

Birds in Art: 1998-99, 2007-08

BORN: 1969, United States
RESIDES: Albany, Oregon
EDUCATION: M.A., Western Oregon University, Monmouth; B.A., University of California, Davis
EXHIBITIONS: *American Miniatures,* 2012, Settlers West Gallery, Tucson, Arizona; *Alaska 2012: A Celebration of Wildlife Art,* 2012, Kenai Visitors & Cultural Center, Kenai
COLLECTIONS: Salem Hospital, Salem, Oregon
REPRESENTATIVES: Wild Wings, Lake City, Minnesota

Most people are familiar with the raucous, honking sounds of geese, but geese also make a lower, guttural call when at rest or feeding in a relaxed state. As I envisioned Silence, *I imagined that if the goose were to call, the mellow sound would echo off the surrounding unseen trees. I wanted to evoke a sense of calm and solitude, not the typical mass of geese. Once the sun is higher in the sky, its warmth will burn off the fog and give this pond an entirely different look and mood; the pond will come to life. For now, in the stillness, the goose is safe and relaxed in peaceful silence.*

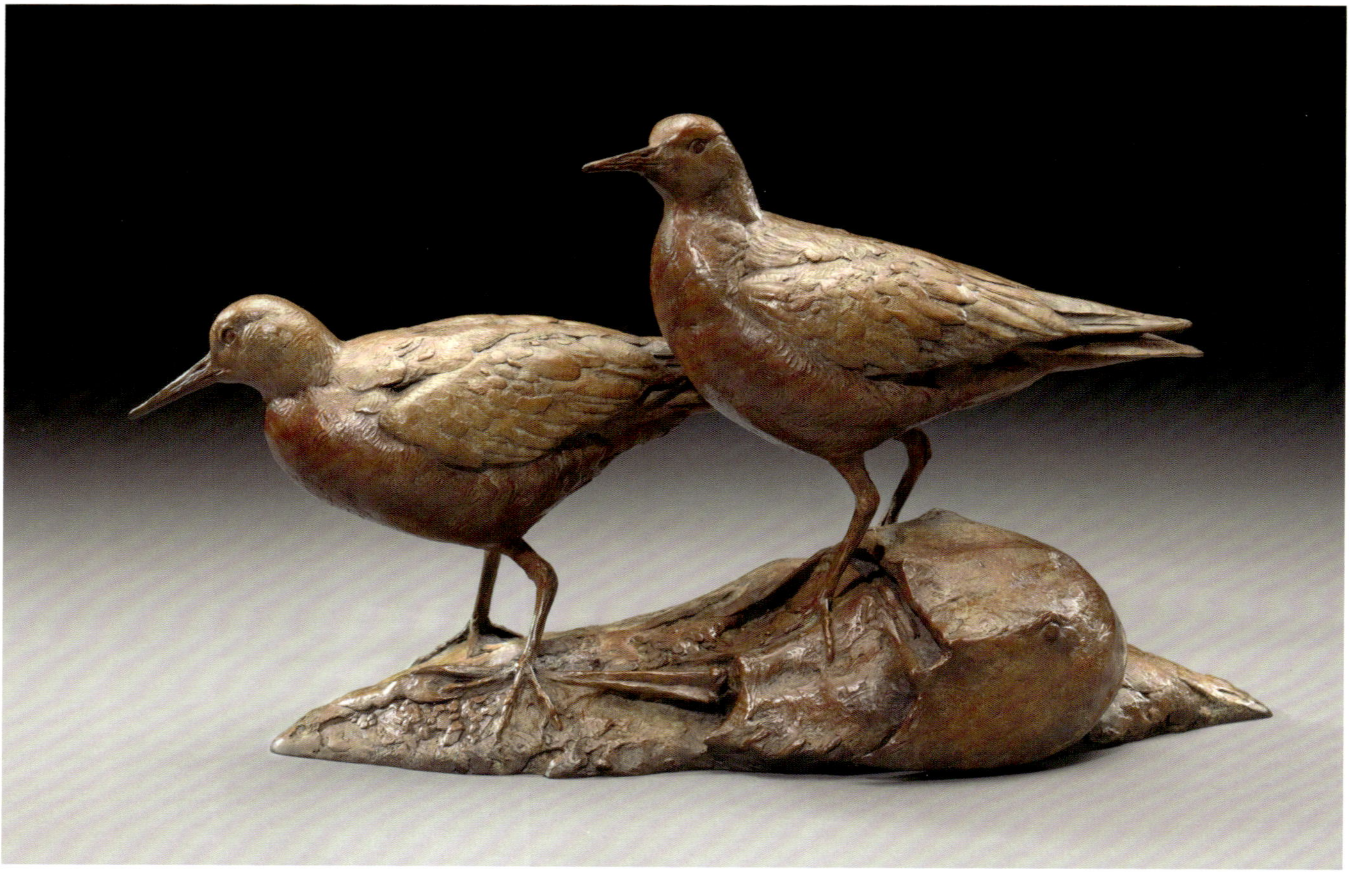

The Tides that Bind (A/P), 2011
Rufa red knot
Bronze
9 x 15 x 6

Collection of the artist

Birds in Art: 1985-86, 1988-91, 1993-94, 1997-11
Master Wildlife Artist: 2007

W

BORN: 1953, United States
RESIDES: Dickerson, Maryland
EDUCATION: B.A., Williams College, Williamstown, Massachusetts
EXHIBITIONS: *Masters of the American West,* 2010-12, Autry National Center, Los Angeles; *American Masters,* 2010-12, Salmagundi Club, New York City; *Art and the Animal,* 2010, San Diego Natural History Museum, 2011, Dennos Museum Center, Northwestern Michigan College, Traverse City, and 2012, Hiram Blauvelt Art Museum, Oradell, New Jersey; *Prix de West Invitational,* 2010 and 2012, National Cowboy & Western Heritage Museum, Oklahoma City; *Light, Form and Reverie,* 2011, Gerald Peters Gallery, Santa Fe, New Mexico; *Collectors' Reserve: Art Exhibition,* 2011, Gilcrease Museum, Tulsa, Oklahoma; *West Select,* 2011, Phoenix Art Museum
AWARDS: Major General and Mrs. Don D. Pittman Wildlife Award, 2011, *Prix de West Invitational*
COLLECTIONS: Brookgreen Gardens, Murrells Inlet, South Carolina
BIBLIOGRAPHY: "Light, Form and Reverie," *Western Art Collector,* June 2011
REPRESENTATIVES: Collectors Covey, Dallas; Gerald Peters Gallery; Meredith Long & Company, Houston

The rufa red knot is a winter resident of Tierra del Fuego, migrating north in May to a critical rendezvous with breeding horseshoe crabs in Delaware Bay. The success of the knots' reproductive cycle is tied to meeting the crabs and doubling their body weight as they gorge on crab eggs before continuing on to their Arctic breeding grounds. Commercial overharvesting of the horseshoe crab population has become a flash point in the conservation of the rufa subspecies because diminished crab stock means reduced availability of eggs. Knot populations number only 15,000 today. The Tides that Bind *was created as a presentation award for the National Fish and Wildlife Foundation, which has funded red knot protection projects.*

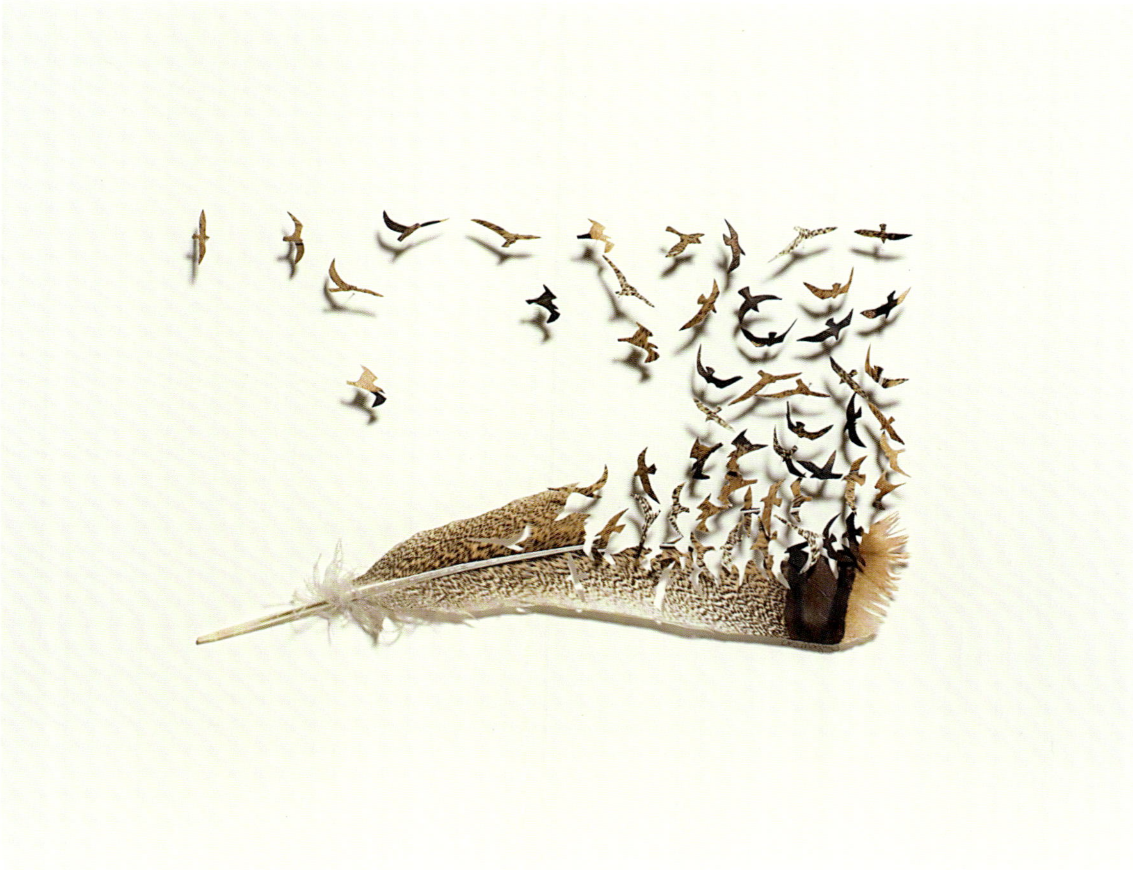

Where Feathers Come From, 2011
Turkey feather on paperboard
21 x 26 x 2

Collection of the artist

BORN: 1954, United States
RESIDES: Olympia, Washington
EDUCATION: B.A., Evergreen State College, Olympia
EXHIBITIONS: Washington State Department of Ecology, 2011, Olympia; Olympia Framemakers, 2012; Evergreen Hospital, 2012, Kirkland, Washington

Where Feathers Come From *is intended to spark curiosity about the complicated and remarkable way feathers grow. I used a molted turkey tail feather because it is large and interestingly patterned. The cutouts from the feather are generic flying birds, though they do remind me of gulls landing on an ocean beach. The turkey breeder raised these birds to sell feathers to fly-tiers who want specific colors and patterns. To accomplish this type of detailed work, I use eye surgery scissors, forceps, scalpels, and magnifiers inherited from my father.*

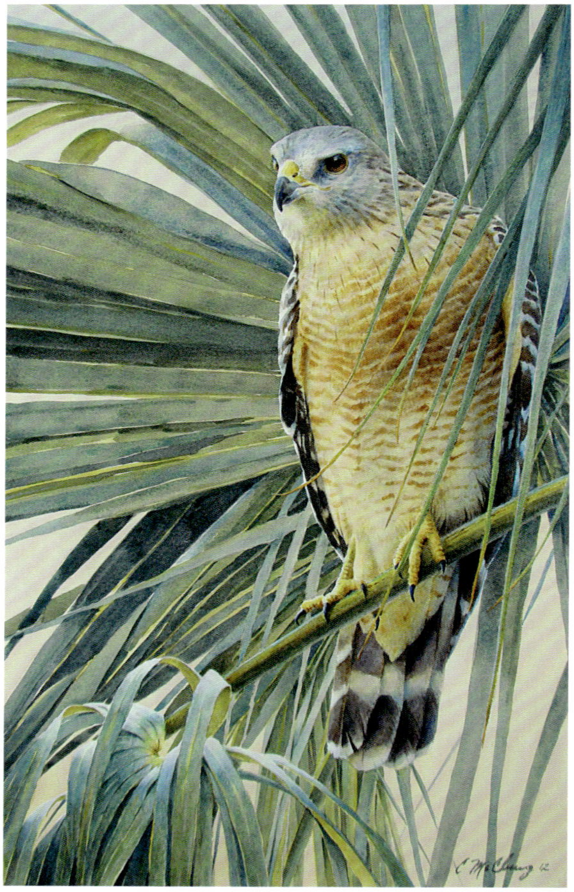

Ready for the Hunt, 2012
Red-shouldered hawk
Watercolor on Winsor & Newton paper
21 x 13

Collection of
Eugene and Rebecca Belknap

Birds in Art: 1982-83, 1985, 1990, 1993, 2009-11

W

BORN: 1951, Canada
RESIDES: Spring Lake, Michigan
EDUCATION: B.S., Eastern Michigan University, Ypsilanti
EXHIBITIONS: Tri-Cities Historical Museum, 2010, Grand Haven, Michigan; *Signs of Spring: Birds and Blooms,* 2010, and *Uniquely West Michigan,* 2011, Gallery Uptown, Grand Haven; *He Has His Eye on the Sparrow,* 2012, Atrium Gallery, Grand Haven; *84th Regional Exhibition,* 2012, Muskegon Museum of Art, Muskegon, Michigan; *Bright, Witty, Bold,* 2012, Gallery Uptown
COMMISSIONS: Lenox China, Bristol, Pennsylvania
REPRESENTATIVES: Gallery Uptown

While on a morning walk in Florida, I saw a beautiful red-shouldered hawk perched about eight feet off the ground. The bird didn't seem to mind my close inspection nor that I tagged along as it moved about hunting for reptiles. Painting palm fronds was a first for me and I delighted in using the element of leading lines to guide the viewer's eye to the main subject. Ready for the Hunt *is all about lines: fat lines, skinny lines, dark lines, light lines, straight lines, curved lines, zig-zag lines, and diagonal lines. What a visual feast!*

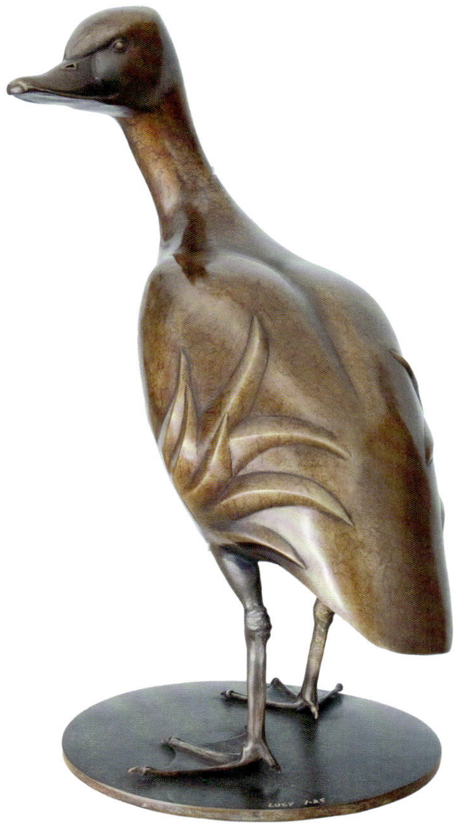

Plumed Whistling Duck
(ed. 25), 2011
Bronze
17 x 12 x 9

Collection of the artist

Birds in Art: 2010-11

BORN: 1981, Australia
RESIDES: Inverleigh, Victoria, Australia
EDUCATION: B.F.A., Monash University, Melbourne, Victoria
EXHIBITIONS: *Season of Birds,* 2010, Purple Noon Gallery, Freemans Reach, New South Wales; *Toorak Village Sculpture Exhibition,* 2010-11, Melbourne; *Cut and Formed on the Plains,* 2011, Roma on Bungil Gallery, Roma, Queensland; *The Waterhouse Natural History Art Prize,* 2011, South Australian Museum, Adelaide; *Backyard Bliss,* 2012, Framed: The Darwin Gallery, Darwin, North Territory
AWARDS: Wine Makers Choice Award, 2011, *Yering Station Sculpture Exhibition,* Yarra Valley Arts, Yarra Glen, Victoria
COLLECTIONS: Yering Station Vineyard, Yarra Glen
BIBLIOGRAPHY: "Carving Out an International Reputation," November 2010, and "Artist Profile: Lucy McEachern," February 2012, *Wildlife Art Society of Australasia*; "Out of the Black," *Yarra Valley and Ranges Magazine,* Autumn 2011
REPRESENTATIVES: Local Images Art Gallery, Penola, South Australia; Purple Noon Gallery; Qdos Art Gallery, Lorne, Victoria

On a frosty, central Queensland morning, we encountered a large number of plumed whistling ducks – tall gooselike birds – sharing their breakfast with a group of Hereford bulls. The closer we got the quicker they scampered, prompting us to hide behind the bulbous bottle tree trunks that surrounded the old cattle yards. A timid bird with buff flank plumes looked over its shoulder and moved in a hurry, probably not impressed that it had been disturbed.

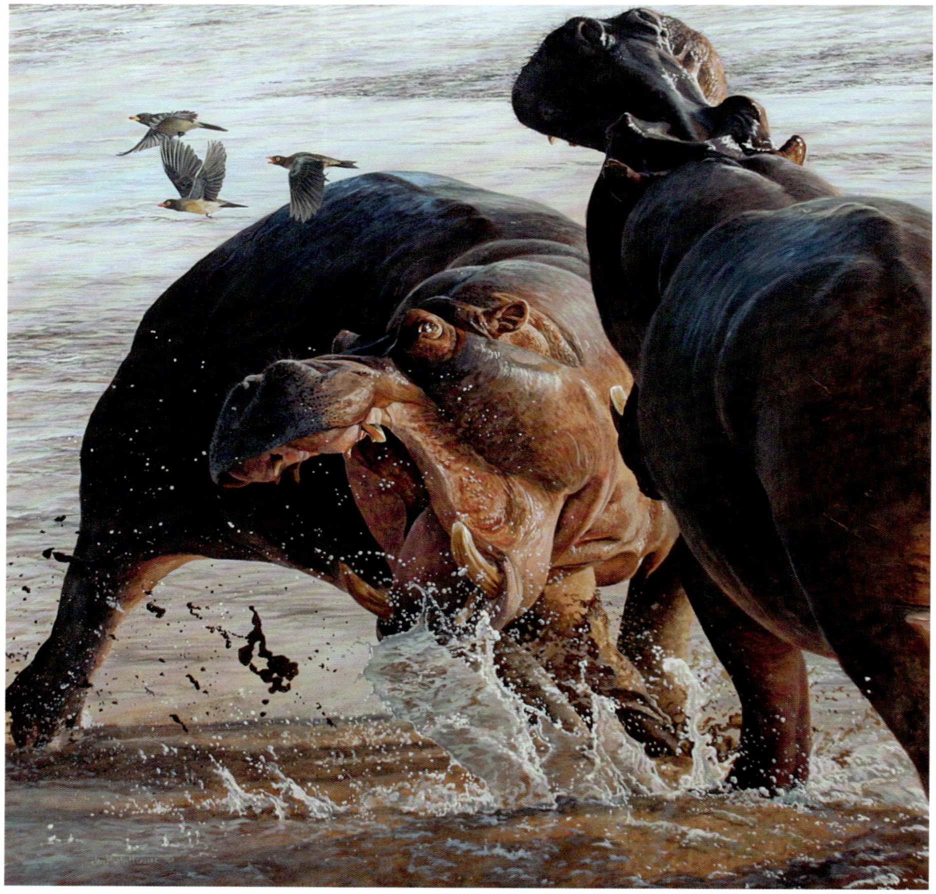

Beastly Battle, 2011
Red-billed and yellow-billed oxpeckers
Acrylic on canvas
45 x 45

Collection of
Lary and Tricia Knowlton

Birds in Art: 1993, 1996-97, 1999-00, 2002, 2004-05, 2007-08, 2010

BORN: 1955, United States
RESIDES: Bartlesville, Oklahoma
EXHIBITIONS: *Collectors' Reserve: Art Exhibition,* 2010-11, Gilcrease Museum, Tulsa, Oklahoma; *American Art in Miniatures,* 2010-12, Settlers West Galleries, Tucson, Arizona; *Art and the Animal Kingdom,* 2010-12, Bennington Center for the Arts, Bennington, Vermont; *Art and the Animal,* 2010, San Diego Natural History Museum, 2011, Dennos Museum Center, Northwestern Michigan College, Traverse City, and 2012, Hiram Blauvelt Art Museum, Oradell, New Jersey; *Night of Artists,* 2012, Briscoe Museum, San Antonio; *Masters in Miniature,* 2012, Trailside Galleries, Jackson, Wyoming
COLLECTIONS: Bennington Center for the Arts; Forbes Magazine, New York City; Raymond James Financial Center, Saint Petersburg, Florida
REPRESENTATIVES: Cultural Heritage Art Centre, Arusha, Tanzania; Settlers West Galleries

During a 2011 trip to Zambia, we stayed just outside North Luangwa National Park in an area rarely visited by tourists. Where the Mwaleshi and Luangwa rivers join, there is a large hippo population. Most of the 'good spots' in the rivers were taken up by herd bulls and their harems; the bachelor bulls, in a group of about 100, were forced into an uneasy alliance at the confluence. Whenever we arrived, they would rise from the sandbars and run en masse toward the river. The bulls became aggressive, and fights broke out almost as far as the eye could see. The roaring, bellowing, grunting, and teeth gnashing was ear splitting! All the birds in the area were disturbed by these battles, especially the oxpeckers perched on the hippos, cleaning them of parasites.

B. Hugh McPeck

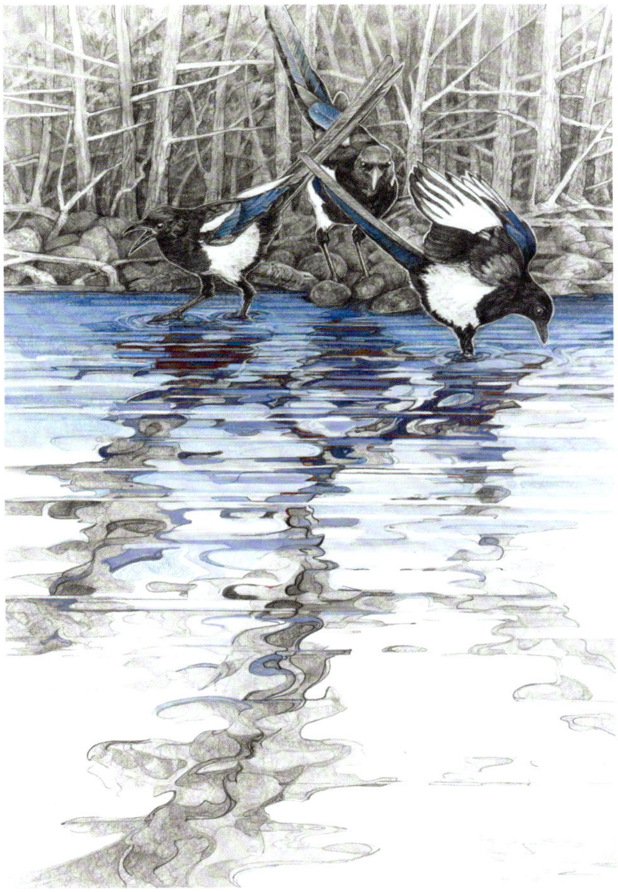

Magpies, 2012
Black-billed magpie
Gouache and graphite on
Strathmore vellum
33 x 24

Collection of the artist

Birds in Art: 2003-04, 2007-11

W

BORN: 1947, United States
RESIDES: Anchorage, Alaska
EDUCATION: M.F.A., Idaho State University, Pocatello; B.F.A., Michigan State University, East Lansing
EXHIBITIONS: University of Alaska, 2011, Kenai; *Intersecting Journeys,* 2011, Kenai Visitors & Cultural Center, Kenai; *Seattle Erotic Art,* 2011, Fremont Studios, Seattle
COLLECTIONS: Anchorage Museum of History and Art; City of Anchorage; Gates of the Arctic National Park, Fairbanks, Alaska
REPRESENTATIVES: Artique, Anchorage

I associate groups of magpies with raucous noise and used the busy water and sharp angles in the background trees to suggest the cacophony of this scene. The Gothic feel of the forest – forbidding and inpenetrable – is intentional. Alaska's forests are raw; getting off a trail by even a few feet can entangle a hiker in all types of undergrowth.

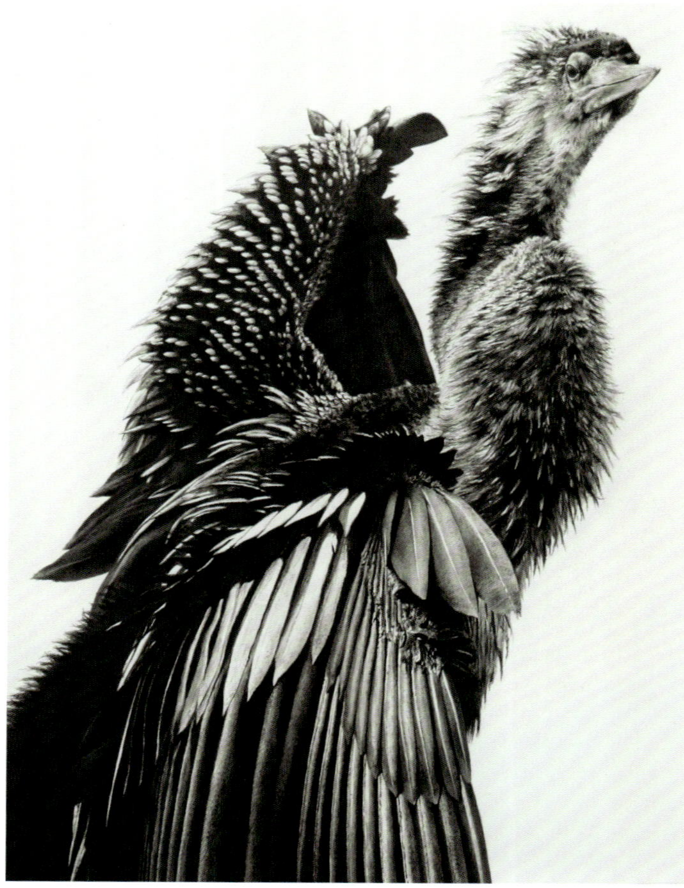

Florezca el Flamenco,
2012
Anhinga
Graphite on Bristol board
16 3/4 x 12 3/4

Collection of the artist

Birds in Art: 1991-96, 1998-11

W

BORN: 1945, United States
RESIDES: Takoma Park, Maryland
EXHIBITIONS: *Art of the Animal Kingdom,* 2010, Bennington Center for the Arts, Bennington, Vermont; *Modern Marine Masters,* 2010, Maritime Gallery, Mystic Seaport, Mystic, Connecticut; *Art and the Animal,* 2010, San Diego Natural History Museum, 2011, Dennos Museum Center, Northwestern Michigan College, Traverse City, and 2012, Hiram Blauvelt Art Museum, Oradell, New Jersey; *Drawing Discourse,* 2011, S. Tucker Cooke Gallery, University of North Carolina, Asheville; *Each One Invites One,* 2011, McBride Gallery, Annapolis, Maryland
AWARDS: Marine Environmental Wildlife Award, 2010, *International Marine Art,* Maritime Gallery
COLLECTIONS: Hiram Blauvelt Art Museum
BIBLIOGRAPHY: "A Fine Line: Artist Terry Miller Drawn to Horses," *Equestrian News,* June/July 2010; *Strokes of Genius 3: The Best of Drawing, Fresh Perspectives,* North Light Books, 2011
REPRESENTATIVES: Howard/Mandville Gallery, Kirkland, Washington; McBride Gallery; Windrush Gallery, Sedona, Arizona

While on a trip to the west coast of Florida, I had a chance to study and photograph an anhinga up close. I watched in fascination while it dried its wings in the morning sun, stretching every now and again and presenting a seemingly disdainful attitude toward me. I was struck, when its wings were spread wide, by just how much its pose reminded me of the haughty swirl of a flamenco dancer and thus the title which, translated, is Flamenco Flourish.

David Milton

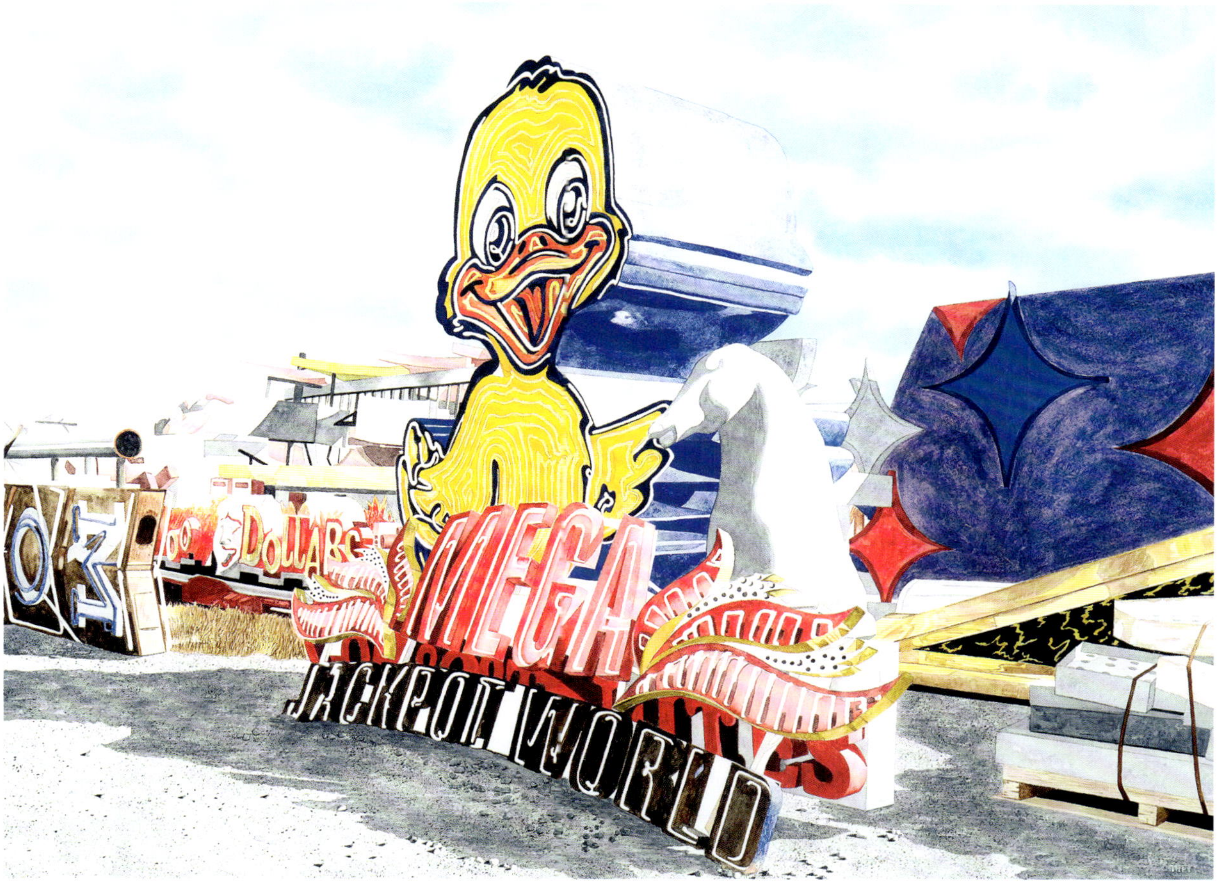

Just Ducky, 2011
Watercolor on Arches paper
22 x 30

Collection of the artist

Birds in Art: 2006-07, 2010

W

BORN: 1947, United States
RESIDES: Laguna Beach, California
EDUCATION: M.F.A., San Jose State University, San Jose, California; B.A., University of California, Santa Cruz
EXHIBITIONS: *Allied Artists of America,* 2011, National Arts Club, New York City
AWARDS: Award for Distinction, 2010, *Taos National Exhibition of American Watercolor,* Millicent Rogers Museum, Taos, New Mexico
COLLECTIONS: Atomic Testing Museum, Las Vegas; Bank of America, San Francisco; 20th Century Fox, Los Angeles
BIBLIOGRAPHY: *Splash 11: New Directions,* 2010; *Splash 12: Celebrating Artistic Vision,* 2011; *Splash 13: Alternative Approaches,* 2012, all North Light Books

I've never recovered from the exhilaration felt when first experiencing the neon signs at Times Square as a young child. Decades later, my quest to find, document, and paint vanishing neon led to a historically significant discovery. In Las Vegas, local preservationists are saving signs that otherwise would be destroyed when a casino or business closes. A two-acre sign graveyard, The Boneyard, is on desert land where signs are informally arranged. The sign featured in Just Ducky *came from a car dealership; the painting is part of a series that has kept me busy for more than thirty years.*

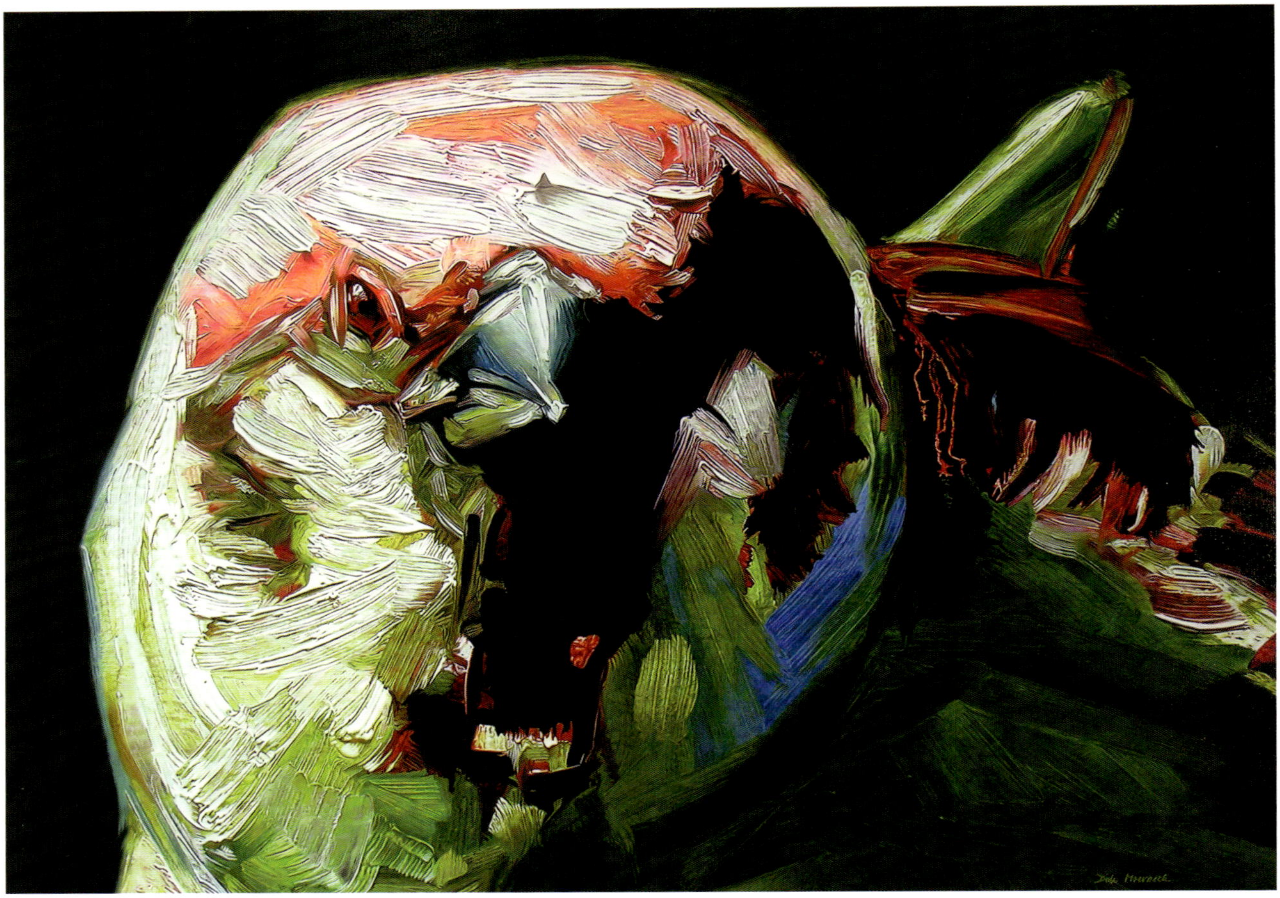

Suzume, 2011
Tree sparrow
Oil on Belgian linen
51 x 71

Collection of the artist

Birds in Art: 2002, 2004-06

W

BORN: 1956, Netherlands
RESIDES: Nieuwolda, Groningen, Netherlands
EDUCATION: M.S., University of Amsterdam; B.A., Koninklijke Academie van Beeldende Kunsten, The Hague
EXHIBITIONS: *Natuurlijk Natuur,* 2010-11, Galerie Staphorsius, Westzaan; *Wild in de Natuur,* 2011, Kunsthuis van het Oosten, Enschede
BIBLIOGRAPHY: *De Kunstenaars van Oost-Groningen,* Stichting Atelierroute Oost-Groningen, 2011

Suzume *is an homage to tree sparrows, little gems with a soft brownish crown, brilliant white cheeks with a bold black spot, and restless behavior and sounds. I feel privileged that these birds visit my garden year round and choose my place to raise their young. I like to think the sparrows do it just for me, but to be honest, the loads of mixed grains I offer them twelve months a year cannot be ruled out as the reason for their presence.*

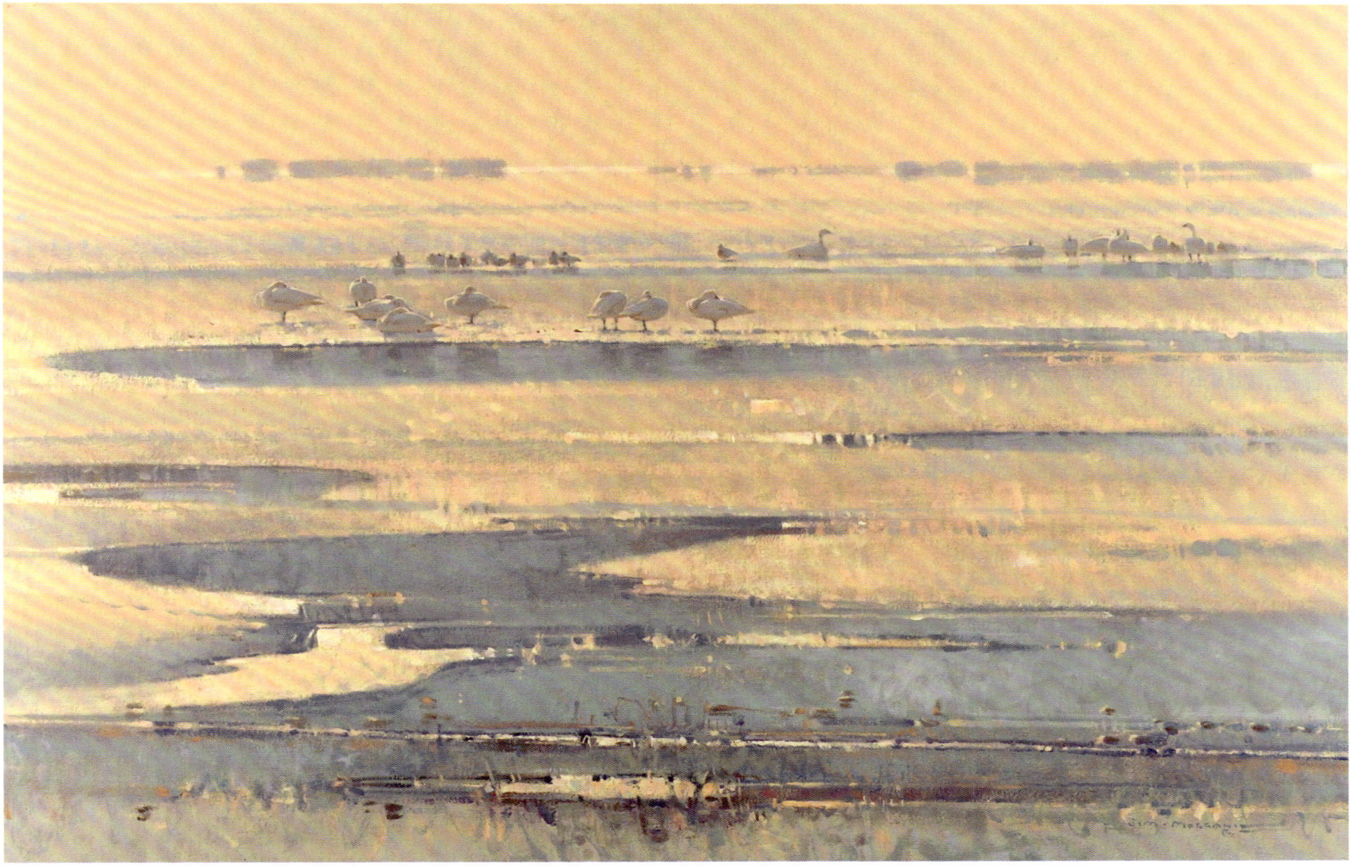

Freeze Up – Early December, 2011
Tundra swan and mallard
Oil on Belgian linen
24 x 36

Collection of the artist

Birds in Art: 1982-83, 1986-94, 1996-11
Master Wildlife Artist: 2008

BORN: 1947, United States
RESIDES: Mendon, Utah
EDUCATION: B.F.A., Utah State University, Logan
EXHIBITIONS: *Masters of the American West,* 2010-12, Autry National Center, Los Angeles; *Prix de West Invitational,* 2010-12, National Cowboy & Western Heritage Museum, Oklahoma City; *American Masters,* 2010-12, Salmagundi Club, New York City; *Wild West: Beauty of the Beast,* 2011, Rockwell Museum of Western Art, Corning, New York; *Romantic Contours, Modern Terrain,* 2011, Gerald Peters Gallery, Santa Fe, New Mexico
COLLECTIONS: Buffalo Bill Historical Center, Cody, Wyoming; Montana Historical Museum, Helena; National Museum of Wildlife Art, Jackson, Wyoming
REPRESENTATIVES: Gerald Peters Gallery; Simpson Gallagher Gallery, Cody; Trailside Galleries, Jackson

I'm fascinated by the distortion and reflective qualities of water in any form: liquid, solid, and even vapor. On a December trip to the Bear River Migratory Bird Refuge near Brigham City, Utah, I found this unusual landscape of salt and fresh water, ice, mud, miragelike reflections, and a mix of late-leaving waterfowl, mostly tundra swans and mallards.

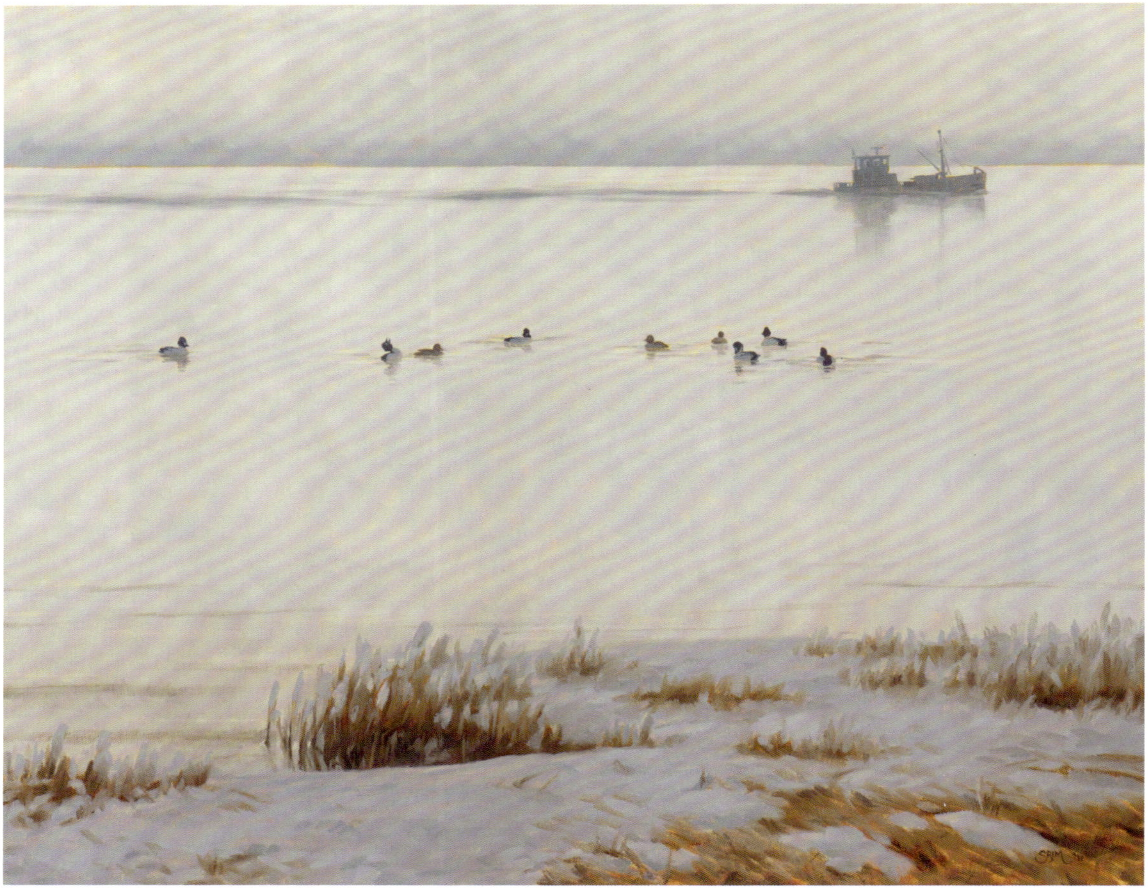

Goldeneyes on a Silver Morning, 2011
Common goldeneye
Oil on linen
24 x 30

Collection of the artist

Birds in Art: 2007

BORN: 1968, United States
RESIDES: Norwalk, Connecticut
EDUCATION: B.F.A., Pratt Institute, Brooklyn, New York
EXHIBITIONS: Greene Art Gallery, 2011, Guilford, Connecticut; *Art of the Animal Kingdom,* 2012, Bennington Center for the Arts, Bennington, Vermont; Audubon Greenwich, 2012, Greenwich, Connecticut
AWARDS: Award of Excellence, 2011, *Art and the Animal,* Dennos Museum Center, Northwestern Michigan College, Traverse City; Award of Excellence, 2011, *Artists for Conservation,* Spirit Gallery, Grouse Mountain, Vancouver, British Columbia, Canada
COLLECTIONS: American Museum of Natural History, New York City; Earthplace, Westport, Connecticut
REPRESENTATIVES: Darien Art & Frame, Darien, Connecticut; Greene Art Gallery

I cut my teeth as both a birder and an artist along the coves and marshes of Long Island's north shore and now continue these pursuits on the Connecticut shoreline. Though there may be more diverse birdlife and less congested landscapes elsewhere, this is my habitat, and I know it in all seasons and weather. Late winter is a favorite time, when the only human intrusions are the hardy oyster boats and birds are plentiful. These common goldeneyes gather to court before flying north to their breeding grounds.

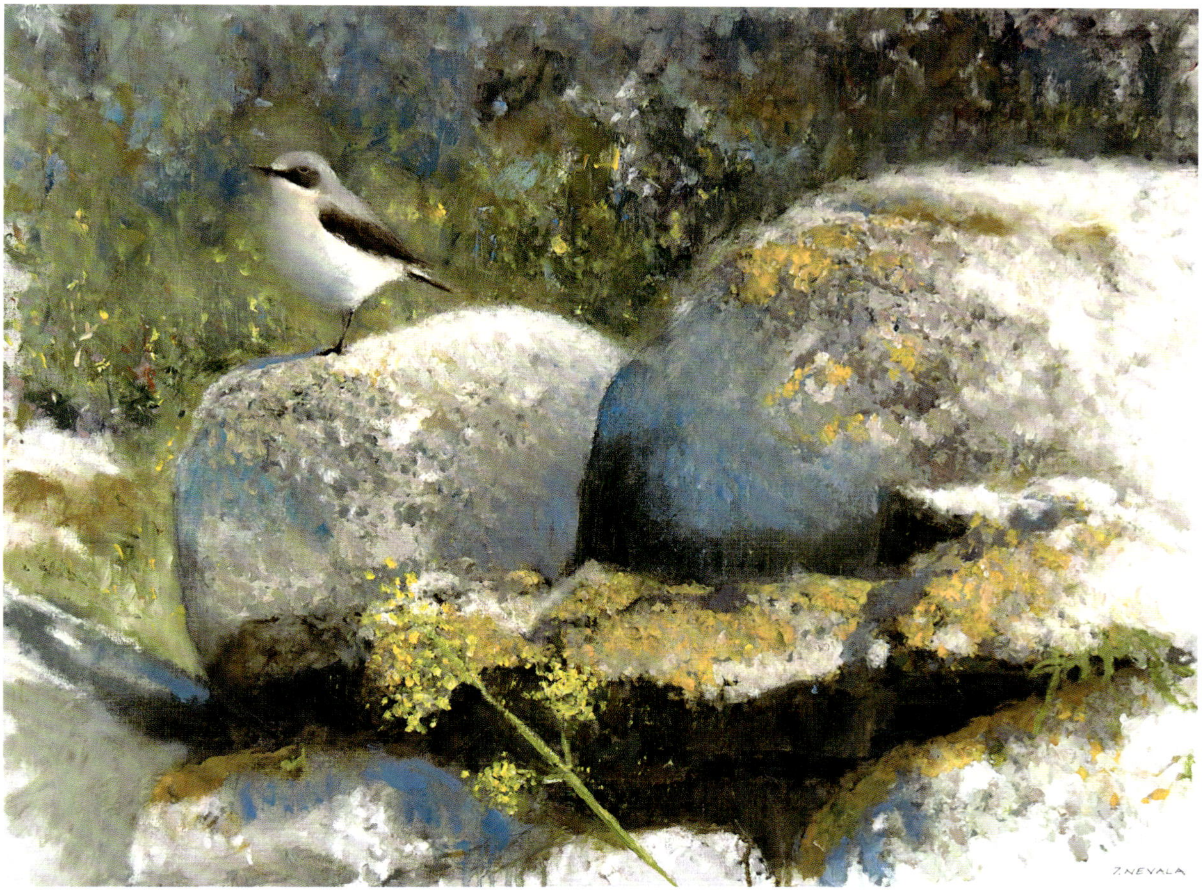

Watchful Eye, 2012
Northern wheatear
Oil on canvas
23 1/2 x 31 1/2

Collection of the artist

Birds in Art: 2003, 2005-06, 2008, 2011

W

BORN: 1966, Finland
RESIDES: Visby, Gotland, Sweden
EDUCATION: M.A., Örebro University, Örebro
EXHIBITIONS: Galleri Karaija, 2010, Inkoo, Finland; Stora Karlsö, 2011, Gotland; Jakobstads Museum, 2011, Jakobstad, Finland; Arkki Satakunnan Museo 2012, Pori, Finland; *Birds 2012,* Galleri Karaija, Inkoo, Finland; *During Migration,* 2012, Falsterbo Art Gallery, Falsterbo; *Open Studio,* 2012, Gotlands Art Museum, Visby
COLLECTIONS: Culture Jakobstad; Jakobstads Museum; Payex, Visby
BIBLIOGRAPHY: "Strandland," *Gotlandica Forlag,* April 2010; "A Day at Stora Karlsö," *Stora Karlsøobladet,* May 2011
REPRESENTATIVES: Galleri Karaija

I favor several different areas where I find both inspiration and subjects for my work. One spot is a large, open, and flat landscape with stone walls. The walls were built by hand more than a hundred years ago to keep farm animals inside the pasture. Nowadays, the landscape is occupied by birds. As I walked along this wall, a wheatear followed my steps with a watchful eye. I, in turn, tried to capture its spirit on the canvas.

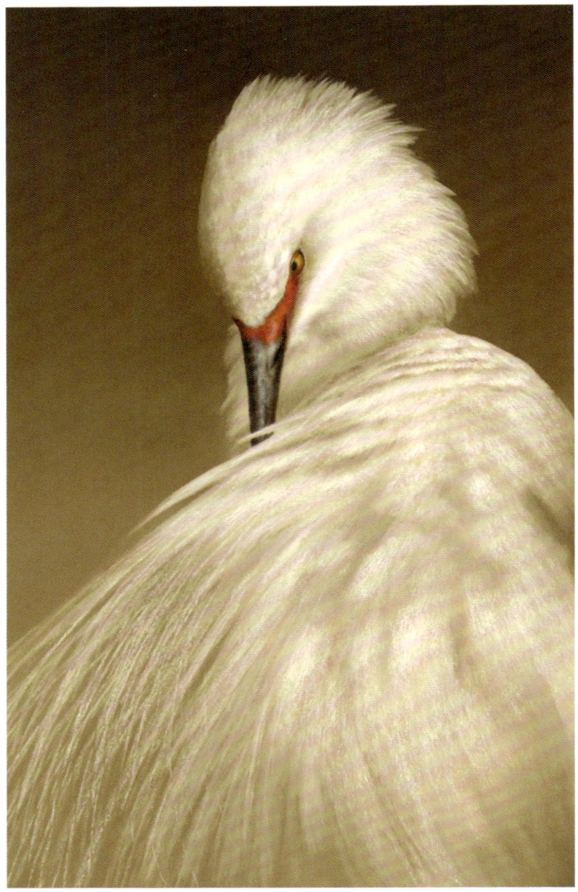

Snowy Egret, 2012
Pastel on Sennelier paper
16 1/2 x 10

Collection of the artist

Birds in Art: 2008-10

W

BORN: 1953, United States
RESIDES: Missouri City, Texas
EXHIBITIONS: *Art and the Animal,* 2011, Dennos Museum Center, Northwestern Michigan College, Traverse City, and 2012, Hiram Blauvelt Art Museum, Oradell, New Jersey

The courtship plumage of the snowy egret made it a sought-after bird by late-nineteenth-century plume hunters; thanks to protective legislation, once decimated populations now flourish. During a Texas Gulf Coast rookery visit last year, the noise and movement of hundreds of egrets, herons, spoonbills, and cormorants created an impression of mass confusion. I focused on a lone snowy egret perched calmly on a branch. Preening, it was seemingly unaffected by the activity. Its long feathers and red lores (the surface between the eyes and the base of the beak) indicated it was in courtship plumage. I made a crude sketch to capture the pose and took reference photos for good measure. In painting this bird, I wanted to convey its calmness.

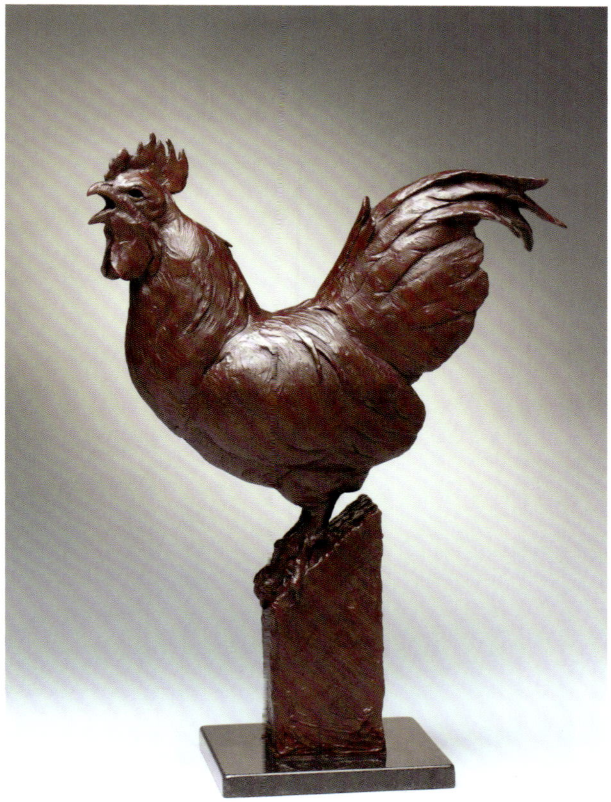

El Pollo Loco (ed. 20), 2011
Bronze
22 x 17 x 6

Collection of the artist

Birds in Art: 2000-01, 2003-04, 2006, 2008

BORN: 1956, United States
RESIDES: Loveland, Colorado
EXHIBITIONS: Nedra Matteucci Galleries, 2010, Santa Fe, New Mexico
AWARDS: Leonard Meiselman Award, 2010, *Audubon Artists Exhibition,* Salmagundi Club, New York City; Ranieri Sculpture Casting Award, 2011, *Allied Artists of America,* National Arts Club, New York City
COLLECTIONS: Crystal Bridges Museum of American Art, Bentonville, Arkansas; Denver Art Museum; National Museum of Wildlife Art, Jackson, Wyoming; Stark Museum of Art, Orange, Texas
BIBLIOGRAPHY: "Dan Ostermiller: Return to the Familiar," *Western Art Collector,* June 2010; "Circle of Life," *Southwest Art,* March 2011; "Outdoor Life," *Western Art & Architecture,* August/September 2012
REPRESENTATIVES: Claggett/Rey Gallery, Vail, Colorado; Nedra Matteucci Galleries

In this rooster's desperate attempt to wake up the world, he could almost fall off his perch!

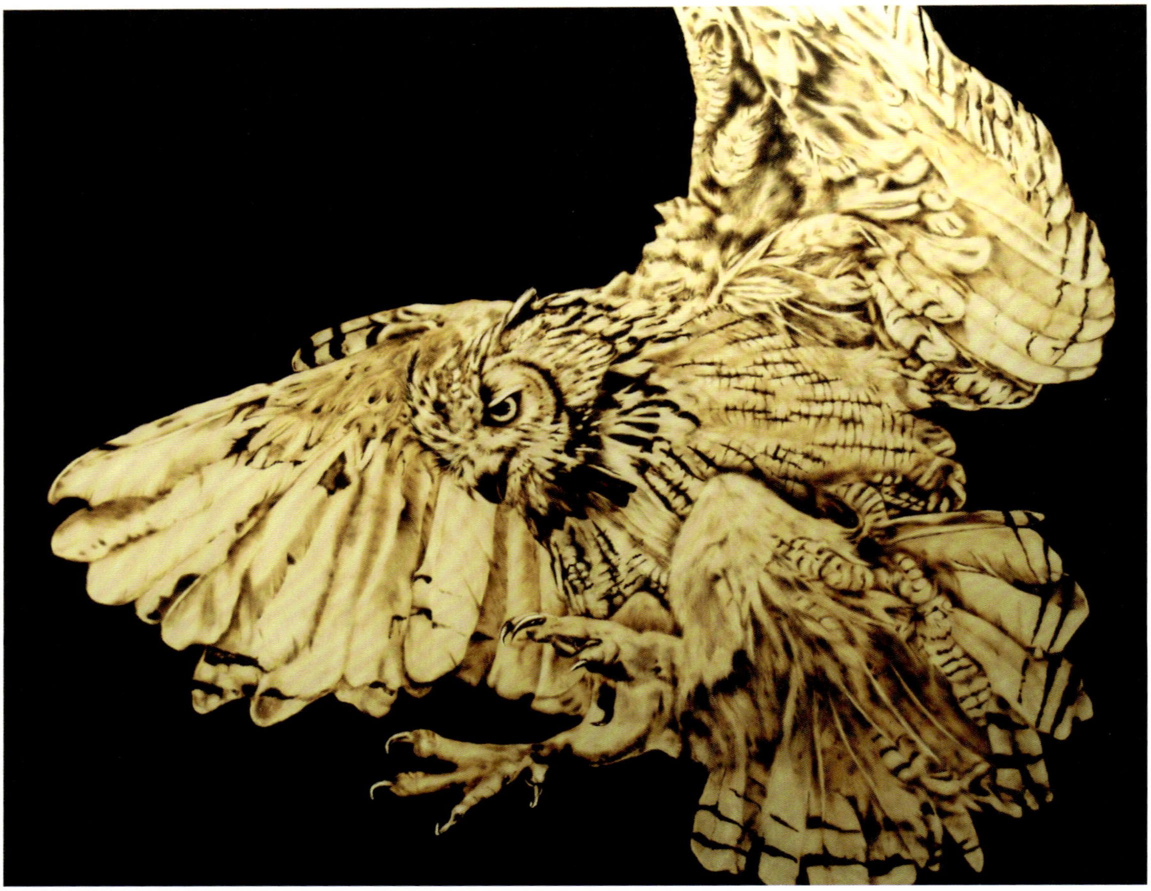

Fire Dancer, 2012
Eagle owl
Pyrography on wood
48 x 60

Collection of the artist

BORN: 1954, United States
RESIDES: Smithville, Tennessee
EDUCATION: B.F.A., Austin Peay State University, Clarksville, Tennessee; A.S., Volunteer State Community College, Gallatin, Tennessee
EXHIBITIONS: Sarratt Gallery, Vanderbilt University, 2010, Nashville; *Red Clay Survey,* 2010, Huntsville Art Museum, Huntsville, Alabama; *Group Exhibit,* 2011, Janine Contemporary Art Gallery, Santa Fe, New Mexico; Diehl Gallery, 2011, Jackson, Wyoming
COLLECTIONS: Blue Cross/Blue Shield, Chattanooga, Tennessee; Huntsville Art Museum; Tennessee State Museum, Nashville
COMMISSIONS: Del Frisco's, New York City; Jackson Hole Airport, Jackson; Terminix Corporation, Dallas
BIBLIOGRAPHY: "30-foot-long Eagle Lands in Revamped Airport," *Jackson Hole News & Guide,* May 26, 2010; "Mixed Media: Light My Fire," *Nashville Scene,* March 2011
REPRESENTATIVES: Diehl Gallery; Janine Contemporary Art Gallery; Studio E Gallery, Palm Beach Gardens, Florida

Fire Dancer *depicts an eagle owl as it is about to strike its prey, eyes fully focused and talons extended. This attack mode is emphasized by the large scale of the work, the cropped left wing, and putting the viewer in the position of the prey. The forcefulness of the pose is my attempt to 're-empower' nature, showing her fully capable of responding to man's continual attacks.*

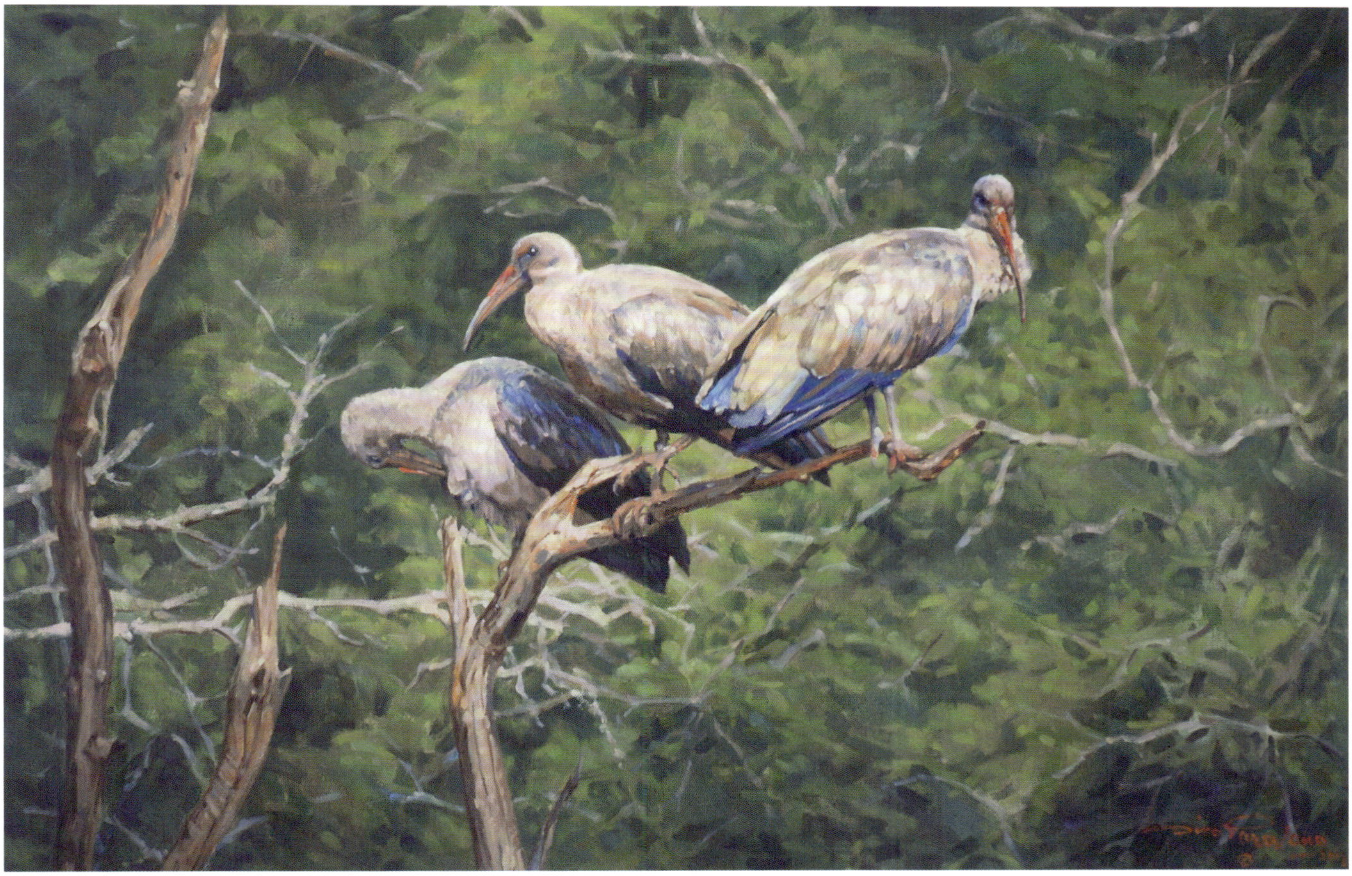

Hadedas, 2012
Hadeda ibis
Oil on canvas
20 x 30

Collection of the artist

Birds in Art: 1985-11
Master Wildlife Artist: 1993

W

BORN: 1935, Italy
RESIDES: Tucson, Arizona
EXHIBITIONS: *Art and the Animal,* 2010, San Diego Natural History Museum
COLLECTIONS: Hiram Blauvelt Art Museum, Oradell, New Jersey; Raymond James Financial, Saint Petersburg, Florida; The Wildlife Experience, Parker, Colorado
REPRESENTATIVES: Bighorn Galleries, Tubac, Arizona; Howard/Mandville Gallery, Kirkland, Washington; Sanders Galleries, Tucson

The hadeda ibis is found in pairs or small groups south of the Sahara to the coast of South Africa. I observed these birds at Mkuze Game Reserve in KwaZulu-Natal. Although the species is not well known in America, when I lived in South Africa these birds would occasionally land on the lawn outside my studio. They announce their arrival with loud, raucous cries that sound like their name, haa-haa-haa-de-dah.

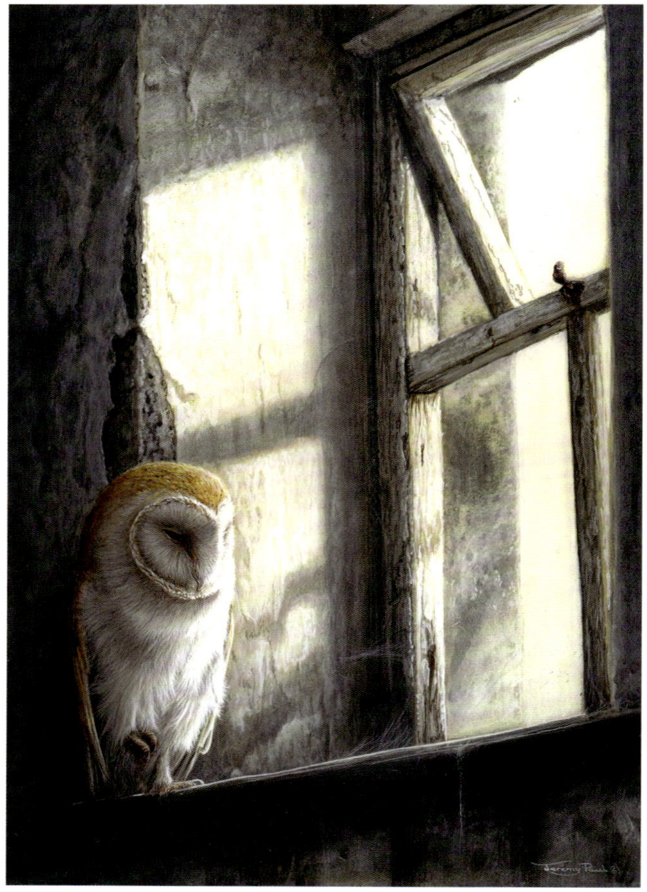

Window Light, 2011
Barn owl
Acrylic on hardboard
16 1/2 x 12

Collection of
Mr. A. Baxendale

Birds in Art: 1994, 2007-09

BORN: 1954, England
RESIDES: Colby, Isle of Man, England
EDUCATION: Ph.D. and B.S., University of Liverpool, Liverpool
EXHIBITIONS: Coach House Gallery, 2010, Guernsey; *Art for Survival,* 2011, Mall Galleries, London; Sayle Gallery, 2011, Isle of Man; *National Exhibition of Wildlife Art,* 2011-12, Gordale Garden Centre, Burton, South Wirral
AWARDS: Category Winner, 2010-12, *Wildlife Artist of the Year,* London
COLLECTIONS: Nature in Art, Twigworth, Gloucester
COMMISSIONS: Isle of Man Post Office

While I've been fortunate to travel the world, I enjoy finding those otherwise unnoticed little bits of landscape – often nearby – and then creating a painting that invites the viewer to look a little closer. An abandoned barn near my home has provided me with a great deal of material and ideas. Wandering around one evening, I noticed how light came through a window onto a whitewashed wall. Occasionally, I saw a barn owl in the area and although I've not found one using the barn, I thought it would make an interesting subject as the owl's colors match the scene almost exactly. I used a limited palette and muted tones, allowing light to be the main subject.

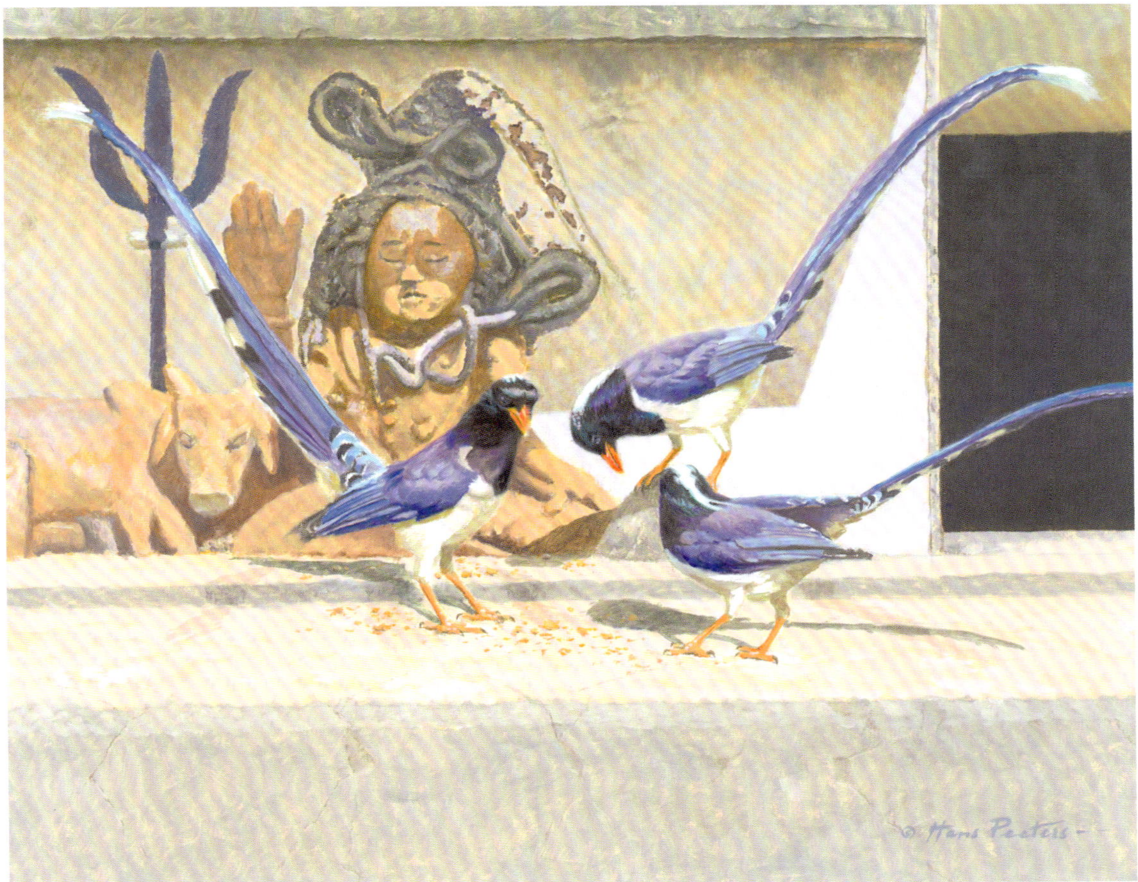

Puja, 2012
Red-billed blue magpie
Oil on canvas
16 x 20

Collection of the artist

Birds in Art: 1981-85, 1987-90, 1993-95

W

BORN: 1937, Germany
RESIDES: Sunol, California
EDUCATION: M.S. and B.A., University of California, Berkeley
EXHIBITIONS: The Bone Room, 2010, Berkeley
AWARDS: Artist of the Year, 2010, Peregrine Fund, Archives of Falconry, Boise, Idaho
COLLECTIONS: Bohemian Club, Puma Camp, Monte Rio, California; Peregrine Fund; San Francisco Public Utilities Commission
COMMISSIONS: Raptor Research and Conservation Foundation, Mumbai, India
BIBLIOGRAPHY: *The Journal of Raptor Research,* Raptor Research Foundation, March 2010 and September 2010; *The Journal, North American Falconer's Association,* 2010 and 2011; *Alameda County Breeding Bird Atlas,* Golden Gate Audubon Society, 2011

Throughout India one finds innumerable temples and shrines where worshippers regularly perform a religious ritual – puja – before statuary devoted to Hindu deities. A puja involves prayers and an offering of flowers, petals, or food such as a handful of grain or lentils. I was delighted to see spectacular magpies in the Himalayan foothills freely helping themselves to these de facto handouts and that the birds were as welcome as curious foreigners. I loved how the corvids in this setting embodied the harmony that exists between the people and the country's countless birds and how the birds' shapes echoed those of the shrine.

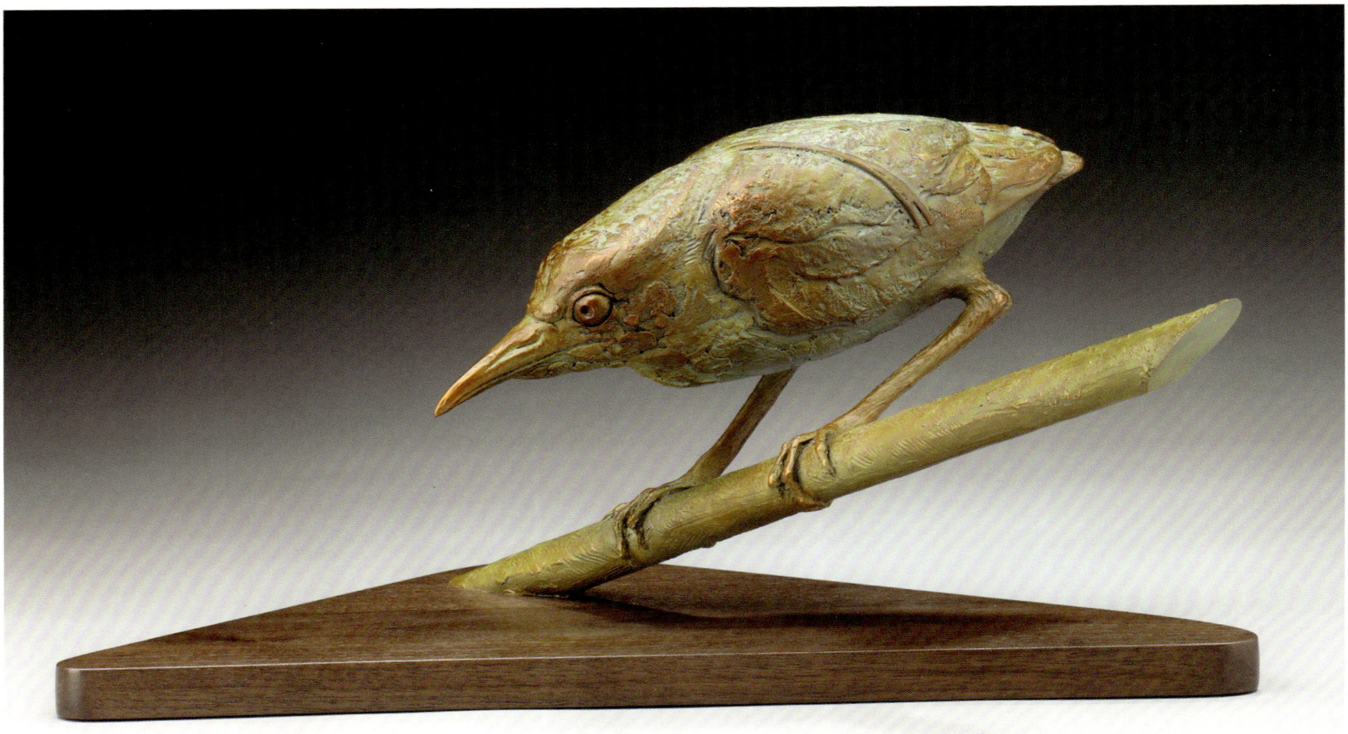

Focus (ed. 19), 2012
Black-crowned night heron
Bronze
8 x 17 x 17

Collection of the artist

Birds in Art: 2006

W

BORN: 1962, England
RESIDES: Guffey, Colorado
EXHIBITIONS: *Art and the Animal,* 2010, San Diego Natural History Museum, and 2011, Dennos Museum Center, Northwestern Michigan College, Traverse City; *Art of the Animal Kingdom,* 2011-12, Bennington Center for the Arts, Bennington, Vermont; *Best of the Best,* 2012, Breckenridge Fine Arts Center, Breckenridge, Texas; *National Sculpture Society Awards Exhibition,* 2012, Brookgreen Gardens, Murrells Inlet, South Carolina
AWARDS: Best in Show, 2010, *Castlegar Sculpturewalk,* Castlegar, British Columbia, Canada; Leonard J. Meiselman Memorial Award, 2011, *Hudson Valley Art Association,* Lyme Academy, Lyme, Connecticut; People's Choice, 2012, *SculptureTour Salina,* Salina, Kansas
COLLECTIONS: Benson Park Sculpture Garden, Loveland, Colorado; Brookgreen Gardens
REPRESENTATIVES: Cavalier Galleries, Nantucket, Massachusetts; SmithKlein Art Gallery, Boulder, Colorado

I was honored to be a sculptor in residence at Brookgreen Gardens in 2009. Behind the studio is a zoo featuring native animals; I challenged myself to sculpt a new subject each day. Black-crowned night herons were perfect models. This one froze for me as it focused on something in the swampy green water while perched on a branch. At the end of the residency, I shipped the clay sculptures home and most still sit on my studio shelves. In 2011, I returned to Brookgreen to teach a workshop and decided to take the clay heron with me. When two students saw it, they claimed the first two castings in the edition. If not for those students the clay model might still be sitting on a shelf in my studio.

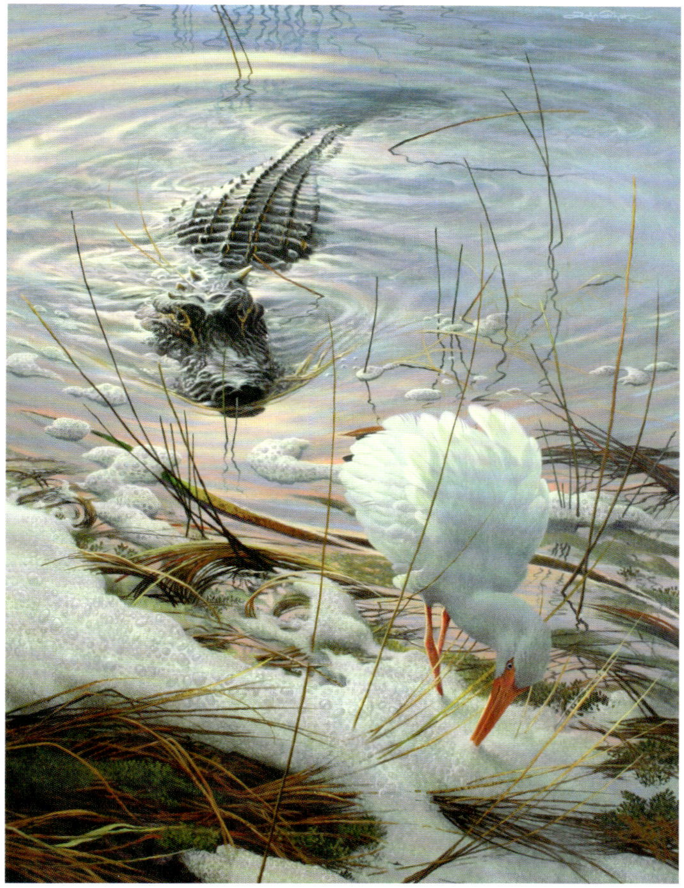

Slow Motion, 2010
White ibis
Acrylic on hardboard
24 x 18

Collection of the artist

Birds in Art: 1978-86, 1994, 2000, 2006, 2008

W

BORN: 1949, United States
RESIDES: Dorset, Vermont
EXHIBITIONS: *Art and the Animal,* 2010, San Diego Natural History Museum; *Today's Legacy,* 2011, Bryan Memorial Gallery, Jeffersonville, Vermont; *WREAF's Boreal Views,* 2012, Catamount Arts Gallery, Saint Johnsbury, Vermont
REPRESENTATIVES: Looking Good Licensing, Manchester, Vermont

It was evening in the Florida Everglades. The air was still. The scene was saturated with color. A small group of white ibises quietly probed for food along the water's edge. Concentrating on them, I barely noticed soft ripples in the water behind the birds. Ever so slowly a gator was moving in. A predator-prey drama was playing out in slow motion.

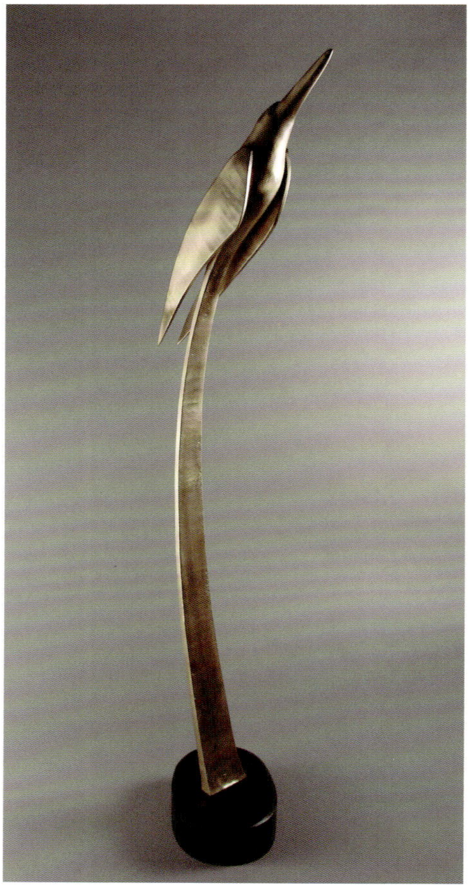

Zenith, 2011
Bronze and steel
27 x 7 x 7

Collection of the artist

BORN: 1970, United States
RESIDES: Memphis, Tennessee
EDUCATION: M.F.A., Southern Illinois University, Carbondale; B.F.A., Memphis College of Art
EXHIBITIONS: Jack Robinson Gallery, 2010, Memphis; *Iron 2010,* National Ornamental Metal Museum, Memphis; Overton Park Gallery, 2011, Memphis; *Alumni Summer Exhibition,* 2012, Memphis College of Art
AWARDS: Purchase Award, 2010, *Toys Designed by Artists,* Arkansas Arts Center, Little Rock; NICHE Award, 2012, Pennsylvania Convention Center, Philadelphia
COLLECTIONS: Arkansas Arts Center; Memphis Botanical Gardens; Shelby County Trustee's Office, Memphis
COMMISSIONS: Arts Memphis; Saint George's Independent School, Collierville, Tennessee

Occasionally my students ask me why I make artwork about birds. Birds exemplify grace, speed, patience, and endurance. Typically, my work begins with a mental snapshot taken while driving or from a brief glimpse of a bird as it perches, takes flight, or hunts. I then distill it all to the bare minimum without losing the integrity of a species. Sometimes my sculptures are simply a reaction to an image or thought about the avian shape. Such compositions are rooted in the formalities of sculpture and metalsmithing, relying on the exaggeration of volume, line, movement, and form. Zenith *speaks to flight, speed, and movement with its elongated tail and beak, animated by an arcing gesture.*

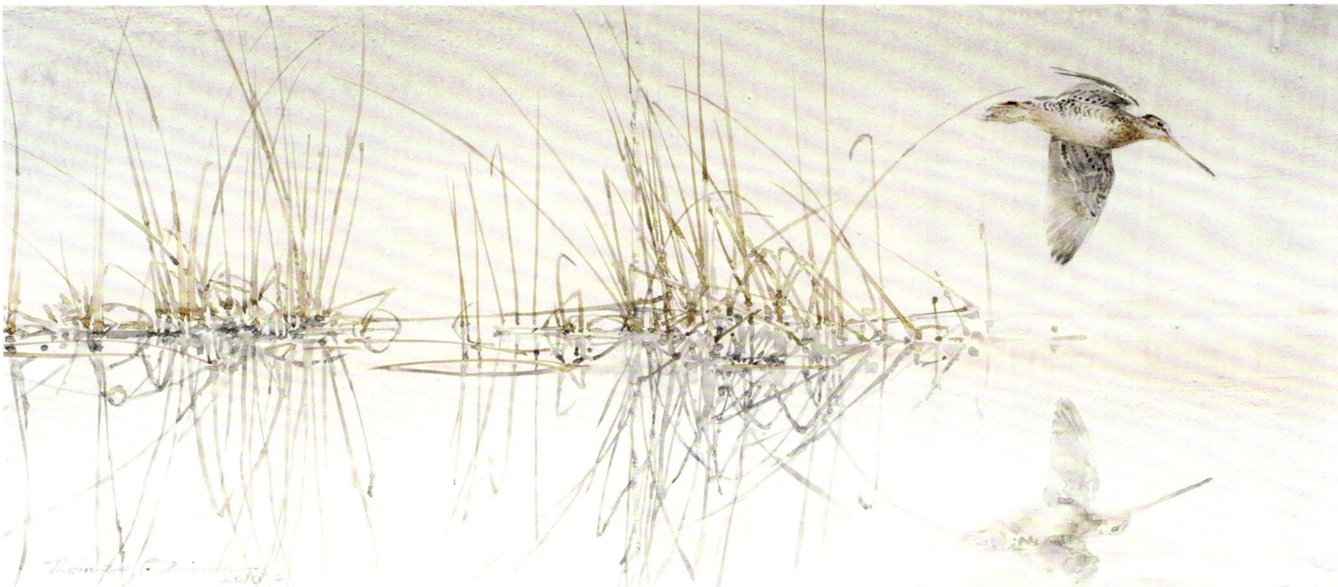

Rhythms of Flight, 2010
Wilson's snipe
Watercolor on gessoed paper
13 3/4 x 30

Courtesy of Hayden Hays Gallery, Colorado Springs

Birds in Art: 1981-82, 1984-91, 1993-11
Master Wildlife Artist: 1998

BORN: 1938, United States
RESIDES: Point Reyes Station, California
EDUCATION: B.P.A., Art Center College of Design, Pasadena, California
EXHIBITIONS: *Prix de West Invitational,* 2010 and 2012, National Cowboy & Western Heritage Museum, Oklahoma City; *Light, Form and Reverie,* 2011, Gerald Peters Gallery, Santa Fe, New Mexico; *Artists for Nature Jubilee,* 2012, Orangerie Landgoed Vollenhoven, De Bilt, Netherlands
COLLECTIONS: National Cowboy & Western Heritage Museum; National Museum of Wildlife Art, Jackson, Wyoming
BIBLIOGRAPHY: "Believable Wonder: The Art of Thomas Quinn," *Western Art Collector,* March 2012; "Thomas Quinn: The Watercolor Samurai," *Wildlife Art Journal,* May 2012 OL
REPRESENTATIVES: Gerald Peters Gallery

A lone jacksnipe sails effortlessly above flooded grasses. Like the arrival of a singular idea, it may with quickening wingbeats dart and sweep, then vanish on the horizon of oblivion.

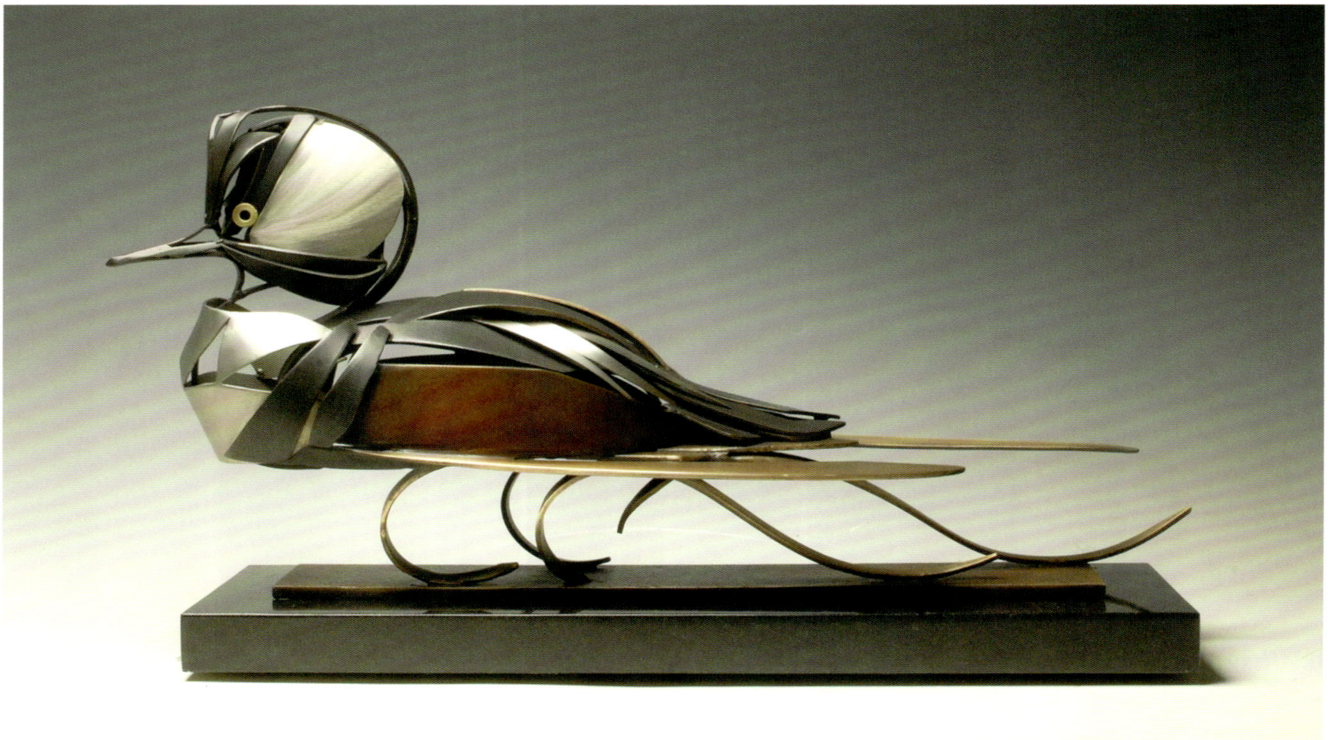

Glide, 2011
Hooded merganser
Bronze and stainless steel
12 x 21 x 7

Collection of
Tom and Alexa Seip

Birds in Art: 1998-99, 2001-02, 2004, 2006-11

W

BORN: 1970, United States
RESIDES: Trevor, Wisconsin
EDUCATION: B.F.A., University of Wisconsin, Milwaukee
EXHIBITIONS: Wendell Gilley Museum, 2010, Southwest Harbor, Maine
AWARDS: Award of Excellence, 2010, *Art and the Animal,* San Diego Natural History Museum; Featured Artist, 2011, *Waterfowl Festival,* Easton, Maryland
COLLECTIONS: Benson Sculpture Garden, Loveland, Colorado; San Diego County Public Library, Fallbrook Branch; Wendell Gilley Museum
COMMISSIONS: Arkansas Children's Hospital, Little Rock; National Museum of Wildlife Art and Teton County Community Pathways, Jackson, Wyoming
BIBLIOGRAPHY: "Expressions of Nature," *Western Art Collector,* July 2011; "Dimensional Expression," *Southwest Art,* July 2011; "Rousing Success," *Western Art Collector,* March 2012
REPRESENTATIVES: Bronze Coast Gallery, Cannon Beach, Oregon; Columbine Gallery, Loveland; Niemi Sculpture Gallery & Garden, Kenosha, Wisconsin

Serendipity can be among an artist's most valuable tools, but you have to be open and ready to embrace it. While finishing a weld on the stainless steel cheek of this merganser, I noticed that if I overlapped and organized the marks left by the sander, it created the perfect visual texture to define the delicate feathering I was trying to achieve. While it wasn't something I set out to do when starting this sculpture, I now have a new technique to use going forward.

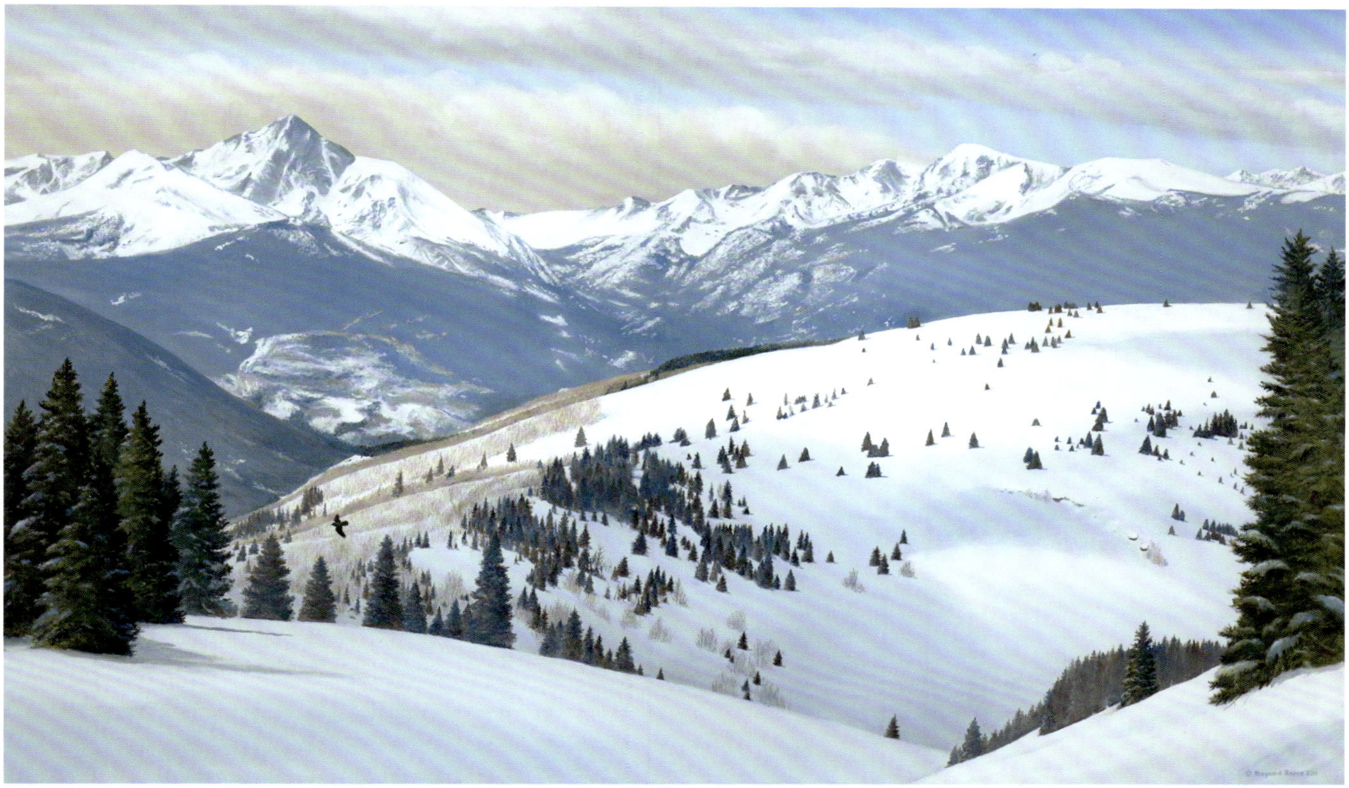

The Raven, 2011
Oil on linen
36 x 60

Private collection

Birds in Art: 1976-11
Master Wildlife Artist: 1989

BORN: 1920, United States
RESIDES: Des Moines, Iowa
COLLECTIONS: Philmont Scout Ranch, Cimarron, New Mexico
REPRESENTATIVES: Mill Pond Press, Venice, Florida

The raven is king over the vast mountainous area near Vail, Colorado, and the only bird that I've seen living at altitudes of 12,000 feet or more. It was a challenge to accurately depict Mount of the Holy Cross towering above the bird, as many people are familiar with the location of every tree and rock in the area. The ski run in the valley below is named Forever, so quote this raven 'Forever More.'

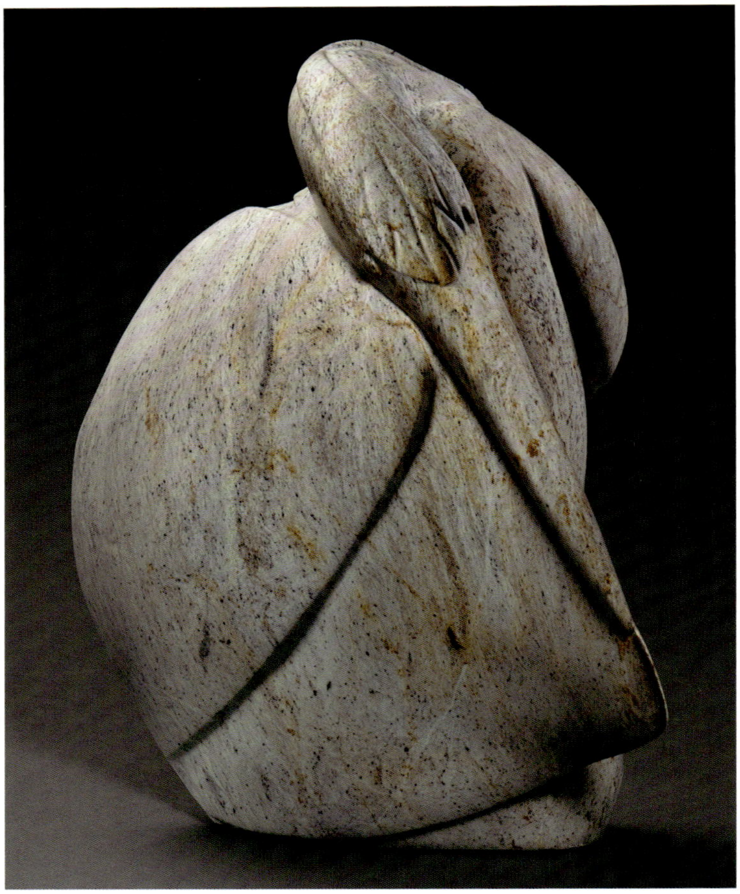

Preening, 2012
Great blue heron
Soapstone
17 x 14 x 6

Collection of the artist

Birds in Art: 2009-10

W

BORN: 1950, United States
RESIDES: Almond, Wisconsin
EDUCATION: B.A., University of Wisconsin, Stevens Point
EXHIBITIONS: *Capturing Horses*, 2011, Riverfront Gallery, Stevens Point; *Stone Sculptures, Paintings & Drawings*, 2011, Tomorrow River Gallery, Amherst, Wisconsin; *Verse & Vision*, 2012, Gallery Q, Stevens Point
COLLECTIONS: River Valley Bank, Wausau; Wausau Homes, Inc.
REPRESENTATIVES: Fineline Designs Gallery, Sister Bay, Wisconsin; Tomorrow River Gallery

A hunter of immense patience stalks the edge of a glacial kettle lake. Her thin legs move almost imperceptibly among the emergent reeds. Armed with a spear, dull yellow in color, this member of the Ardea tribe searches the shallows for her favorite prey. She has three hungry young ones at home. Her stealthy movements are almost painfully slow when her sharp spear flashes and another small bluegill is added to her bag. At her return she is greeted with a raucous clamor. After the young ones breakfast on regurgitated bluegills, the great blue heron preens her slate-gray feathers in preparation for another hunt.

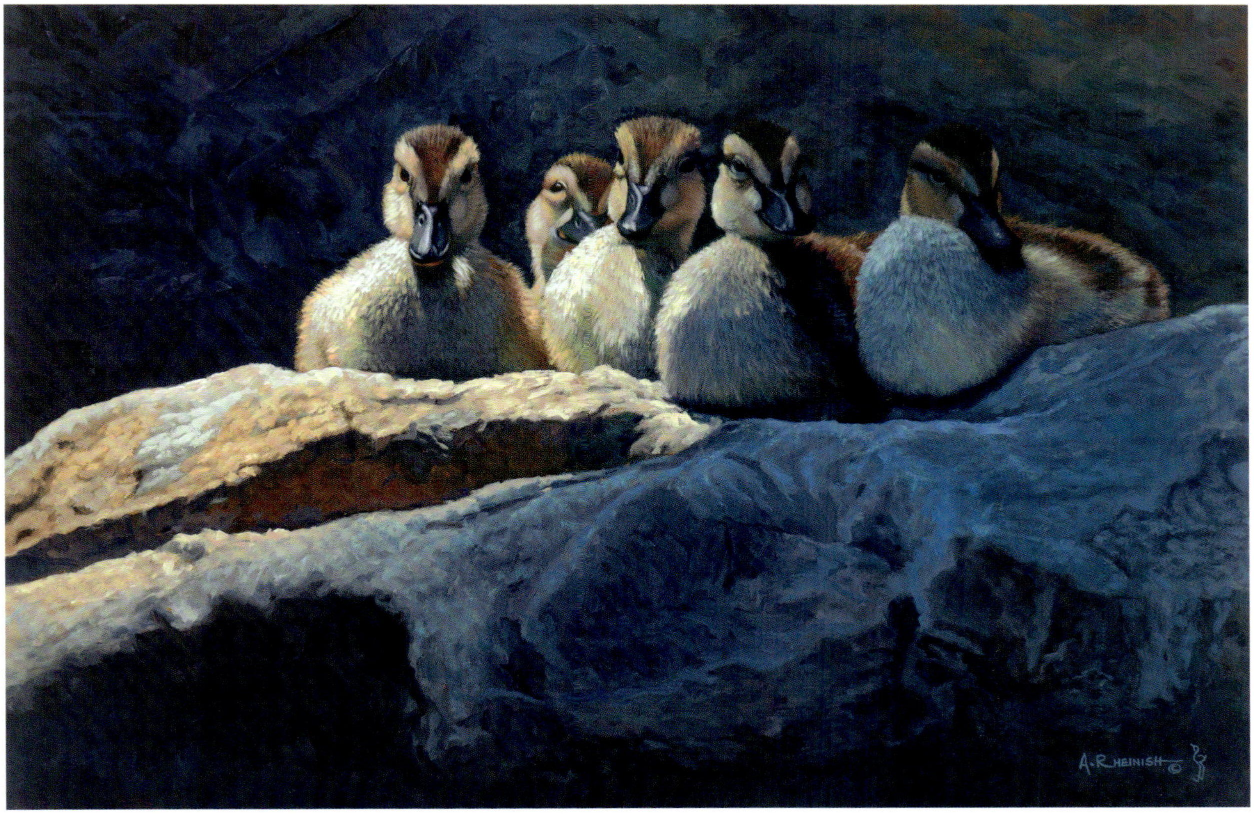

Ducklings 4 + 1, 2012
Mallard
Oil on linen
16 x 24

Collection of the artist

Birds in Art: 2008, 2010-11

BORN: 1962, United States
RESIDES: Trabuco Canyon, California
EXHIBITIONS: *Art-A-Fair Festival,* 2010 and 2012, Laguna Beach, California; *Art and the Animal,* 2011, Dennos Museum Center, Northwestern Michigan College, Traverse City, and 2012, Hiram Blauvelt Art Museum, Oradell, New Jersey
AWARDS: First Place, 2010, *Catalina Festival of Art,* Avalon, California
BIBLIOGRAPHY: "California Artist: Arlene Rheinish," *Catalina Festival of Art,* 2010

The theatrical effect of light against dark can guide the eyes of a viewer through a painting. I was excited to see this piece come to life with each paint stroke; the little subjects made it all the more enjoyable as they took center stage. A vacation to Lake Tahoe provided an opportunity to observe mallard ducklings following their mother to the lake's shoreline rocks. As the little ones made themselves comfortable, mom flew off to forage on her own. The display of sunlight was captivating as it played across these young ones enjoying their outing.

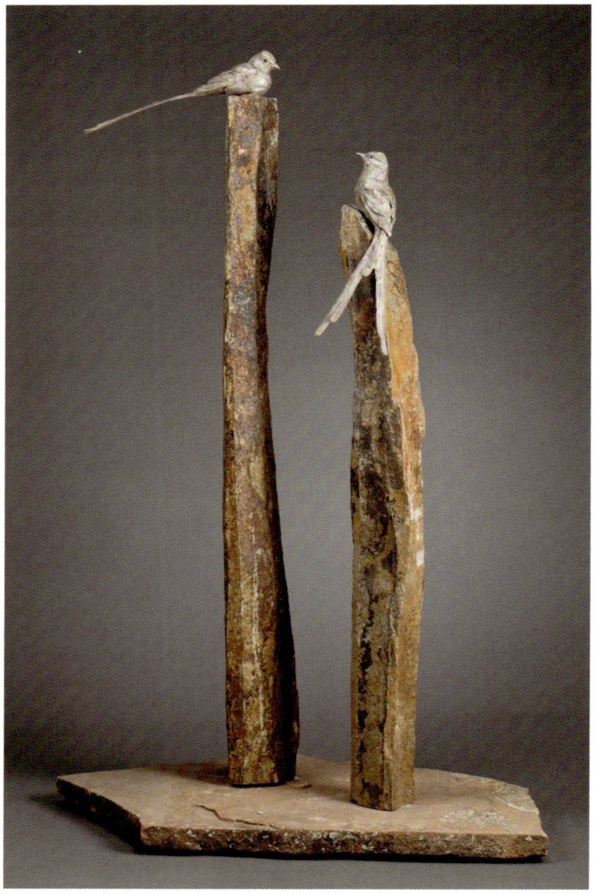

Skydancers (ed. 25), 2011
Scissor-tailed flycatcher
Bronze on basalt
48 x 18 x 18

Collection of the artist

Birds in Art: 2008-11

W

BORN: 1962, United States
RESIDES: Point of Rocks, Maryland
EXHIBITIONS: *About Face,* 2011, Annmarie Sculpture Garden & Art Center, Dowell, Maryland; *Art and the Animal,* 2011, Dennos Museum Center, Northwestern Michigan College, Traverse City, and 2012, Hiram Blauvelt Art Museum, Oradell, New Jersey; *National Sculpture Society Awards Exhibition,* 2012, Brookgreen Gardens, Murrells Inlet, South Carolina
AWARDS: Best of Show, Three Dimensional, 2010 and 2012, *NatureWorks,* Tulsa, Oklahoma; Best of Show, Wildfowl Sculpture, 2011, *Ward World Championship Wildfowl Carving Competition,* Ocean City, Maryland
COLLECTIONS: Denver Zoo; Smithsonian National Museum of Natural History, Washington
COMMISSIONS: NatureWorks
BIBLIOGRAPHY: "Associate Profile: Paul Rhymer," *National Sculpture Society,* May/June 2011; "Monumental Milestone," *Western Art Collector,* July 2011
REPRESENTATIVES: Audubon Gallery, Charleston, South Carolina; Lovetts Fine Art Gallery, Tulsa; Manitou Galleries, Santa Fe, New Mexico

As an artist I'm always trying to balance the desire to create something meaningful and the need to earn a living. Ideally, both can be accomplished. Skydancers *was inspired by many miles of travel on the roads of Oklahoma where I saw scissor-tailed flycatchers on fences and telephone wires. This piece combines my experience with a beautiful bird and provides a perfect sculpture for those living in Oklahoma, where the scissor-tailed flycatcher is the state bird. Known by the nickname 'skydancer,' these birds engage in an amazing aerial courtship dance.*

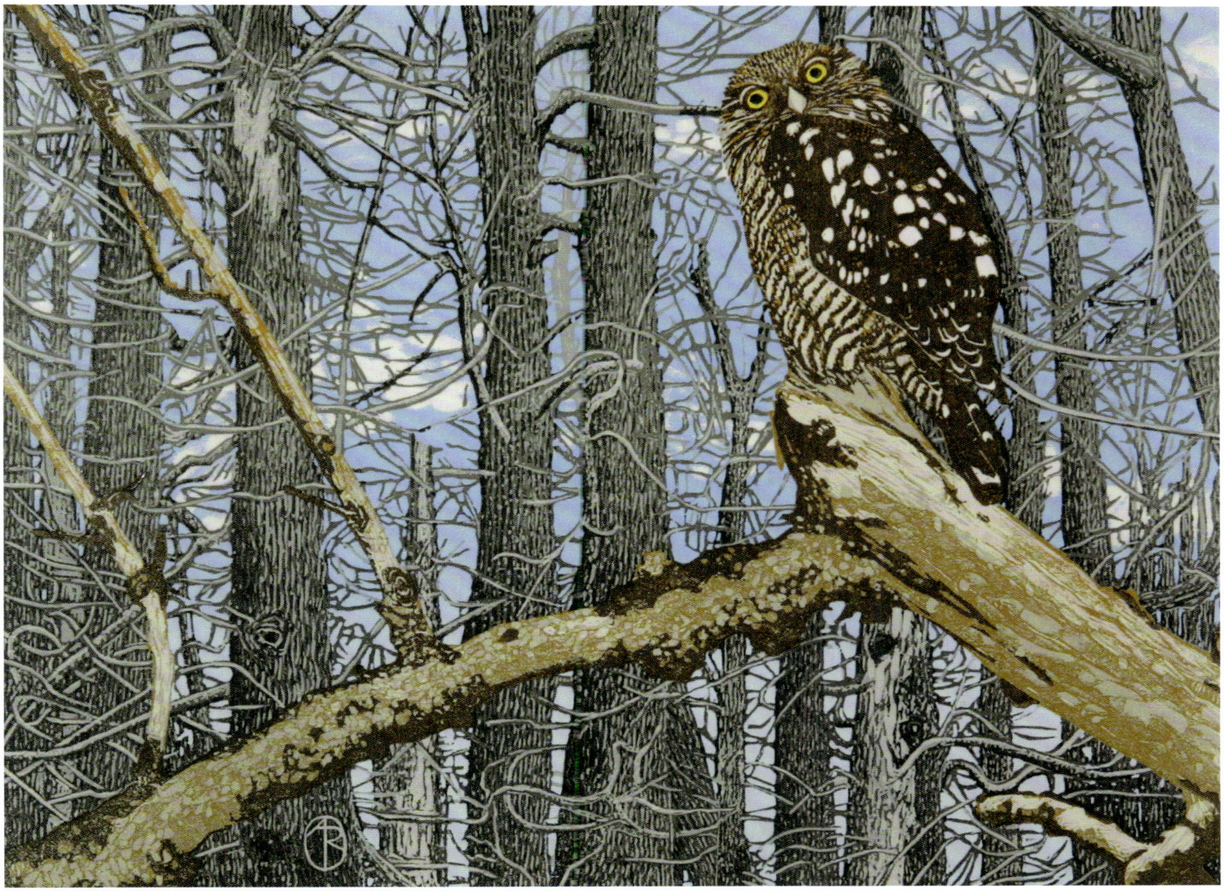

Northern Hawk Owl
(5/30), 2011
Woodcut on mulberry paper
12 x 16

Collection of the artist

Birds in Art: 1989, 1991-95, 1997-11
Master Wildlife Artist: 2006

W

BORN: 1954, United States
RESIDES: Santa Cruz, California
EDUCATION: B.S., University of Wisconsin, Whitewater
EXHIBITIONS: *Art of the Animal Kingdom,* 2010-12, Bennington Center for the Arts, Bennington, Vermont; *Drawing Inspiration from the Hula Valley,* 2011, Agamon Park Gallery, Upper Galilee, Israel; *Paper in Particular,* 2012, Columbia College, Columbia, Missouri; Woodson Art Museum, 2012; *Artists for Nature Jubilee,* 2012, Orangerie Landgoed Vollenhoven, De Bilt, Netherlands
AWARDS: Medal of Excellence, 2011, *Artists for Conservation,* Spirit Gallery, Grouse Mountain, Vancouver, British Columbia, Canada
COLLECTIONS: Brown University, Providence, Rhode Island; Hiram Blauvelt Art Museum, Oradell, New Jersey; Mass Audubon Visual Arts Center, Canton, Massachusetts
BIBLIOGRAPHY: *Drawing Inspiration from the Hula Valley,* Society for the Protection of Nature in Israel, 2011
REPRESENTATIVES: Gallery M, Half Moon Bay, California; Wildlife Art Gallery, Lavenham, Suffolk, England; Williams Gallery West, Oakhurst, California

Carving the blocks for a woodcut is the most fun part of the process. For this northern hawk owl, I carved three separate blocks and used a reduction process to print them multiple times. I especially enjoyed the complex patterns created by the bare branches in the trees. I spotted this owl in Alaska at Thanksgiving; the memory is linked to the moose served by our friends as part of their traditional dinner.

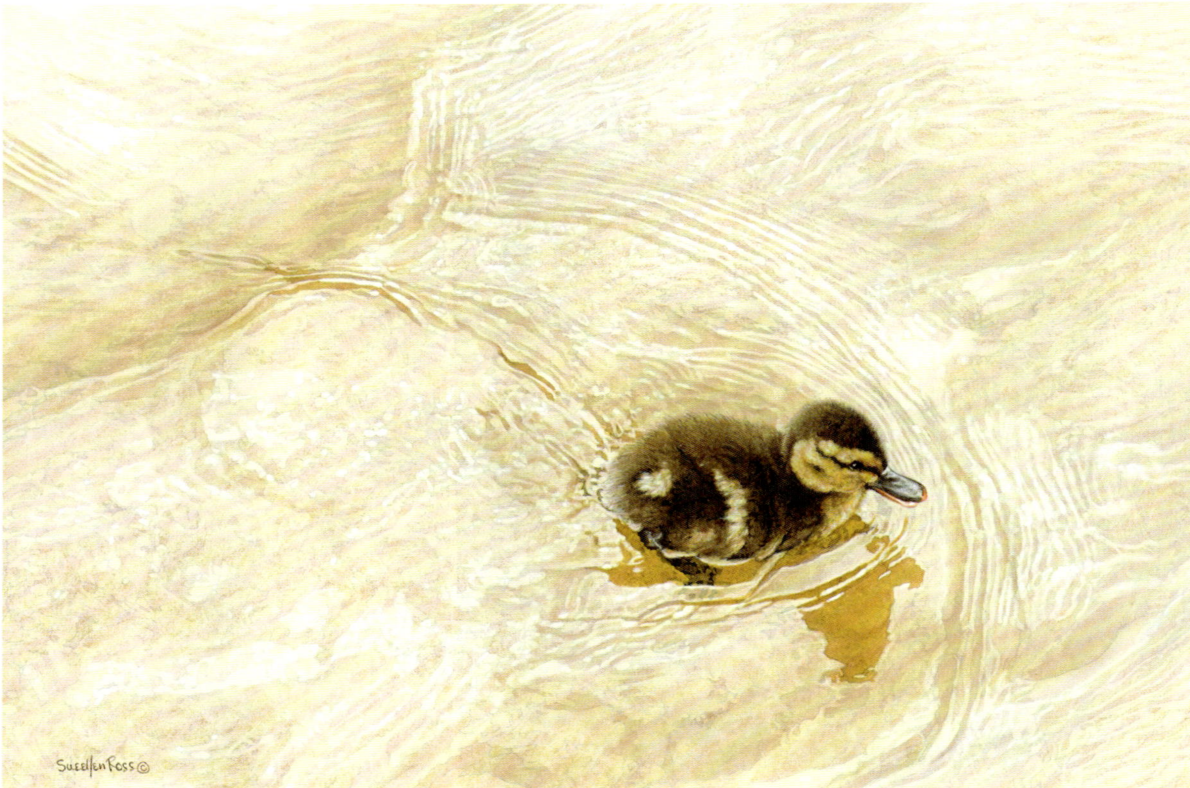

Very Small Duck, 2012
Mallard
India ink, watercolor, and colored pencil on Arches paper
10 1/2 x 15 1/2

Private collection

Birds in Art: 1987, 1989, 1991-95, 1997, 1999-04, 2007, 2009-11

W

BORN: 1941, United States
RESIDES: Seattle
EDUCATION: B.A., University of California, Berkeley
EXHIBITIONS: *American Miniatures,* 2010-12, Settlers West Galleries, Tucson, Arizona; *Invitational Small Works,* 2010-12, Howard/Mandville Gallery, Kirkland, Washington; *Masters in Miniature,* 2011-12, Trailside Galleries, Jackson, Wyoming
COLLECTIONS: Bank of America, Seattle; Shell Oil Company, Houston
REPRESENTATIVES: Howard/Mandville Gallery; Trailside Galleries, Jackson, Wyoming, and Scottsdale, Arizona

Very Small Duck *could be any mallard duckling on any body of water. Its identity is not as important as its size and condition; it takes up very little space in the painting and is alone. The title is purposely vague and doesn't answer questions about the duckling's destination, safety, or whether its mother and siblings are nearby. Although the overall theme is isolation, this little one is making a purposeful wake in a featureless, overcast waterscape.*

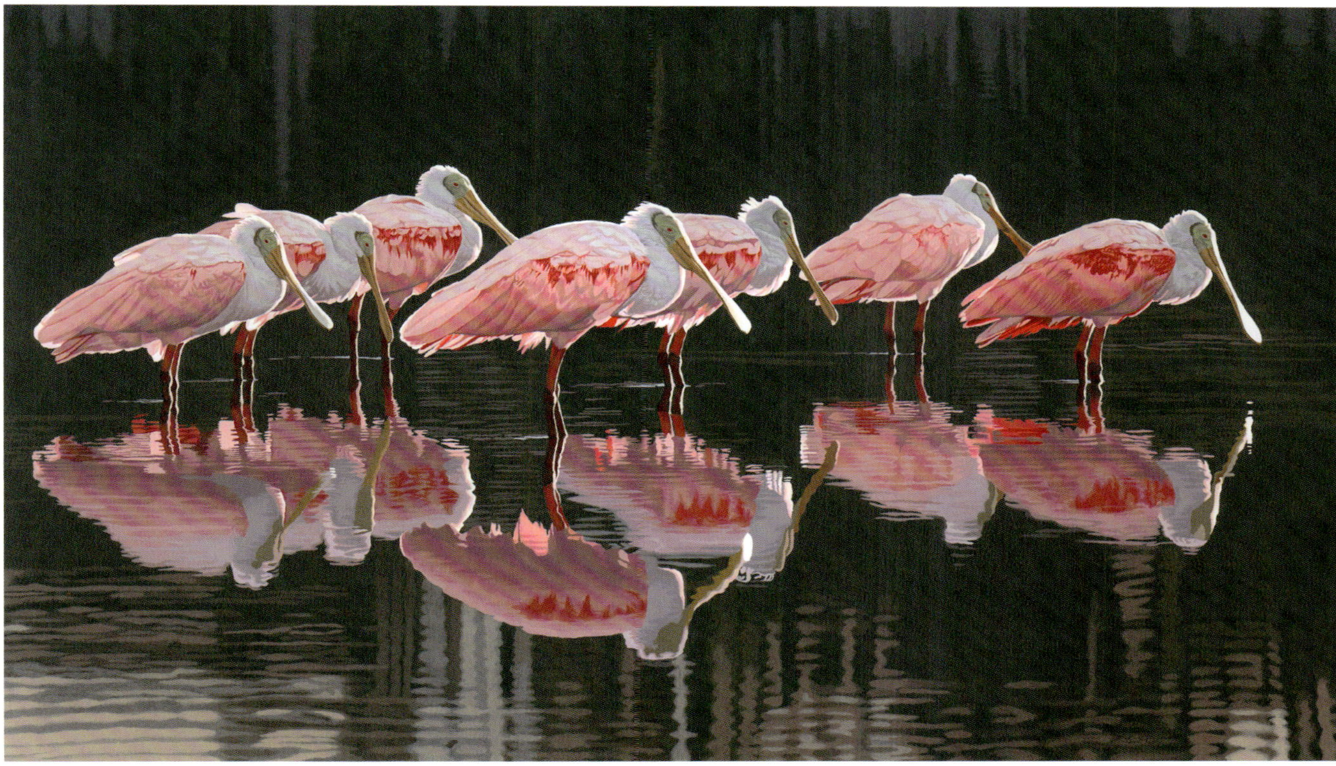

Roseate Spoonbills, 2010
Acrylic on gessoed hardboard
28 x 48

Private collection

Birds in Art: 1992-94, 1996-02, 2004-05, 2008, 2010-11

W

BORN: 1968, United States
RESIDES: Greenbank, Whidbey Island, Washington
EDUCATION: B.A., University of Kentucky, Lexington
EXHIBITIONS: *Art and the Animal,* 2011, Dennos Museum Center, Northwestern Michigan College, Traverse City; *Masters in Miniature,* 2011-12, Trailside Galleries, Jackson, Wyoming; *Focus on Nature,* 2012, New York State Museum, Albany
AWARDS: Poster Artist, 2010, *Skagit Valley Tulip Festival,* Mount Vernon, Washington; Teacher Excellence Award, 2010, University of Washington Educational Outreach, Seattle; Gold Medal, 2010, International Festivals and Events Association, Boise, Idaho
COLLECTIONS: Bennington Center for the Arts, Bennington, Vermont; Mass Audubon Society, Lincoln, Massachusetts; Skagit Valley Tulip Festival
COMMISSIONS: Island Adventures, Anacortes, Washington
BIBLIOGRAPHY: "The Magnificent Bald Eagle," *Harbors Magazine,* Spring 2012

I was inspired to paint these roseate spoonbills during a trip to Ding Darling National Wildlife Refuge in Florida. Large flocks of spoonbills gathered every afternoon, providing interesting interactions and group compositions. The refuge has plenty of eye-catching water birds, but the spoonbills always diverted my attention when they flew in. The backlighting on these colorful birds, framed by the dark green background, was too attractive for me to resist, capped by the fact that I really enjoy painting groups of birds.

Jonathan Sainsbury

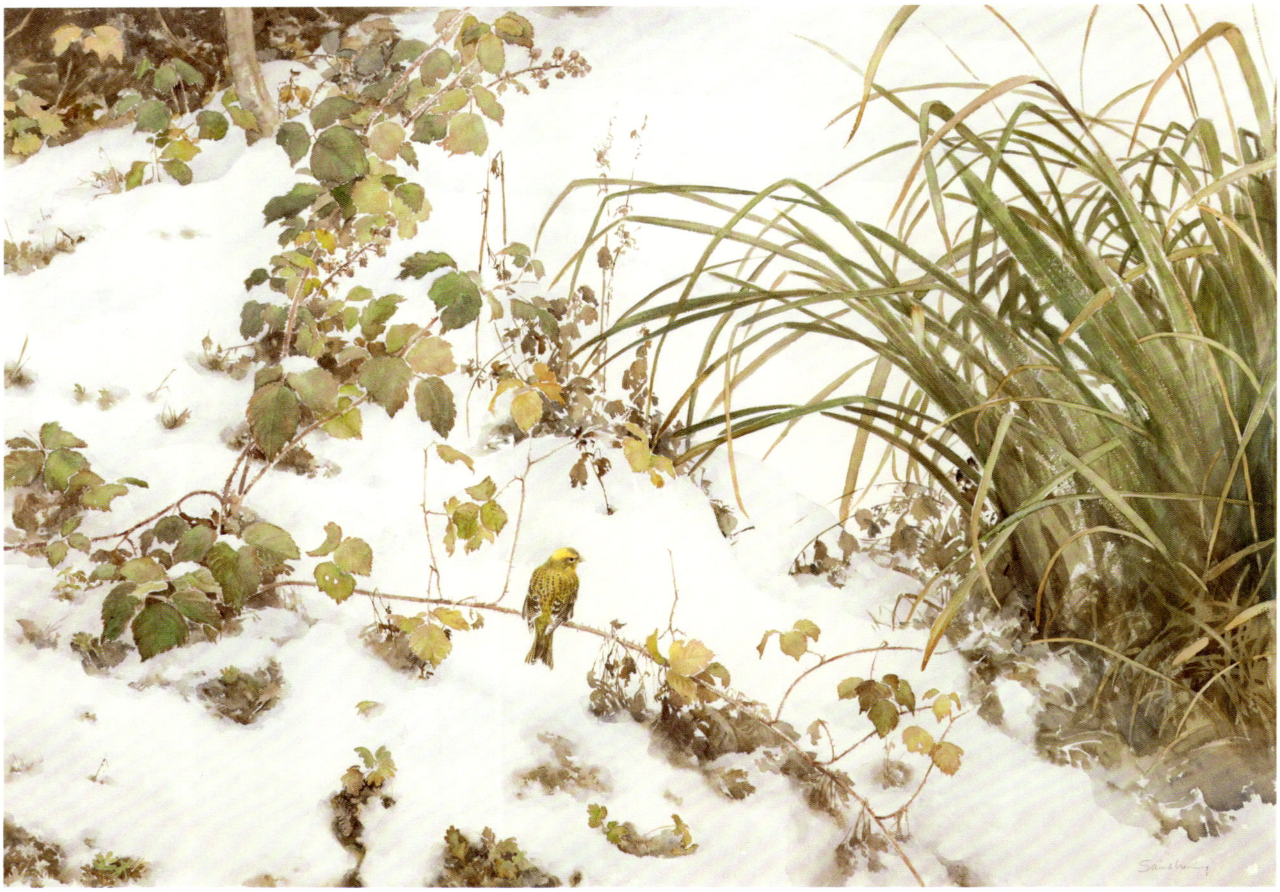

Freedom, 2012
Canary
Watercolor on Arches Aquarelle paper
29 x 41

Collection of the artist

Birds in Art: 1994, 1996-97, 2009

W

BORN: 1951, England
RESIDES: Comrie, Perthshire, Scotland
EDUCATION: B.A., Leeds College of Art, Leeds, England
EXHIBITIONS: *The Natural Eye,* 2010-11, Mall Galleries, London; *Art and the Animal,* 2010, San Diego Natural History Museum, 2011, Dennos Museum Center, Northwestern Michigan College, Traverse City, and 2012, Hiram Blauvelt Art Museum, Oradell, New Jersey; *Royal Society of Painters in Watercolours,* 2010 and 2012, Royal Scottish Academy, Edinburgh

Tweet, my canary, is confined to a cage in my studio. Knowing she would perish if I set her free, I decided to paint her in the world outside my window, giving her an imagined freedom. I understood that Tweet would be in a state of apprehension and wonder; that is why she looks half back to the home she has left that is boring but safe, and forward to the arch of reeds that leads to a path as yet untaken. The parallels with childhood cannot be ignored. Tweet is about to experience nature. Who amongst us could forget the first time we felt the warmth of a living creature, the sting of nettles, or the scent of roses. These thoughts swirled in my head as I painted with few challenges. I had a still life outside my window and a model in the studio.

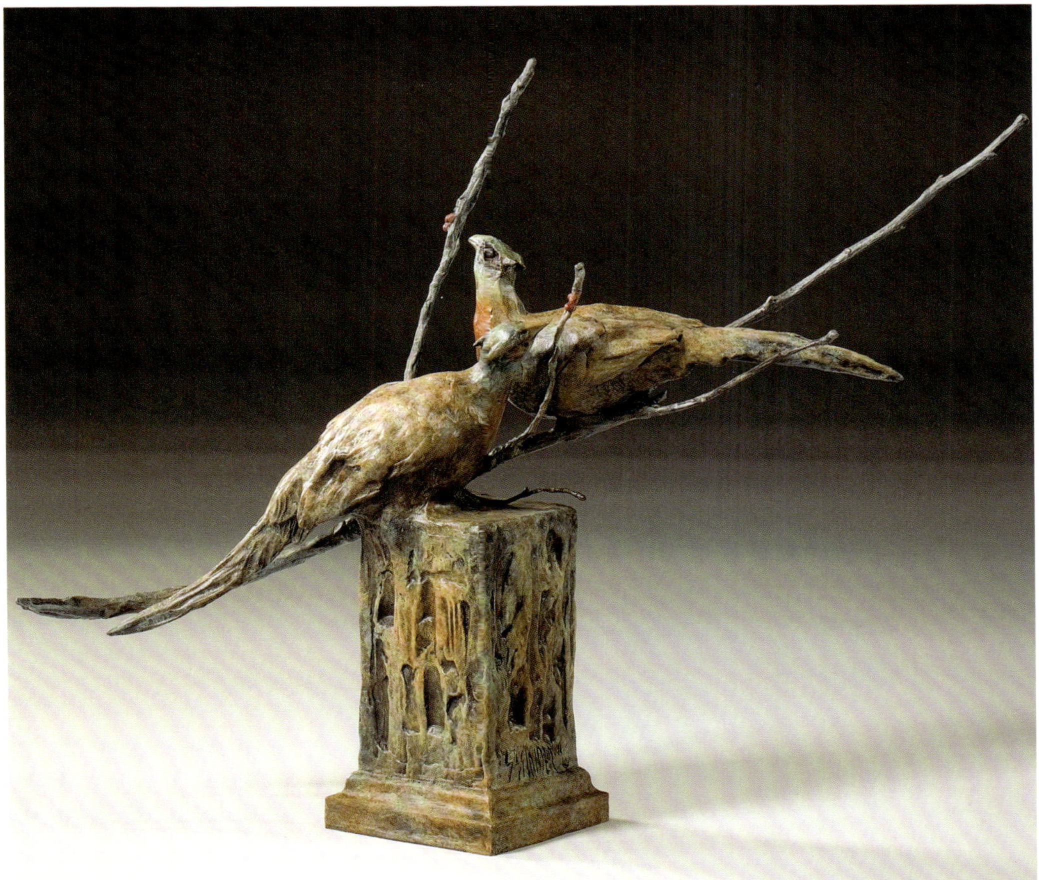

Berries in the Snow
(ed. 35), 2011
Ring-necked pheasant
Bronze
12 x 12 x 6

Collection of the artist

Birds in Art: 1989-90, 1992, 1994-96, 1998-99, 2002, 2007, 2011

W

BORN: 1941, United States
RESIDES: Kalispell, Montana
EXHIBITIONS: *Prix de West Invitational,* 2011-12, National Cowboy & Western Heritage Museum, Oklahoma City; *Art and the Animal,* 2011, Dennos Museum Center, Northwestern Michigan College, Traverse City, and 2012, Hiram Blauvelt Art Museum, Oradell, New Jersey
AWARDS: Award of Excellence, 2010, *Art and the Animal*, San Diego Natural History Museum; First Place Three-Dimensional Art, 2010-12, *Cowgirl Up!,* Desert Caballeros Western Museum, Wickenburg, Arizona; Pietro and Alfrieda Montana Memorial Award, 2011, *Allied Artists of America,* National Arts Club, New York City; Artists Choice Award, 2012, *Night of Artists,* Briscoe Museum, San Antonio
COLLECTIONS: Buffalo Bill Museum, Cody, Wyoming; Leanin' Tree Museum of Western Art, Boulder, Colorado; National Museum of Wildlife Art, Jackson, Wyoming
REPRESENTATIVES: Greenhouse Gallery of Fine Art, San Antonio; Meyer Gallery, Park City, Utah; Trailside Galleries, Jackson, Wyoming, and Scottsdale, Arizona

Just beyond my studio window grows a splendid mountain ash. Its berries tenaciously cling throughout the fierce winds of approaching winter, remaining long after the leaves have fallen and decayed under the snow. The deep red against a background of white creates a visual richness on a gray day. Turkeys wobble on the thinner branches trying to pick at berries beyond their reach. Pheasants feast as chickadees dart in and out. The chattering of squirrels completes the ensemble. While this is a visual gift to me, it is immensely important to those needing energy to endure the cold months ahead.

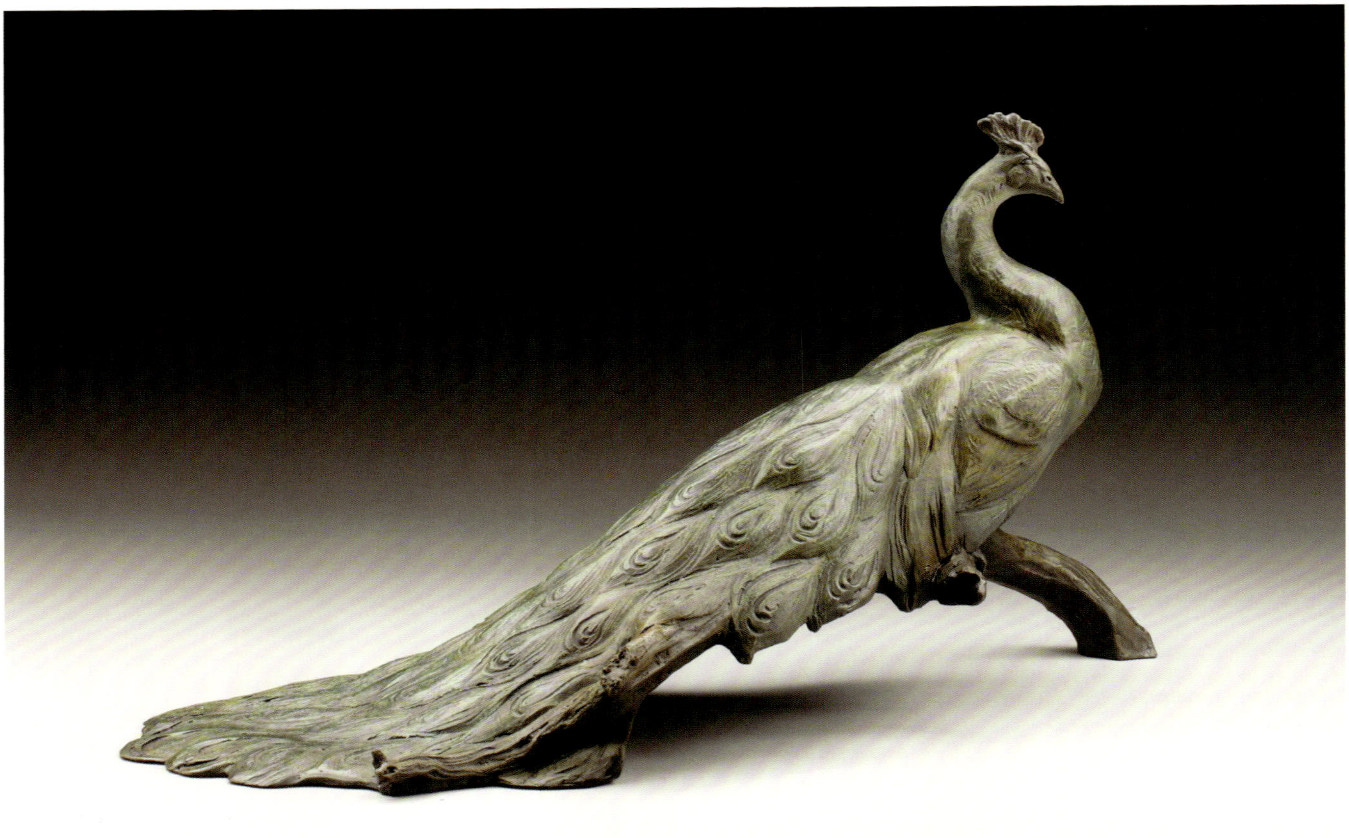

Shade of Paradise (ed. 65), 2011
Peacock
Bronze
13 x 23 x 11

Collection of the artist

Birds in Art: 1996, 1998, 2003

BORN: 1943, United States
RESIDES: Lander, Wyoming
EDUCATION: Kansas City Art Institute, Kansas City, Missouri
EXHIBITIONS: *Art and the Animal,* 2010, San Diego Natural History Museum; *Masters of the American West,* 2012, Autry National Center, Los Angeles; *Prix de West Invitational,* 2012, National Cowboy & Western Heritage Museum, Oklahoma City
AWARDS: Award of Excellence, 2011, *Art and the Animal,* Dennos Museum Center, Northwestern Michigan College, Traverse City
COLLECTIONS: Brookgreen Gardens, Murrells Inlet, South Carolina; National Cowboy & Western Heritage Museum; National Museum of Wildlife Art, Jackson, Wyoming
BIBLIOGRAPHY: "Wild and Domestic," April 2011, and "Inside-Out," July 2012, *Western Art Collector*; "Prominent People," *Southwest Art,* May 2012
REPRESENTATIVES: Trailside Galleries, Scottsdale, Arizona; Whistle Pik Gallery, Fredericksburg, Texas; Wilcox Gallery, Jackson

The sensual and elegant Art Nouveau *movement of the 1800s was influenced by Japanese art, and exotic birds such as peafowl were often a source of inspiration. Years ago I owned peafowl. Although noisy, these birds are so magnificently beautiful that their earsplitting screams were easy to ignore. I focused on their ornate and luxurious qualities in* Shade of Paradise, *a maquette for a larger, life-sized sculpture that will be more than seven feet long.*

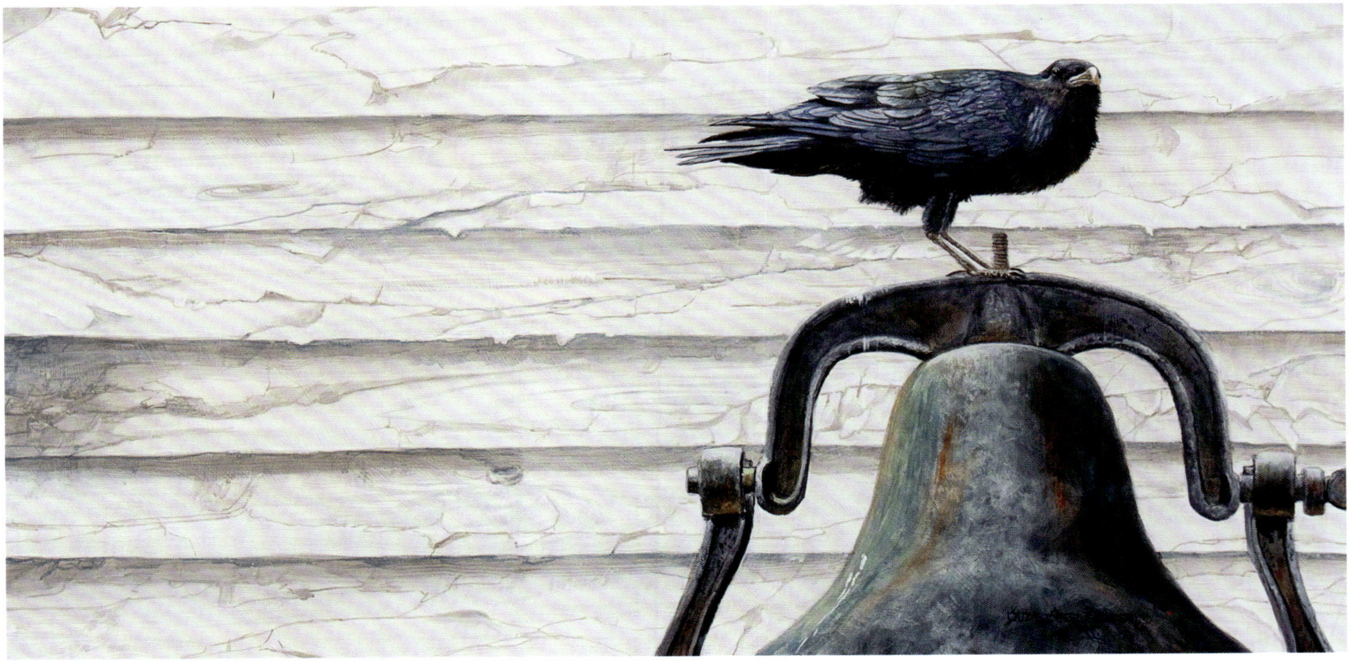

School Belle, 2011
Common raven
Acrylic on hardboard
12 x 24

Collection of the artist

Birds in Art: 2004, 2006, 2010-11

BORN: 1955, United States
RESIDES: Osprey, Florida
EDUCATION: B.S., George Mason University, Fairfax, Virginia
EXHIBITIONS: Final Touch Frame & Gallery, 2010, Venice, Florida; *Wildlife Discovery,* 2010, and *Invitational Miniature Show,* 2012, Trailside Galleries, Jackson, Wyoming; *America the Beautiful,* 2012, Hueys Fine Art, Santa Fe, New Mexico
AWARDS: Honorable Mention, 2012, *The Artist's Magazine*
COLLECTIONS: Bennington Center for the Arts, Bennington, Vermont; Raymond James Financial Center, Saint Petersburg, Florida
BIBLIOGRAPHY: "A Woman's Place," *Sporting Classics,* March/April 2010; "Suzie Seerey-Lester: The 'Secret' Life of an Artist," *SKB Legacy News,* Winter 2010
REPRESENTATIVES: Hueys Fine Art; Plainsmen Gallery, Clearwater, Florida; Trailside Galleries

We have an old school bell in our yard that is the perfect perch for a bird. I knew my choice of bird had to be one with enough weight to offset the bell. A reference photo of a raven taken in Yellowstone National Park years ago was what I was looking for. Since both the bell and the bird were black, I needed a light background. A drive through a neighborhood of great old homes in our hometown yielded a wood building that caught my eye. It was white, but the paint was cracked and peeling. It had character. Three distinct components came together in School Belle.

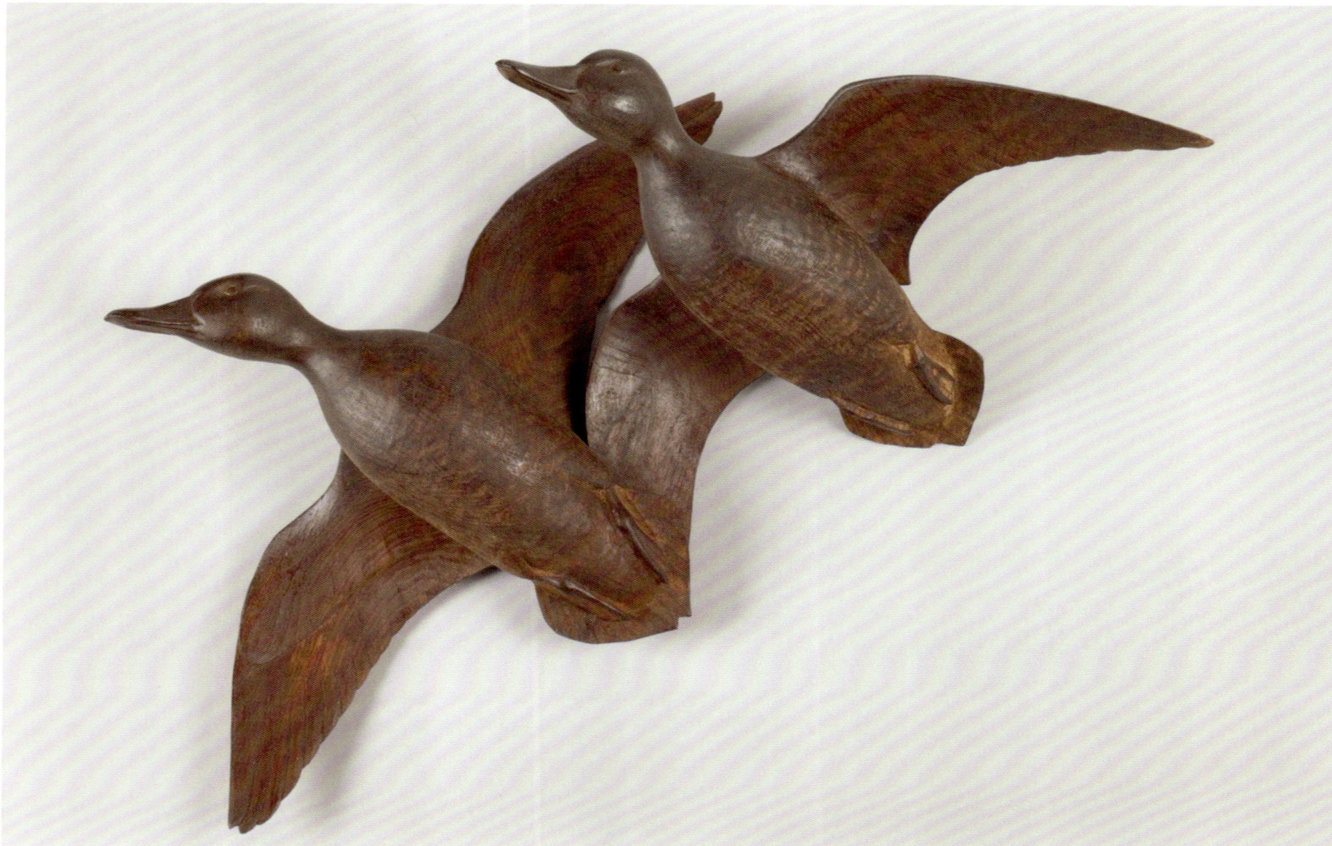

Teal Study, 2010
Black walnut
22 x 24 x 12

Collection of the artist

Birds in Art: 1982, 1984-91, 1993, 1995-11
Master Wildlife Artist: 1996

W

BORN: 1943, United States
RESIDES: Kent, Ohio
EXHIBITIONS: *Light, Form and Reverie,* 2011, Gerald Peters Gallery, Santa Fe, New Mexico
COLLECTIONS: Cleveland Museum of Natural History; Nature in Art, Twigworth, Gloucester, England; Ward Museum of Wildfowl Art, Salisbury University, Salisbury, Maryland
REPRESENTATIVES: Gerald Peters Gallery

I carved these two birds intact from a section of walnut, finished in linseed oil. The grain direction is horizontal, running through the length of the birds' bodies – somewhat of a departure, as I usually carve in a vertical grain attitude. The right wing of the upper bird passes over and attaches to the top of the lower bird's tail, while the right wing of the lower one mounts to the wall, suspending Teal Study.

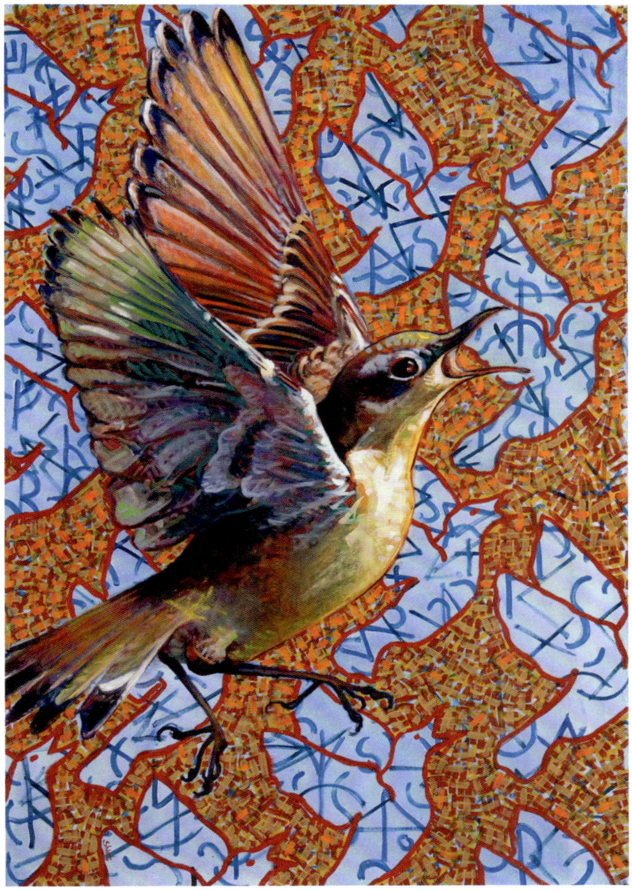

Danger Right**,** 2011
American robin
Oil on Lanaquarelle cold press paper on Belgian linen
60 x 40

Collection of the artist

Birds in Art: 2009-10

BORN: 1950, United States
RESIDES: Cincinnati
EDUCATION: B.F.A., University of Cincinnati
EXHIBITIONS: *Contemporary Realism Biennial,* 2010, Fort Wayne Museum of Art, Fort Wayne, Indiana; *Here's Looking at You,* 2011, Riffe Gallery, Columbus, Ohio; *Ohio Annual Exhibition,* 2011, Zanesville Museum of Art, Zanesville; *Mid-Year Exhibition,* Butler Institute of American Art, 2011, Youngstown, Ohio; *Fresh Ohio,* 2011, Willard Winkelman Gallery, Bowling Green State University, Bowling Green
AWARDS: Second Place, 2012, *National Juried Exhibition,* Customs House Museum, Clarksville, Tennessee
COLLECTIONS: Four Entertainment Group, Cincinnati; Trindle Wealth Management, Morgan Stanley/Smith Barney, Cincinnati
BIBLIOGRAPHY: "Dog Daze," *The Artist's Magazine,* June 2012
REPRESENTATIVES: Cincinnati Art Gallery; Leider's Creek Gallery, Franklin, Tennessee

Danger Right *is the left half of a pair of robins crying out a warning. They are from a series about dizygotic or fraternal twins, using mirrored images of animals. The robin, my de facto 'canary in the coal mine,' sounds the warning because this bird is ubiquitous in the United States. The background pattern – birds going in the same direction – represents those that might be acolytes, lemmings, or sycophants. The viewer must decide how to translate the 'pattern' of behavior. I intend 'left' and 'right' in my titles as well as the relative position of the halves to be both political and directional.*

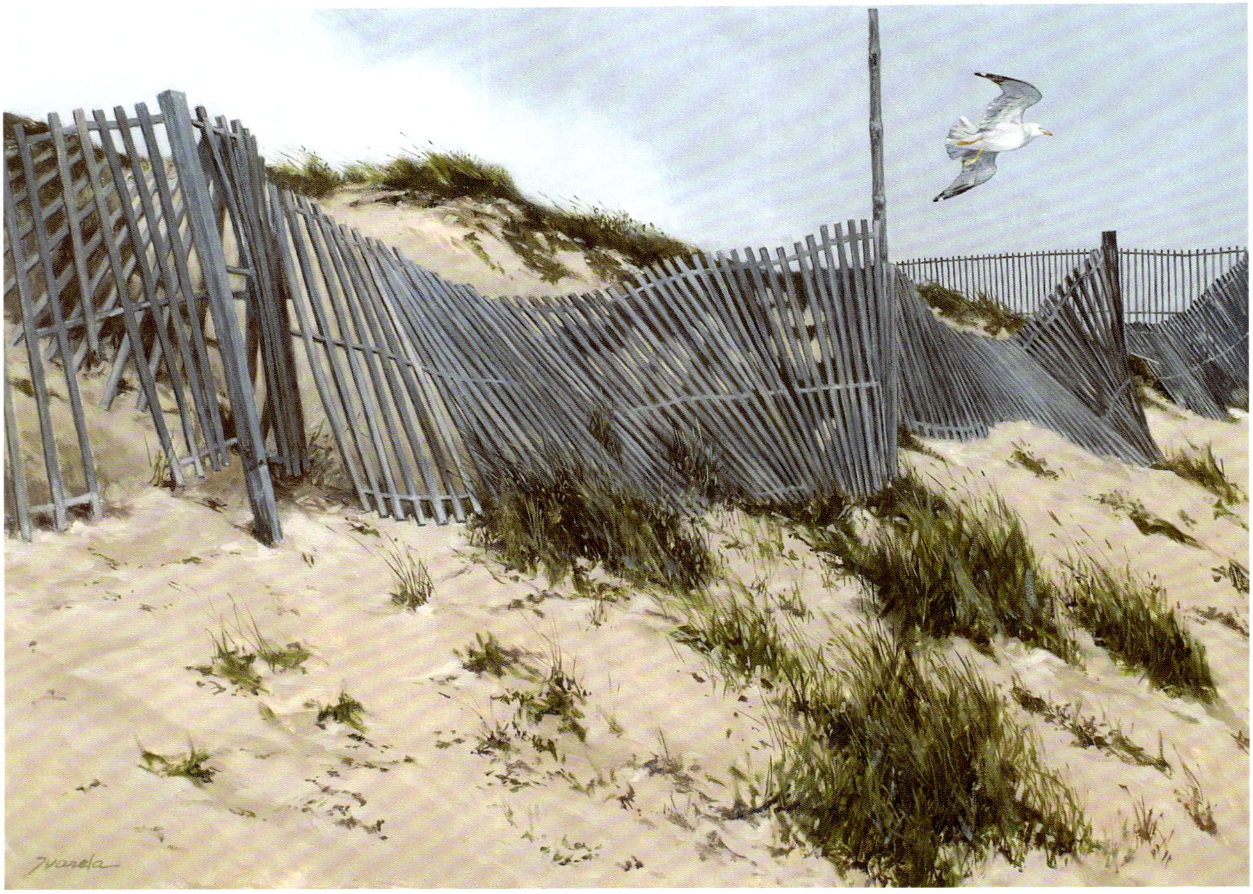

West Wind, 2012
Herring gull
Oil on canvas
23 1/2 x 31 3/4

Private collection

Birds in Art: 2002, 2011

W

BORN: 1950, Spain
RESIDES: Madrid, Spain
EDUCATION: M.S., Madrid University
EXHIBITIONS: Museu de Ciències Naturals, 2010, Lleida; Jardín Botánico de Córdoba, 2011, Córdoba; *Drawing Inspiration from the Hula Valley,* 2011, Agamon Park Gallery, Upper Galilee, Israel; *Artists for Nature Jubilee,* 2012, Orangerie Landgoed Vollenhoven, De Bilt, Netherlands
COLLECTIONS: Fundación Sa Nostra, Mallorca; Fundació Territori i Paisatge, Barcelona
COMMISSIONS: International Union for Conservation of Nature, Malaga
BIBLIOGRAPHY: *Entre Mar y Tierra/Between Sea and Land,* Lynx Edicions, 2010; *Las Aves en el Museo del Prado,* SEO/BirdLife, 2010; "Five Questions/Five Artworks: Meet Spaniard Juan Varela," *Wildlife Art Journal,* February 2011 OL; *Drawing Inspiration from the Hula Valley,* Society for the Protection of Nature in Israel, 2011

I had this coastal landscape in mind for several years after a visit to the Portuguese Algarve. The wind's rhythm, movement, and force are suggested by the sinuous shape of the fence and the struggling gull. The continuity of the fence speaks to the passage of time. The sand and vegetation are permanent elements, yet continuously renewed. The gull is both a passenger and a casual visitor. The most alive and active element in the composition, the gull is therefore the most fragile.

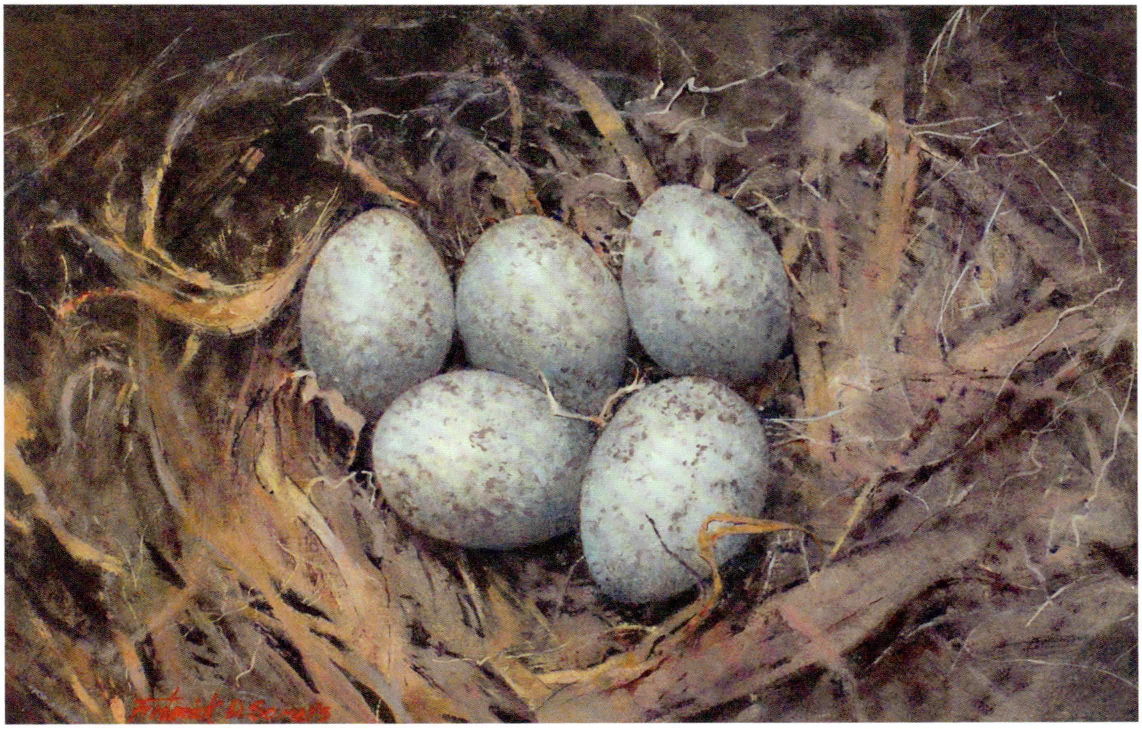

A Crow's Eye View, 2012
Oil on linen
8 x 12

Collection of the artist

Birds in Art: 1997, 2003, 2006

W

BORN: 1942, United States
RESIDES: Northfield, Minnesota
EDUCATION: M.A. and M.F.A., University of Iowa, Iowa City; B.F.A., University of Nebraska, Omaha
EXHIBITIONS: *Oil Painters of America,* 2010, Legacy Gallery, Scottsdale, Arizona; *International Association of Pastel Societies,* 2010, Butler Institute of American Art, Youngstown, Ohio
AWARDS: First Place, Landscape, 2011, *The Artist's Magazine*; Pastel Journal Award, 2011, *Pastels Only,* National Arts Club, New York City; Second Place, Landscape and Honorable Mention, Abstract, 2011, *Pastel Journal*
COLLECTIONS: Acuity Insurance, Sheboygan, Wisconsin; Mayo Foundation, Rochester, Minnesota
COMMISSIONS: Sisters of Saint Joseph of Carondelet, Saint Paul, Minnesota
BIBLIOGRAPHY: *Art Journey America: Landscapes,* F&W Publishing, 2011; "The Pastel 100 Winners Circle," *Pastel Journal,* April 2011; "The 28th Annual Competition: 30 Winners," *The Artist's Magazine,* December 2011
REPRESENTATIVES: Edgewood Orchard Galleries, Fish Creek, Wisconsin; DH Art and SpiritOne Gallery, Wayzata, Minnesota

Nests are always a happy discovery. From the window at church I first noticed the crows, then the nest. It was early spring and the leaves had not yet covered the box elder tree. I hiked across a horse pasture and climbed the tree – some thirty-five feet or so in the air – to take a photo only to discover that the film in my camera was spoiled. I had to climb the tree a second time to get the photo reference. The parent birds left the nest as I approached, but I stayed only a few minutes. What a find – these crows had lined their nest with the clean, fragrant inner bark of cedar trees, woven together with long horse hair.

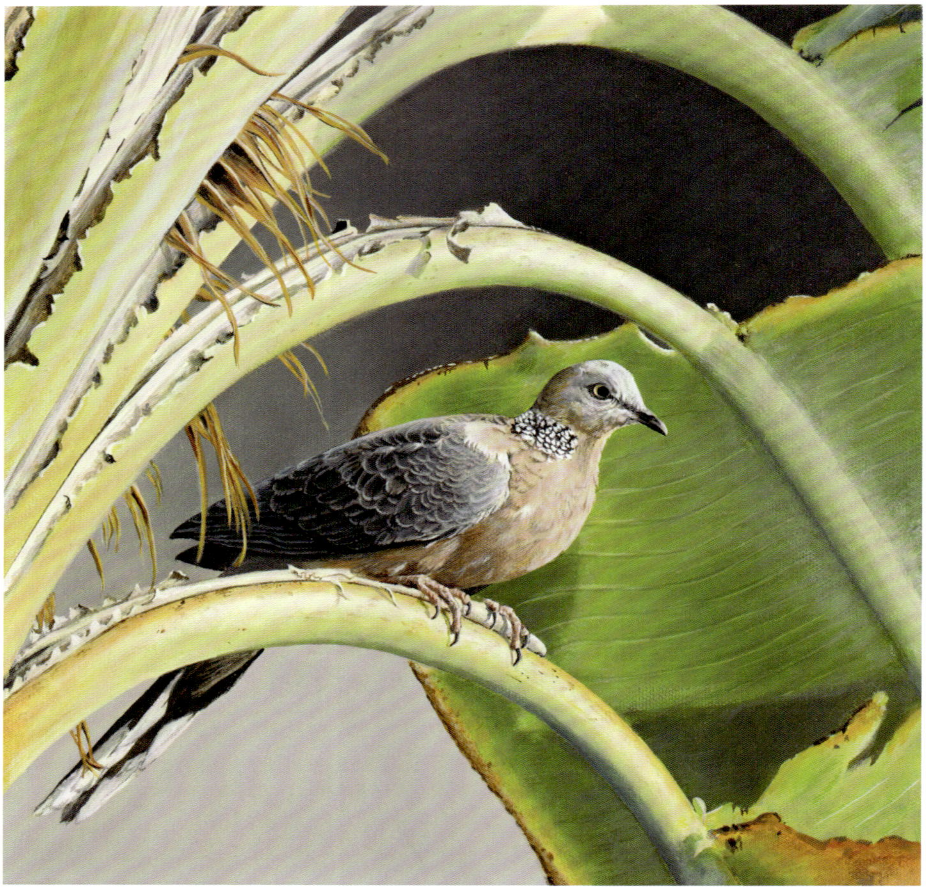

Spotted Dove, 2011
Acrylic on canvas
12 x 12

Collection of the artist

BORN: 1953, United States
RESIDES: Norway, Michigan
EXHIBITIONS: *Great Lakes Showcase,* 2010, Michigan Technological University, Visual and Performing Arts, Houghton; *Northern Exposure,* 2011, William Bonifas Fine Arts Center, Escanaba, Michigan
AWARDS: Honorable Mention, 2010, *Northern Exposure*
REPRESENTATIVES: ArtWorks Gallery, Iron Mountain, Michigan

On a recent trip to the island of Hawaii, I enjoyed a daily morning walk that took me past a grove of small trees filled with birds. During one of these walks, I observed a spotted dove peacefully resting on a banana palm. The subtle colors, graceful arch of palm leaves, bright sunlight, and the way the bird was naturally framed suggested this painting. My intent was to portray a tranquil scene, just as I had experienced it. Often, upon completing a painting, I feel I would change something on another attempt. When I finished Spotted Dove *I felt I accomplished exactly what I envisioned.*

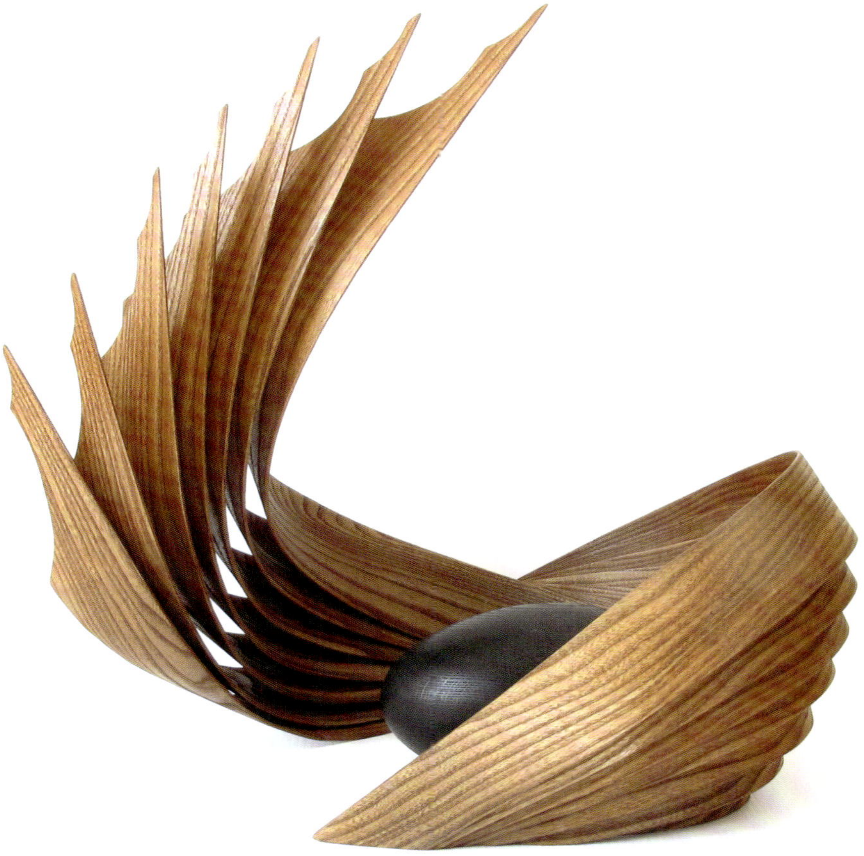

The Nest, 2011
Red elm
20 x 22 x 16

Collection of the artist

BORN: 1965, Canada
RESIDES: Gatineau, Quebec
EXHIBITIONS: *Autumn Art Exhibition,* 2010, McMichael Canadian Art Collection, Kleinburg, Ontario; Iris Art Gallery, 2010, Baie-Saint-Paul, Quebec; Espace Pierre-Debain, 2011, Gatineau; Shenkman Arts Centre, Ottawa, Ontario; *Nature into Sculpture,* 2011, Canadian Museum of Nature, Ottawa
AWARDS: Second Prize, 2011, Symposium Art and Garden, Vincent d'Indy Park, Boucherville, Quebec
COLLECTIONS: Royal Canadian Mint, Ottawa
REPRESENTATIVES: Blue Heron Gallery, Wellfleet, Massachusetts

Inspired by nature as well as the Indians of Quebec and Western Canada, I am intrigued by the expressive possibilities of wood. For fifteen years, I've used a non-traditional steam-bending technique to arrive at a singular form of expression to suggest the elegant and graceful movement and form of birds. However, the figure is for me only a starting point, and it cannot fully communicate my vision without the evocativeness of abstraction. As a metaphor, my sculptures become a way to capture the flight of birds as well as to represent the bird itself.

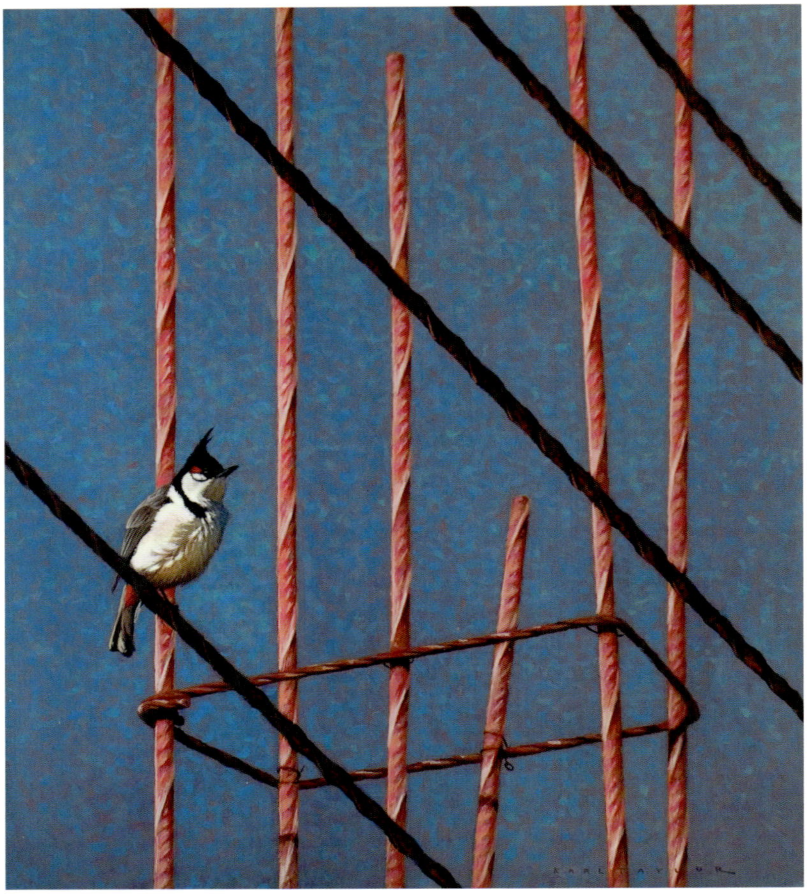

Bulbul on Rebar, 2011
Red-whiskered bulbul
Acrylic on gessoed hardboard
18 x 16

Collection of the artist

Birds in Art: 1998, 1999, 2002-03, 2005, 2011

W

BORN: 1963, England
RESIDES: Axminster, Devon, England
EDUCATION: Higher National Diploma, Carmarthen College of Technology and Art, Carmarthen, Dyfed, Wales
EXHIBITIONS: Alexander Gallery, 2010, Bristol, Avon; *Choughed,* 2010, Nature in Art, Twigworth, Gloucestershire; *Winter Exhibition,* 2011, Martin's Gallery, Cheltenham
COLLECTIONS: Bristol City Museum, Bristol; Walls Ice Cream, Gloucestershire
REPRESENTATIVES: Alexander Gallery; Gloss Gallery, Exeter, Devon

Several years ago my family and I went to Kerala, India, where we observed the culture, customs, and, of course, birds. We visited the small town of Kumily, high in the beautiful hills of the Western Ghats. Though surrounded by tropical forest, I found myself drawn to the drama of the region's more urban areas. Bulbul on Rebar *was inspired by a group of birds perched on reinforcement bars protruding from a building. The contrast of the long, rusty metal forms with the seemingly exotic bulbuls was an irresistible combination. I cropped the image to create a dynamic geometric pattern of verticals and diagonals, with the bird providing a subtle yet important diagonal line.*

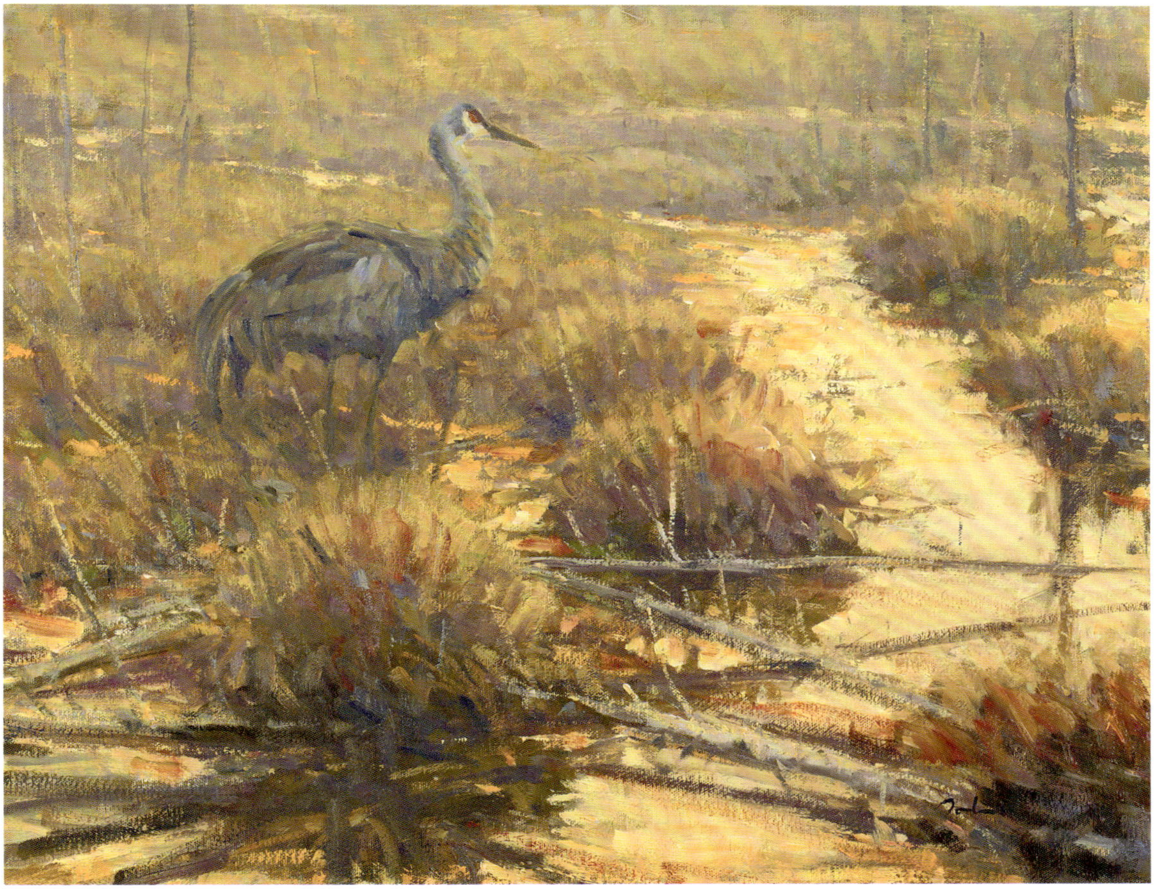

March Light, 2010
Sandhill crane
Oil on canvas
16 x 20

Collection of the artist

Birds in Art: 1993, 1998-99, 2004, 2006-07, 2011

W

BORN: 1958, United States
RESIDES: Whitmore Lake, Michigan
EDUCATION: B.F.A., University of Michigan, Ann Arbor
EXHIBITIONS: *Art of the Animal Kingdom,* 2010, Bennington Center for the Arts, Bennington, Vermont
REPRESENTATIVES: Bier Art Gallery, Charlevoix, Michigan; Treeline Gallery, Suttons Bay, Michigan

I look forward to the return of sandhill cranes each March, always a welcomed sight after winter. March Light *is about the landscape and my feelings toward that time of year – the first warm evenings when the chorus frogs and red-winged blackbirds start calling and join the cranes in their courtship displays. This canvas resulted from numerous* plein-air *studies of the wetlands near my home. Over the years I've learned to work fast and on a small scale while in the field. It's the only way I can gather enough information to get at the essence of a place and capture fleeting light.*

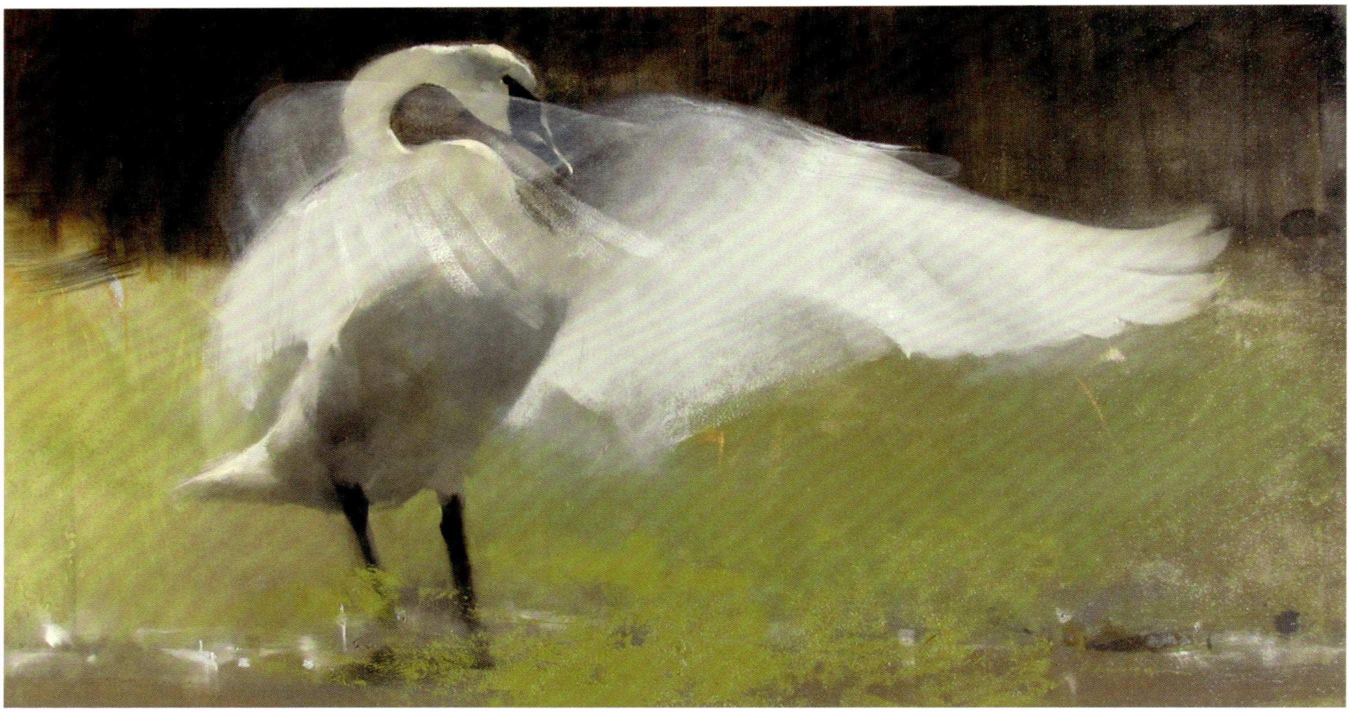

As with Breath, 2011
Trumpeter swan
Oil on canvas
27 3/4 x 50

Private collection

Birds in Art: 2010

BORN: 1971, United States
RESIDES: Jackson, Wyoming
EDUCATION: M.A., University of Virginia, Charlottesville; B.A., University of Notre Dame, South Bend, Indiana
EXHIBITIONS: Trio Fine Art, 2010-12, Jackson
AWARDS: Contemporary Art Award, 2010, *National Academy of Equine Art,* International Museum of the Horse, Lexington, Kentucky; Air Float System Award, 2010, *PaintAmerica Mini Top 50,* Southwind Gallery, Topeka, Kansas; Best of Show, 2011, *American Impressionist Society*, Mountain Song Galleries, Carmel, California
COLLECTIONS: National Museum of Wildlife Art, Jackson; Saint John's Hospital, Jackson; University of Notre Dame
BIBLIOGRAPHY: "Painting God's Country," *Images West: The Guide to the Arts in Jackson Hole,* 2010; "The Art of Women," *Wyoming Women Magazine,* Spring 2011; "Artist Captures Essence of Moment in Siena," *Jackson Hole News and Guide,* November 9, 2011
REPRESENTATIVES: Long View Gallery, Washington; Mountain Song Galleries; Trio Fine Art

In the real world, birds are anything but static! My desire to communicate movement took me beyond photographs to the anatomical mechanics of birds. I began by drawing the bone structure of skeletal models. To learn musculature and feather patterns, I spent long visits with a neighbor's pet macaw and made sketches of the patients at a local bird rehabilitation center. Video recordings of birds in flight taught me about wing movement; I could slow the frames per second or hit replay until I understood the mechanics of flight. My goal is to portray the gracefulness of wing movement in a single frame.

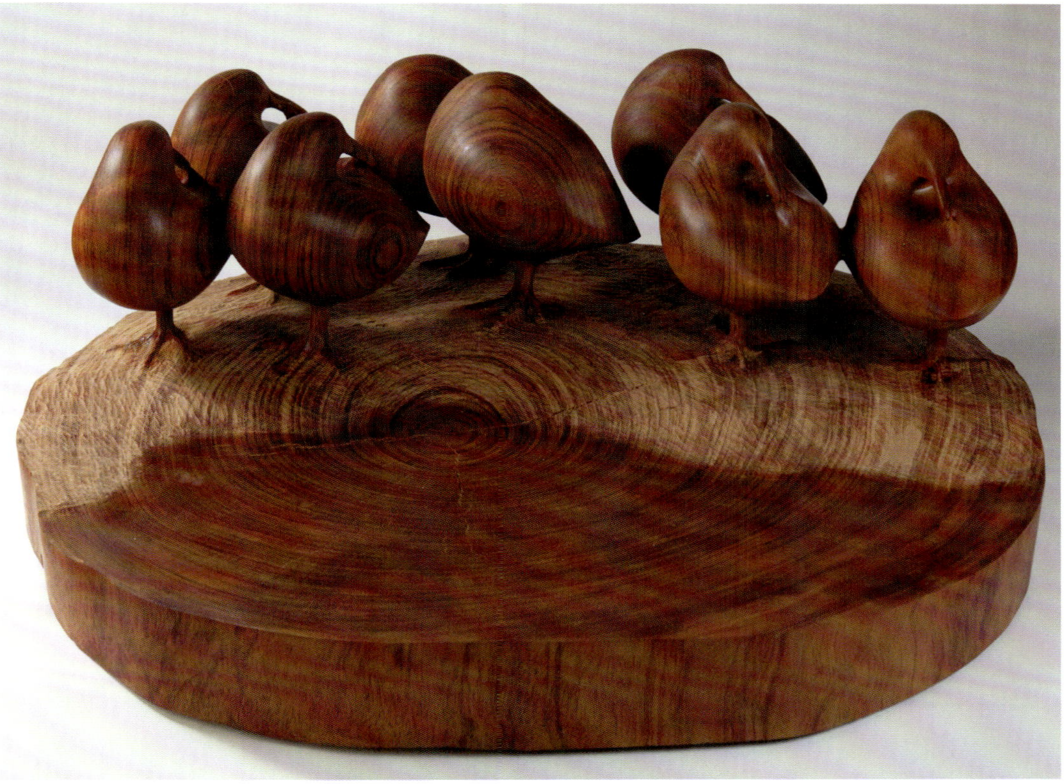

Dunlin Sandpiper Family, 2012
Bubinga
10 x 24 x 24

Collection of the artist

Birds in Art: 1984-88, 1992, 1995, 1997, 2000-01, 2003, 2005, 2011

W

BORN: 1944, United States
RESIDES: Hallowell, Maine
EDUCATION: M.A., Oregon State University, Corvallis; B.A., University of New Hampshire, Durham
EXHIBITIONS: *Member Exhibition*, 2010-11, Harlow Art Gallery, Hallowell; *Art of the Animal Kingdom*, 2011, Bennington Center for the Arts, Bennington, Vermont

Growing up on the rocky Maine coast, an appreciation for the diversity of forms and shapes of shorebirds came with the territory. Dunlins quickly pass by on their northward migration; however, they linger to feed in the mudflats of Maquoit Bay in Brunswick during their autumn flight south. Their appealing plump size and slightly down-curved bills combined with the contrast of mud textures and water led to this complex design. Bubinga – a hard West African wood – was a logical choice because of its variety of grain patterns and lustrous, rich colors.

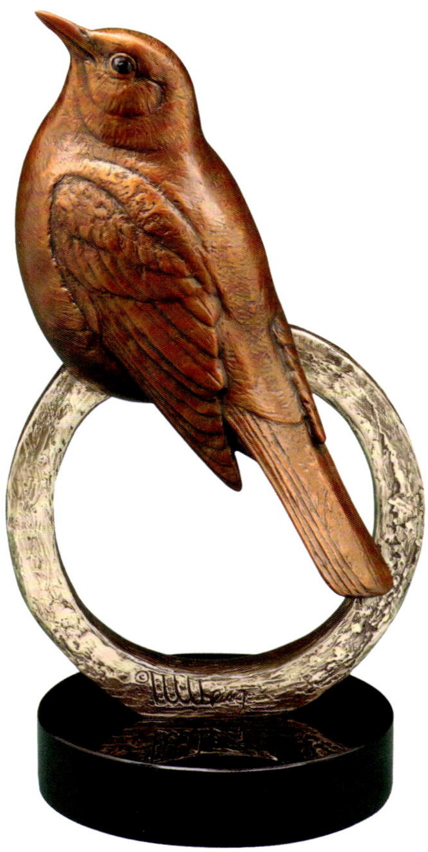

Round Robin (ed. 50), 2011
American robin
Bronze
17 1/2 x 11 x 8

Collection of the artist

Birds in Art: 1982-07, 2009-11
Master Wildlife Artist: 1987

W

BORN: 1945, Sweden
RESIDES: Corpus Christi, Texas
EXHIBITIONS: *Prix de West Invitational,* 2010-12, National Cowboy & Western Heritage Museum, Oklahoma City; *Masters of the American West,* 2010-12, Autry National Center, Los Angeles; *Art of the Dive: Portraits of the Deep,* 2011, Fishing Hall of Fame & Museum, Dania Beach, Florida; *Sharks!,* 2012, Museum of Art, Fort Lauderdale, Florida
AWARDS: Briscoe Legacy Award and People's Choice Award, 2010, *Night of Artists,* Briscoe Museum, San Antonio
COLLECTIONS: City of Lake Charles, Lake Charles, Louisiana; First National Bank of Omaha, Omaha, Nebraska; University of North Texas, Denton; University of Texas Marine Science Institute, Port Aransas
COMMISSIONS: Saint Louis Zoo
BIBLIOGRAPHY: "Soaring Heights," *Western Art Collector,* July 2010
REPRESENTATIVES: Helena Fox Fine Art, Charleston, South Carolina; Sportsman's Gallery, Atlanta; Trailside Galleries, Jackson, Wyoming

A beautiful male robin relaxed and puffed up to a rounded shape as it sat on its circular nest in the backyard of my Colorado studio. I used this inspiration to play with the forms – as well as the theme – turning the nest edge vertically to create a polished bronze circular perch. An eighteenth-century Swedish Royal Navy term, also used in contemporary competitive sports, suggested the title, Round Robin.

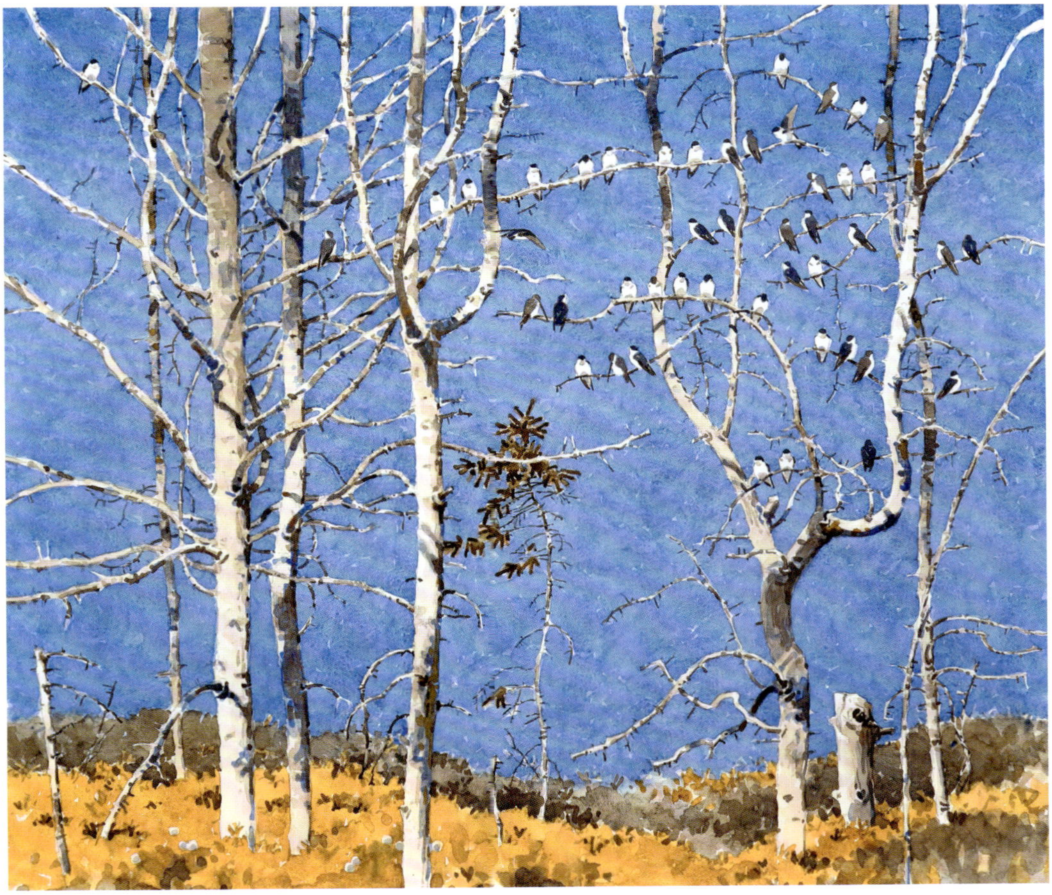

The Gathering Place, 2012
Tree swallow
Watercolor on Lanaquarelle hot press paper
22 x 25 1/2

Collection of the artist

Birds in Art: 1991-92, 1994, 1996, 1998-99, 2001-02, 2004, 2007-08, 2011

W

BORN: 1954, United States
RESIDES: Princeton, Massachusetts
EDUCATION: B.A., University of Massachusetts, North Dartmouth
EXHIBITIONS: Fruitlands Museum, 2010, Harvard, Massachusetts; *Focus on Nature,* 2010, New York State Museum, Albany; Jamaica Bay National Wildlife Refuge, 2010, Brooklyn, New York; *Art of the Animal Kingdom,* 2010, Bennington Center for the Arts, Bennington, Vermont; Vermont Institute of Natural Science, 2011, Quechee; *Drawing Inspiration from the Hula Valley,* 2011, Agamon Park Gallery, Upper Galilee, Israel; *Artists for Nature Jubilee,* 2012, Orangerie Landgoed Vollenhoven, De Bilt, Netherlands; Petersham Art Center, 2012, Petersham, Massachusetts
AWARDS: Artist-in-Residence, 2011, Coastal Maine Botanical Gardens, Boothbay
COLLECTIONS: Fruitlands Museum; Mass Audubon Visual Arts Center, Canton, Massachusetts
BIBLIOGRAPHY: *Drawing and Painting Birds,* Crowood Press, 2010; *There and Back,* Langford Press, 2011; *Drawing Inspiration from the Hula Valley,* Society for the Protection of Nature in Israel, 2011

Some of my watercolors are born in a matter of minutes, while others may take years. The Gathering Place *represents the latter, resulting from field sketches and color studies stretching back more than a decade. On many occasions, I've hauled my canoe to a tamarack bog near my home where hundreds of tree swallows gather before their southward migration. A canoe isn't ideal for field sketching; the slightest breeze sets everything spinning. At the bog I can paddle onto submerged water lily beds to stabilize the boat. The canoe's low vantage point yields the clear, blue sky backdrop. I combined studies of the ghostly tamarack 'skeletons' with drawings of the swallows, and this larger composition gradually took form in the studio.*

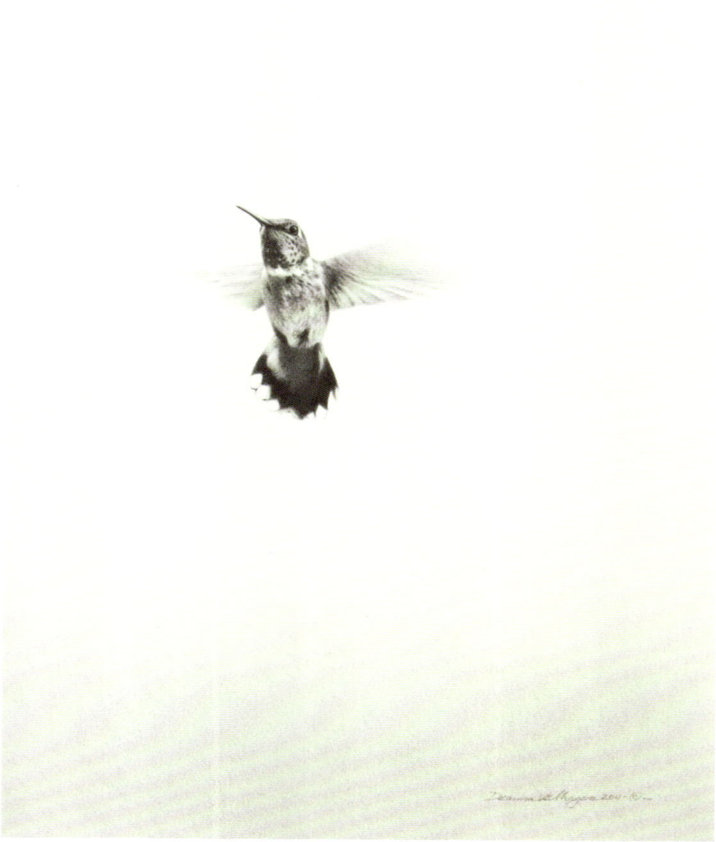

Little Wings, 2011
Rufous hummingbird
Graphite on Stonehenge paper
12 1/2 x 9 3/4

Collection of the artist

BORN: 1966, United States
RESIDES: Albuquerque, New Mexico
EDUCATION: A.D., Colorado Institute of Art, Denver
AWARDS: Second Place, Wildlife & Animal, 2011, *Pastel 100 Competition,* The Pastel Journal
BIBLIOGRAPHY: "The 12th Pastel 100 Competition/Animal & Wildlife," *The Pastel Journal,* April 2011; "Artisan Art Talk/Featured Artist," *Artisan,* September 2011

Although the rufous hummingbird is quite colorful, displaying orange and green colors, I was inspired to capture the essence of the movement of this female's wings in a black and white drawing. I wanted the viewer to understand the delicacy and airiness of the wings in motion. Upon completion, the title Little Wings *seemed appropriate for such a delicate little bird.*

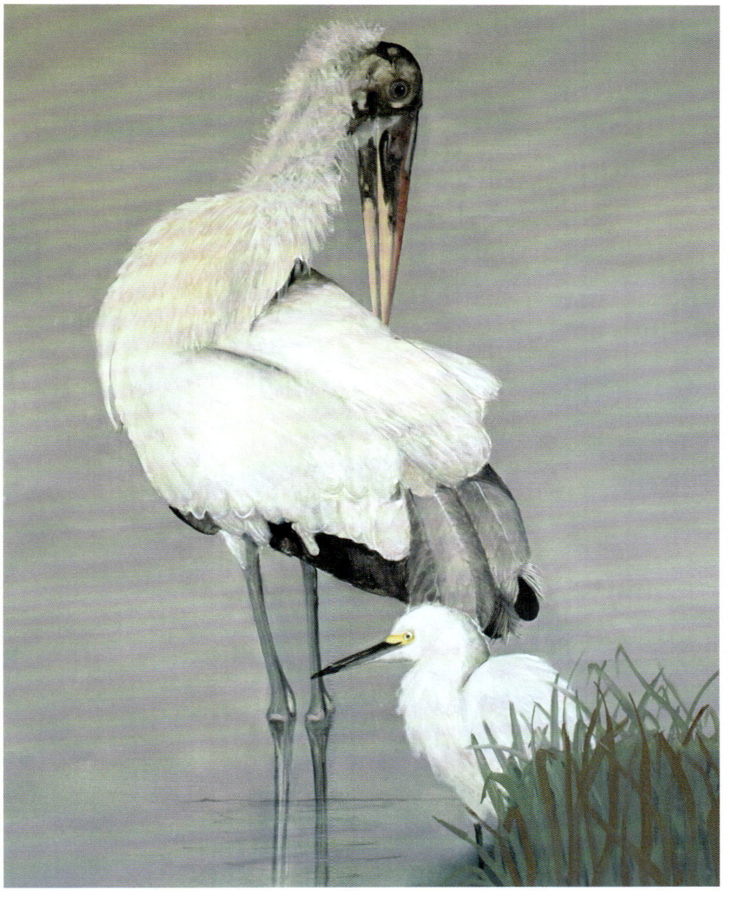

Wood Stork & Egret, 2011
Oil on canvas
60 x 48

Collection of the artist

BORN: 1940, United States
RESIDES: New York City
EDUCATION: M.F.A., Hunter College, New York City; B.A., University of California, Berkeley
COLLECTIONS: Metropolitan Museum of Art, New York City; Yale University School of Architecture, New Haven, Connecticut

It is always rewarding to be with my camera in a place where there are wild birds. It's sheer fun and nothing like the challenge of making an interesting painting once back in the studio. There, I am faced with the dichotomy of being a figurative painter in a post-modernist art world. My teachers were abstractionists who strove for monumentality. Though in my bird paintings I have embraced the reality of what I see in the world, the lessons of my early training inform and become the structural base for everything I do. It's a challenge to reconcile these experiences. When I painted Wood Stork & Egret *I was looking at Édouard Manet's palette and did several paintings using the subdued grays, creams, and pinks of the* Bar at the Folies-Bergère.

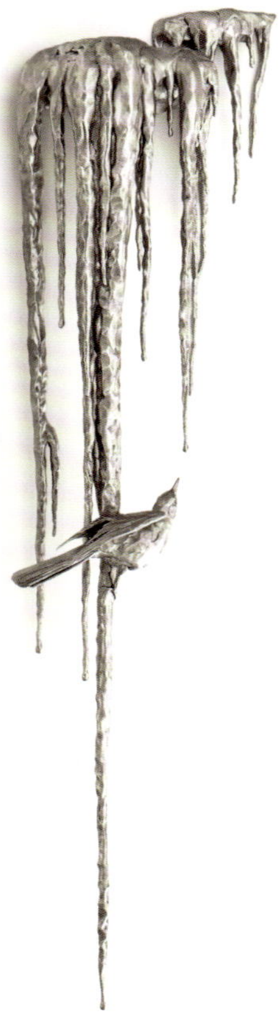

Climate Change II (ed. 6), 2011
Bronze
41 x 14 x 7

Private collection

Birds in Art: 1986, 1989, 1991-92, 1998-99, 2001-02, 2004, 2006, 2011

W

BORN: 1958, United States
RESIDES: Westminster, Maryland
EDUCATION: B.A., Hiram College, Hiram, Ohio
EXHIBITIONS: African Wildlife Foundation, 2011, Washington; *National Sculpture Society*, 2010-12, Brookgreen Gardens, Murrells Inlet, South Carolina; Ella Sharp Museum of Art, 2012, Jackson, Michigan; *Solitary Pursuits*, 2012, Gerald Peters Gallery, Santa Fe, New Mexico
AWARDS: Silver Medal, 2011, *National Sculpture Society*, New York City; Featured Artist, 2011, *Western Visions*, National Museum of Wildlife Art, Jackson, Wyoming; J.J. Turner Award, 2012, Hiram College
COLLECTIONS: Canton Museum of Art, Canton, Ohio; Ella Sharp Museum of Art; The National Zoo, Washington
COMMISSIONS: Chattanooga Zoo, Chattanooga, Tennessee
BIBLIOGRAPHY: "The Soul of Wildlife," *Southwest Art*, April 2011; "Reports from the Field," September 2011, and "Solitary Pursuits," July 2012, *Western Art Collector*
REPRESENTATIVES: Astoria Fine Art, Jackson, Wyoming; Gerald Peters Gallery; Rehs Gallery, New York City

Several years ago, Maryland experienced two snowstorms in quick succession. Amid wind, swirling snow, and sub-freezing temperatures, I encountered an astonishing sight: gigantic icicles hanging almost to the ground from my roof. Wanting a three-dimensional record of this rare event, I worked rapidly in clay, wondering if I should leave it as a study or add a focal point and create something more. I remembered seeing a chickadee perched on an icicle, stretching out to drink from a droplet forming on an adjacent ice dagger, but a chickadee didn't possess enough mass. I worked on an avian form from imagination, and after weeks of internal debate, decided simply to finish the bird as what it most resembled – a catbird.

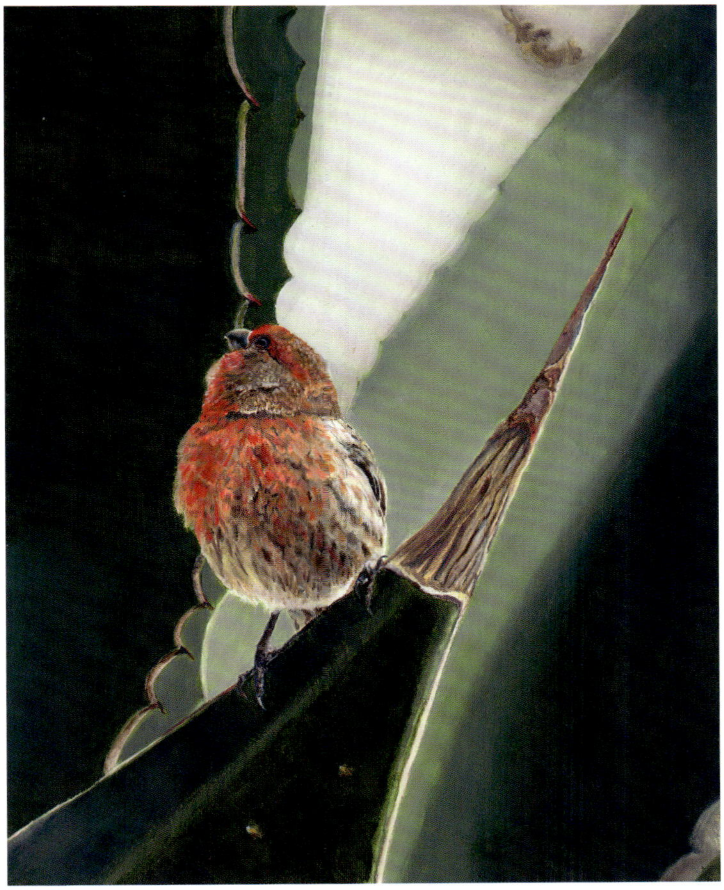

Safe Haven, 2011
House finch
Oil on canvas board
14 x 11

Collection of the artist

BORN: 1944, United States
RESIDES: Tucson, Arizor.a
EDUCATION: B.F.A. anc B.Ed., University of Arizona, Tucson
EXHIBITIONS: Long Gallery at Academy Village, 2010, Tucson; *Four Hands Show,* 2010, Agua Caliente Ran:h House Gallery, Tucson; *Contemporary Western Art Show,* 2011, Mountain Oyster Club, Tucson
AWARDS: Best in Show, 2011, *Art of the Alum and Friends,* Northern Tr.ıst, Tucson

This little house finch came most mornings to a small fountain I could see from my bedroom window. Its color caught my eye – a rich orange-red complemented by the intense green-blue of the agave. I was intrigued that the finch would freely take a bath or boldly stand on the agave in plain sight. His fragile puffiness against the morning cold contrasted perfectly with the fierce spikes of the leaves. It seemed impossible the two could be found together. As I watched, it made perfect sense; the finch had found the ultimate safe haven.

Paula Waterman

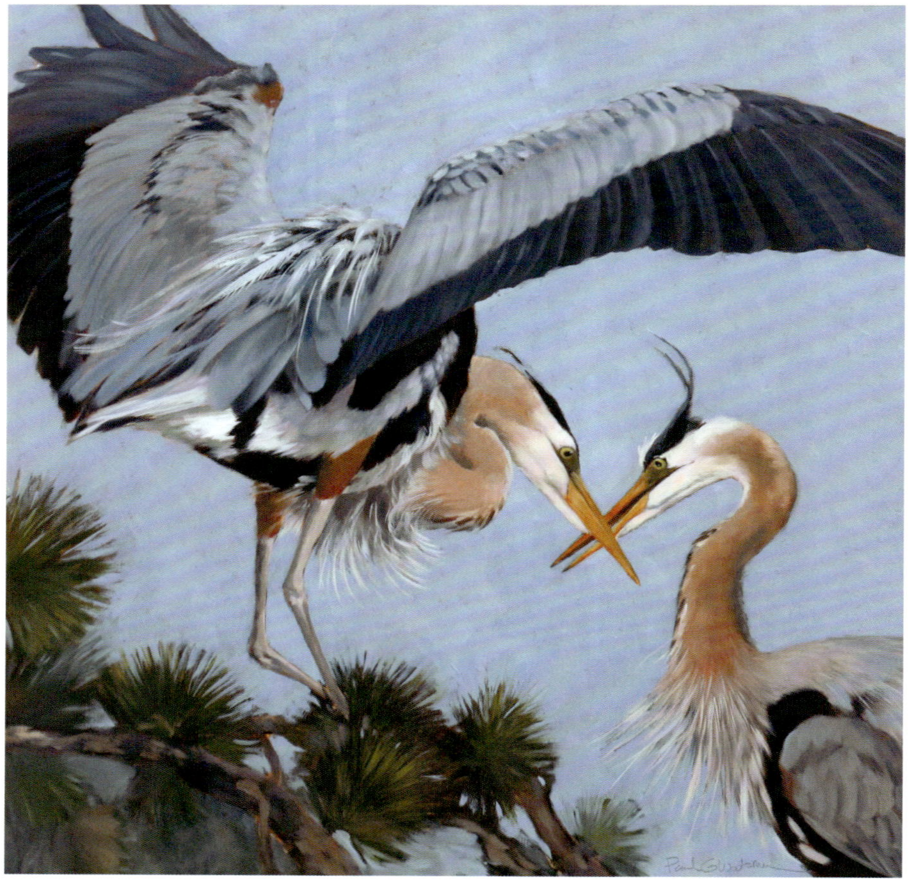

Offering, 2011
Great blue heron
Oil on canvas
30 x 30

Collection of the artist

Birds in Art: 1992, 1994, 1996-02, 2004-11

W

BORN: 1954, United States
RESIDES: Eldersburg, Maryland
EDUCATION: R.N., Washington Hospital Center School of Nursing, Washington
EXHIBITIONS: *Anniversary Show,* 2010, and *Each One Invites One,* 2011, McBride Gallery, Annapolis, Maryland
COLLECTIONS: Bennington Center for the Arts, Bennington, Vermont; RAC Solutions, Bethesda, Maryland
REPRESENTATIVES: McBride Gallery; Mystic Seaport Gallery, Mystic, Connecticut; Troika Gallery, Easton, Maryland

Offering *resulted from a short and rewarding trip to Florida a couple of winters ago. Egrets and herons are a subject I return to again and again as I feel they are in many ways the most beautiful birds. Great blue herons have metallic-looking wing feathers; I almost expect to hear the feathers sound against one another when the birds interact during the late-winter breeding season.*

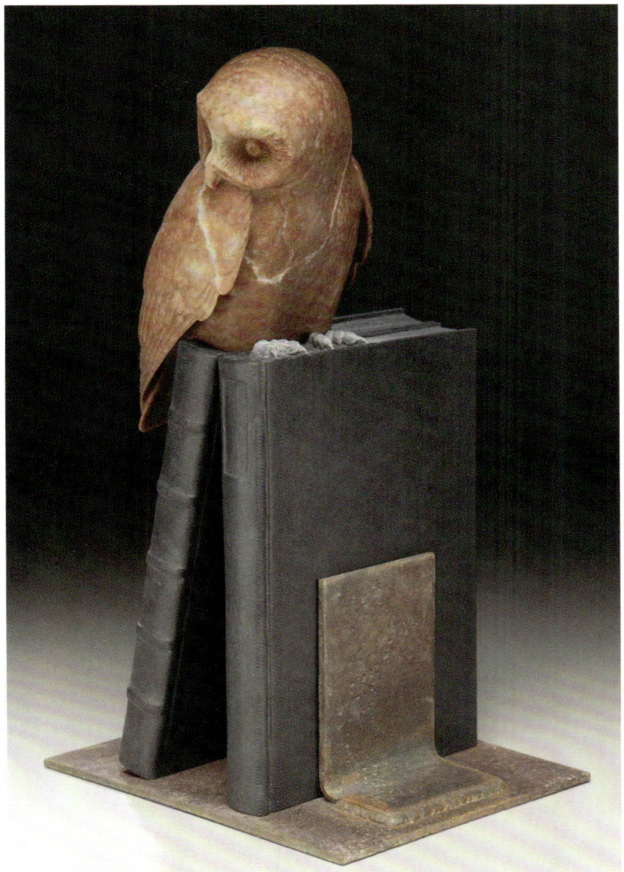

Higher Learning, 2011
Southern boobook owl
Alabaster on Virginia steatite and steel
20 x 11 x 9

Collection of the artist

Birds in Art: 1999-02, 2009-11

W

BORN: 1947, United States
RESIDES: Tryon, North Carolina
EDUCATION: M.B.A., Boston University; M.S., University of Florida, Gainesville; B.S., Lehigh University, Bethlehem, Pennsylvania
EXHIBITIONS: Holden Gallery, Warren Wilson College, 2010, Swannanoa, North Carolina; Warm Springs Gallery, 2010, Warm Springs, Virginia; Gallery Minerva, 2010, Asheville, North Carolina; *Art and the Animal,* 2010, San Diego Natural History Museum, and 2012, Hiram Blauvelt Art Museum, Oradell, New Jersey; *Out of the Wild: Animals in Sculpture,* and *Cold Blooded Art: Reptiles, Amphibians, Fish and Insects,* 2011, and *National Sculpture Society Awards Exhibition,* 2012, Brookgreen Gardens, Murrells Inlet, South Carolina
COLLECTIONS: Brookgreen Gardens; Hiram Blauvelt Art Museum
BIBLIOGRAPHY: "An Artist's Vision of the Unseen," *Hunting & Fishing Collectibles,* January/February 2012
REPRESENTATIVES: Collette Fine Art, Highlands, North Carolina; Russell A. Fink Gallery, Lorton, Virginia; Stephen O'Brien Jr. Fine Arts, Boston

The inspiration for Higher Learning *came from the bird's perch – two beautiful slabs of Virginia steatite. The dimensions were perfect for books; to determine the configuration, I tried stacking, turning, laying down, and, finally, leaning the slabs. The stone – an exquisite, modestly sized piece of light brown alabaster with cream veining – directed me to the bird, a boobook owl from Australia. Fitting the pieces together so they were stable and meshed seamlessly without using mechanical fasteners was a puzzle. Achieving the precarious balancing effect created by the books was essential. The title speaks to my research and thought process, while paying homage to the sculptural elements.*

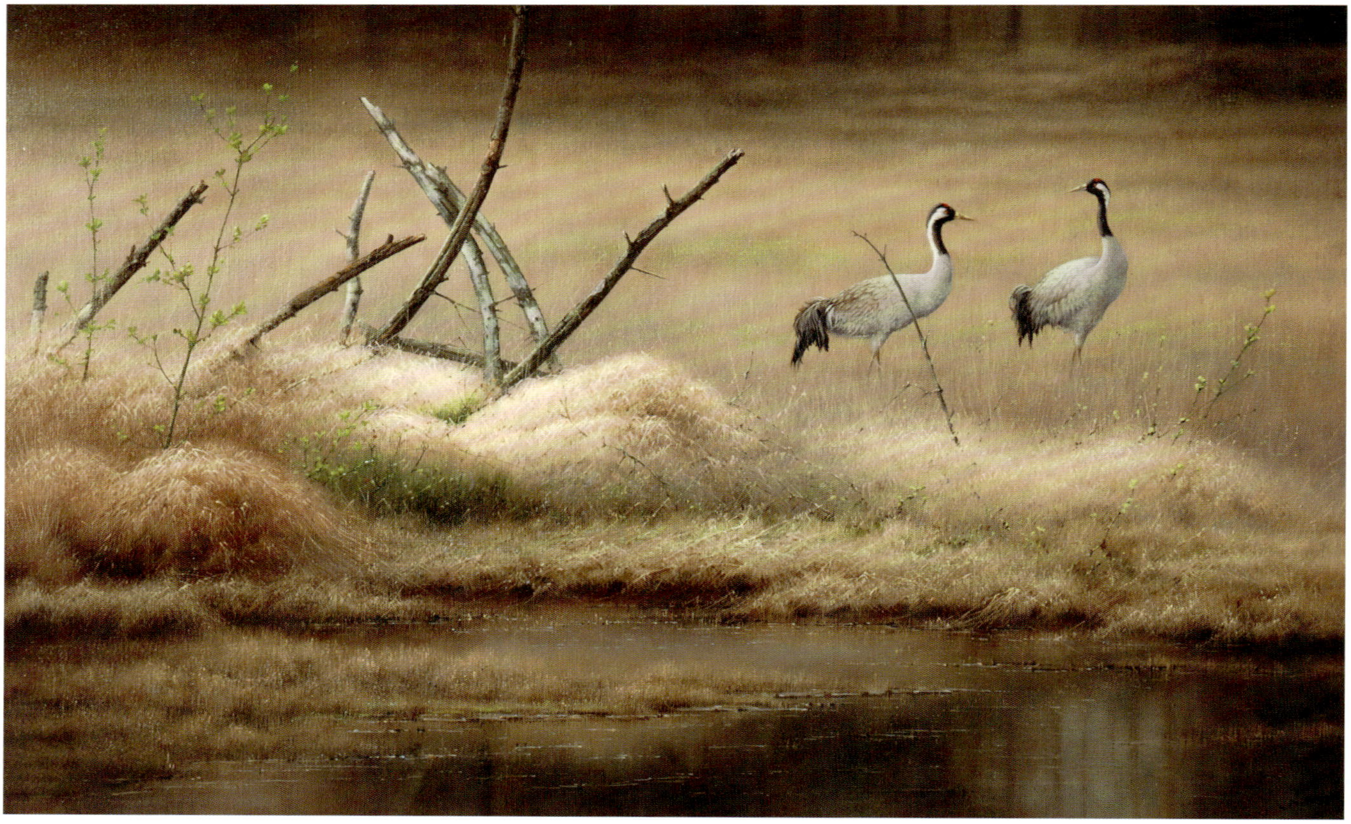

Peat-moor Visitors, 2011
European crane
Oil on canvas
22 x 35

Collection of the artist

Birds in Art: 1998, 2000, 2004-05, 2008

W

BORN: 1945, Netherlands
RESIDES: Hengelo, Overÿssel, Netherlands
AWARDS: Best of Show, 2010-11, *Wild in de Natuur,* Kunsthuis van het Oosten, Enschede
COLLECTIONS: Manly Art Museum, Sydney, Australia; Kunsthuis van het Oosten
BIBLIOGRAPHY: "De mooie ziekte van Jan Wessels," *Tubantia,* January 2011; "Atelier van de Kunstschilder," *Landleven,* February 2011

In the eastern part of the Netherlands where I live, cranes are not common. These birds do visit the old moors where peat once was harvested. Since being designated as nature preserves, the moors are rather quiet, which suits the cranes just fine. Painting the landscape with its limited colors and subtle nuances was a challenge; the presence of two cranes made the composition complete.

Sue Westin

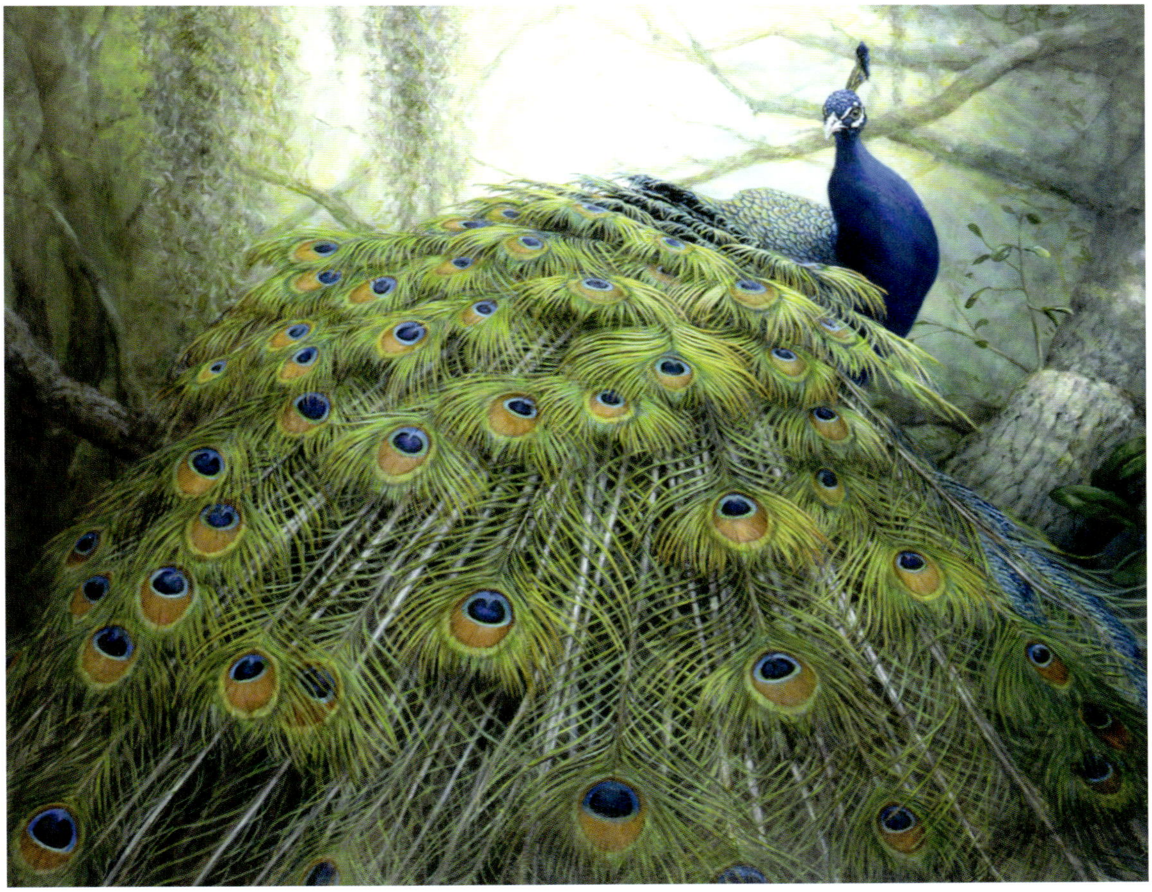

Cascade, 2010
Black-shouldered peafowl
Oil on gessoed hardboard
24 x 30

Collection of the artist

Birds in Art: 1987-89, 1992-97, 1999-01, 2004, 2007, 2009

W

BORN: 1950, United States
RESIDES: Dorset, Vermont
EDUCATION: B.A., Hartwick College, Oneonta, New York
EXHIBITIONS: *Art and the Animal,* 2010, San Diego Natural History Museum; *Seeing Through an Artist's Eye,* 2012, Germanton Gallery, Germanton, North Carolina
AWARDS: Southwest Art Magazine Editor's Choice Award, 2011, *Art and the Animal,* Dennos Museum Center, Northwestern Michigan College, Traverse City
COLLECTIONS: Bennington Center for the Arts, Bennington, Vermont
REPRESENTATIVES: Germanton Gallery

Artists can learn much by studying the work of other artists and their different genres and styles. Cascade *was an experiment in composition inspired by the works of N.C. Wyeth, who often employed dramatic, pyramidlike compositions and loosely painted, glowing backgrounds. N.C. Wyeth's paintings* Hands Up *and* Mexican Shepherd *– though a far cry from a peacock portrait – were particularly inspirational.*

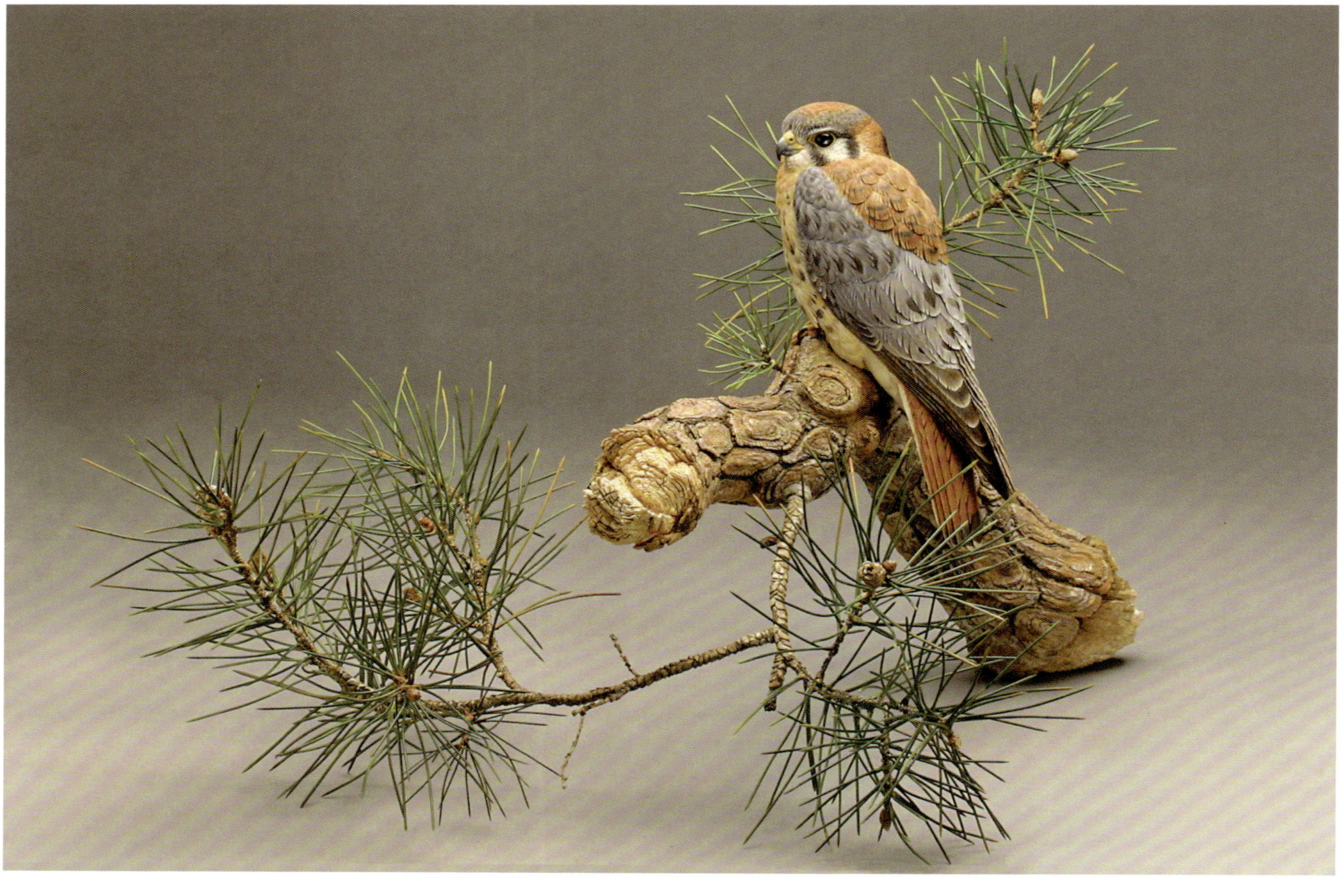

Kestrel, 2012
Oil on basswood
13 x 18 x 26

Private collection

Birds in Art: 1989, 1991, 1994, 2000-01, 2003-07

W

BORN: 1968, United States
RESIDES: Appleton, Wisconsin
EDUCATION: B.F.A., University of Wisconsin, Stevens Point
EXHIBITIONS: *Wisconsin Wildlife Biennial,* 2011, Miller Art Museum, Sturgeon Bay
AWARDS: Second, Best in World, 2011, Ward World Championship Wildfowl Carving Competition, Ocean City, Maryland
COLLECTIONS: Ella Sharp Museum of Art, Jackson, Michigan; Ward Museum of Wildfowl Art, Salisbury University, Salisbury, Maryland

I started carving birds after my parents brought me to see Birds in Art *when I was twelve years old. More than thirty years later, I work in advertising with a focus on packaging. Working with proportions and negative spaces in two dimensions is a helpful exercise for the three dimensions of woodcarving. Getting away from my studio to go to work helps me take a fresh look at my sculpture when I return. What seems problematic at the end of a long studio session often is resolved by directing my focus elsewhere. The satisfaction upon completing this kestrel came from the use of steel needles to balance two of the three contact points, giving the sculpture an airy look.*

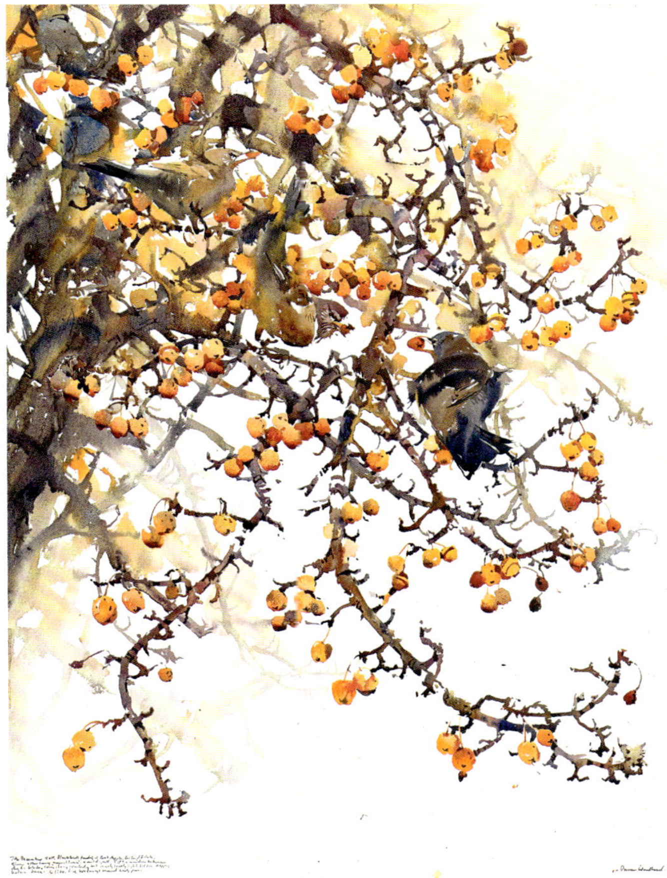

Eurasian Blackbirds among Crab Apples, 2011
Watercolor on Arches paper
30 x 22

Collection of the artist

Birds in Art: 2000-01

W

BORN: 1971, England
RESIDES: Haddington, East Lothian, Scotland
EDUCATION: M.A., Royal College of Art, London
EXHIBITIONS: Birdscapes Gallery, 2010, Norfolk, England; *Society of Wildlife Artists*, 2010-11, Mall Galleries, London; *India Artists for Nature Foundation*, 2011, Donald Watson Gallery, Aberlady, East Lothian; Donald Watson Gallery, 2011; *Drawing Inspiration from the Hula Valley*, 2011, Agamon Park Gallery, Upper Galilee, Israel; *Artists for Nature Jubilee*, 2012, Orangerie Landgoed Vollenhoven, De Bilt, Netherlands
COLLECTIONS: HRH The Duke of Edinburgh
BIBLIOGRAPHY: *Drawing Inspiration from the Hula Valley*, Society for the Protection of Nature in Israel, 2011

I never work in a studio, instead finding excitement and inspiration working directly from the subject. While the unpredictability of Scottish weather affects paint intensely, I use this to my advantage in pushing the pigments on the paper. I look for areas where I can be inspired to work for days on end. Finding a small group of crab apple trees that were holding onto their fruit in early winter, I knew it would be exciting. Day after day, small birds and especially migrant blackbirds became oblivious to my presence and would often feed at arm's length, rapidly stripping the trees of their golden fruit. On this particular day, an overly aggressive female took up residence in the center of the tree and became the controller at the gate, so to speak.

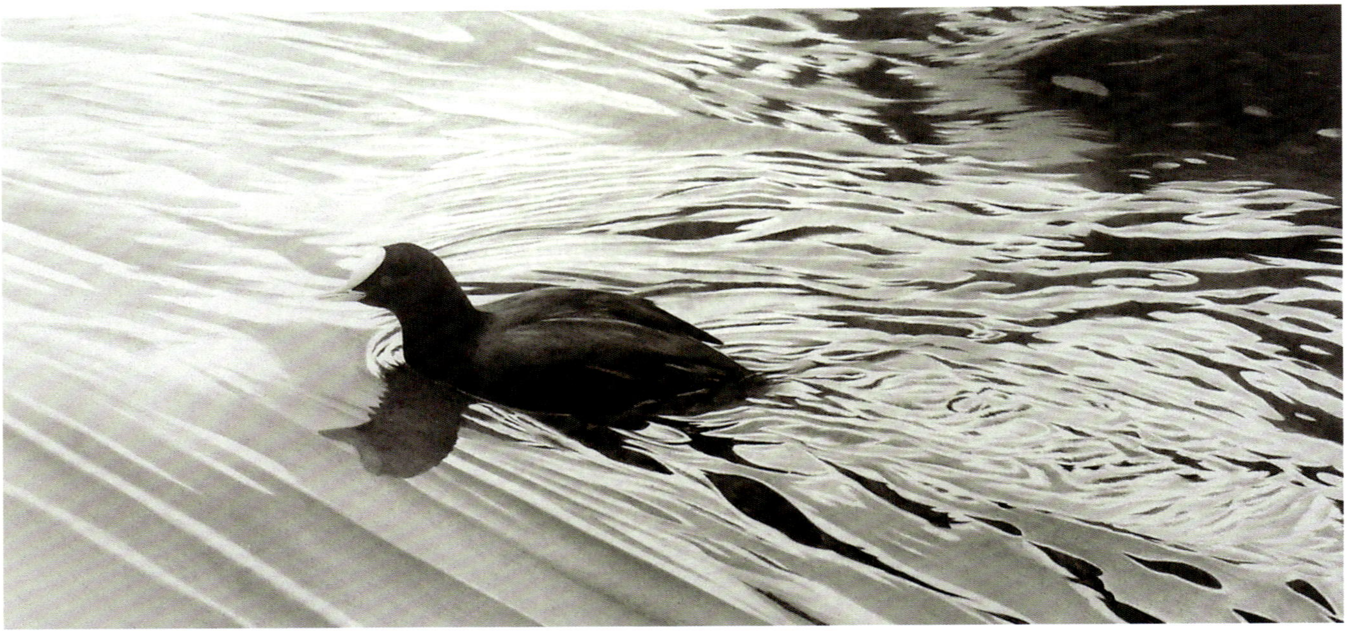

Swimming Coot, 2011
European coot
Graphite on Fabriano paper
16 x 25

Collection of the artist

Birds in Art: 2011

BORN: 1964, Great Britain
RESIDES: Maidstone, Kent, England
EXHIBITIONS: *National Exhibition of Wildlife Art,* 2010-2012, Gordale Garden Centre, Burton, South Wirral
REPRESENTATIVES: Francis Iles Gallery, Rochester, Kent

The movement of water and the movement of birds within it have become a growing fascination for me in the last year or so. Both have found their way into my work on many occasions. Water is a demanding subject and requires a high degree of concentration and application. In Swimming Coot, *I tried to capture the way that water becomes a constantly shifting canvas of abstract shapes, all the result of movement across its surface by a common, yet captivating bird.*

Sherrie York

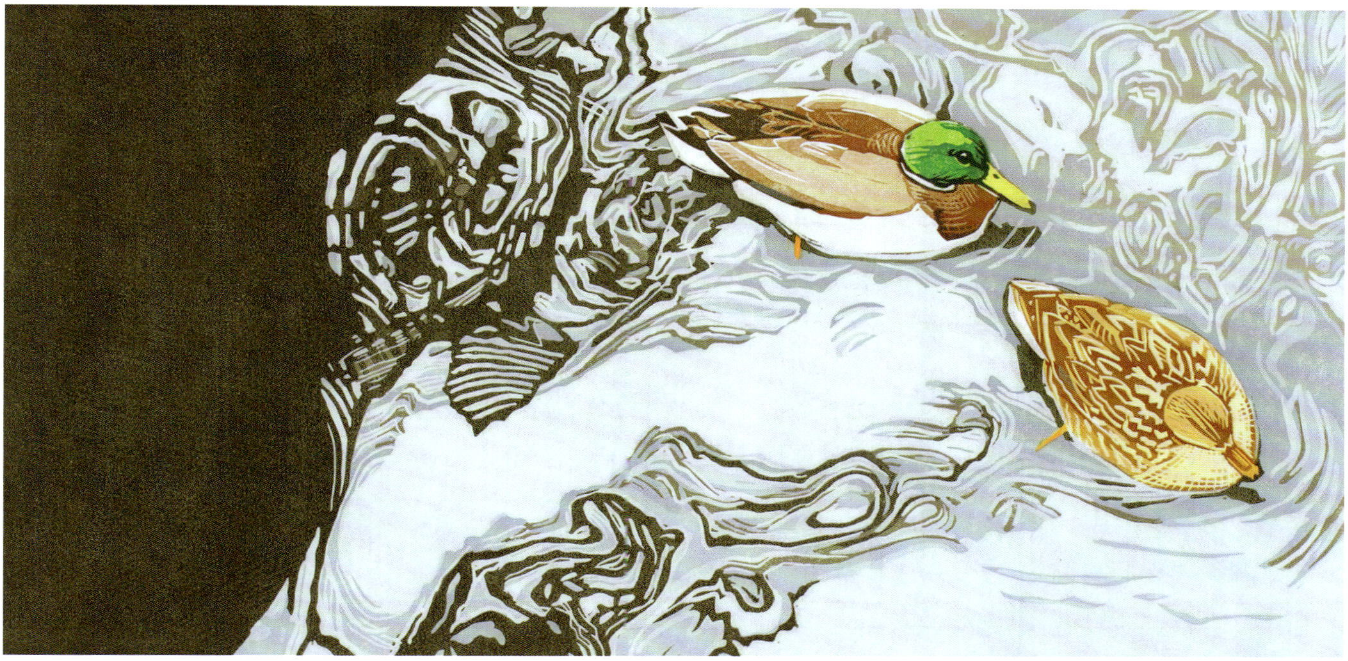

Pas de Ducks (2/10), 2012
Mallard
Linocut on Awagami kozo paper
8 x 16

Collection of the artist

Birds in Art: 1991, 1997, 2011

BORN: 1962, United States
RESIDES: Salida, Colorado
EDUCATION: B.S., Concordia University, Seward, Nebraska
EXHIBITIONS: *Drawing on Nature,* 2010, New Mexico Museum of Nature and Science, Albuquerque; *National Print Exhibition,* 2010, Artlink Gallery, Fort Wayne, Indiana; Paquette Gallery, 2010 and 2012, Salida; *Come With Me to the Birch Forest,* 2011, Art Museum Timisoara, Timisoara, Romania; *National Small Print,* 2011, Creede Repertory Theatre Gallery, Creede, Colorado; Dos Chappell Bathhouse, 2011, Denver; *Artists for Nature Jubilee,* 2012, Orangerie Landgoed Vollenhoven, De Bilt, Netherlands
AWARDS: First Place, 2012, *National Small Print*
COLLECTIONS: Heart of the Rockies Regional Medical Center, Salida
BIBLIOGRAPHY: *Printmakers Today,* Schiffer Publishing, 2010; *Drawing Lab for Mixed Media Artists,* Quarry Books, 2010; "Five Questions/Five Artworks: Denis Clavreul Interviews Sherrie York," *Wildlife Art Journal,* December 2011 OL
REPRESENTATIVES: Abend Gallery, Denver; Maverick Potter Gallery, Salida

My best work stems from personal observation. What's easier to observe in the field than the ubiquitous mallard? A fishing pier crafted from old concrete bridge sections and iron fence railings juts into a pond near my home. Through the winter it's a favorite hangout for a gang of unruly mallards that lie in wait for well-meaning providers of donuts and other questionable foodstuff. Come spring the band disperses, driven more by the urge to mate than by their bellies. Mallard courtships can be as rowdy as their food squabbles, with a great deal of splashing and squawking. From time to time, though, I spot a pair twirling the water below the pier in a quiet pas de deux.

Production Notes

TYPOGRAPHY: Officina Sans Bold, Berkeley, Berkeley Black Italic

PAPER: Cover, Neenah Classic Columns Duplex, 120# Cover, Canyon Brown/Natural White; Endpaper, Neenah Classic, 70# Text, Classic White; Text, Stora Enso Gusto Satin, 100# Text, White

PRINTING: Cover, foil-stamped, die-cut; Text, four-color process, plus one match color and spot gloss varnish, offset lithography

DESIGN: Richard Wunsch, Wausau, Wisconsin

COLOR SEPARATIONS AND PRINTING: Reindl Printing, Inc., Merrill, Wisconsin

PHOTOGRAPHY: Art & Soul Photo, Seattle: 102; Art on Giclee, Inc, Lake Forest, California: 99; Allan Carlisle, Palm Beach Gardens, Florida: 51; Chromatics, Nashville: 42; Classic Art Prints, Thomas Zarnoth, Milwaukee: 27, 97; Colourgenics Inc., Toronto, Ontario, Canada: 13; Christopher Coville, Twinsburg, Ohio: 108; Rolant Dafis, Aberystwyth, Wales, United Kingdom: 49; Bruce L. deGraaf, Shrewsbury, Massachusetts: 119; Wes Demarest, Sussex, New Jersey: 16; DPI Art Services, Minneapolis: 28; Bill Duffy, Bradford, New Hampshire: 117; Patrick E. Fraser, Wilmette, Illinois: 18; Anne Garcia, Julian, California: 44; Dror Gilboa, Kiryat, Tivon, Israel: 67; The Image Loft, Manchester, Vermont: 56; The Image Maker, Marcia Ward, Loveland, Colorado: 87; The Imagery Group, Barry Levin, Union City, California: 91; Rick Lang, Laguna Beach, California: 81; Heather Martinez, Durango, Colorado: 50; John McKenzie, Ormiston, East Lothian, Scotland: 129; T. C. Miller, Saint Augustine, Florida: 54; Peter James Millson, Bridport, Dorest, England: 114; Richard Nicol, Seattle: 38; Chuck Osborne, Tulsa, Oklahoma: 78; C. Otting, Veenendaal, Netherlands: 70; Jafe Parsons, Loveland, Colorado: 45, 60, 92, 106, 118; Eddie Phillips, Angus, Scotland: 104; Phototec, Gilbert Wideawske, Rutland, Vermont: 127; Photographic Solutions, Daniel Tilton, Billings, Montana: 25; Quicksilver Photographers, Mark Gulezian, Takoma Park, Maryland: 74; Re-Art, M. Salome, Almere, Netherlands: 65; Reed Photo-Imaging, Denver: 131; Lee Rolfe, Lake Forest Park, Washington: 11; Larry Sanders, Milwaukee: 98; John Seerey-Lester, Osprey, Florida: 107; Bruce Shippee, Santa Rosa, California: 95; Skylark Images, Darren Briggs, Sebastopol, California: 14; Steve Stayton, Tucson, Arizona: 123; The Studio, Peter Vance, Weston, Wisconsin: 15, 36, 43, 64, 79, 112, 115, 120; Kevin Sturges, Geelong, Victoria, Australia: 77; Tim Barnwell Photography, Asheville, North Carolina: 125; Tony Walsh Photography, Cincinnati: 109; Trevon Baker Photography, Somers, Montana: 105; Timothy Wampler, Paso Robles, California: 100; Wild Wings, Lake City, Minnesota: 73

Unless otherwise specified, images have been provided courtesy of the artists.

Printed in the United States of America

Leigh Yawkey Woodson Art Museum
700 North Twelfth Street
Wausau, Wisconsin 54403-5007
USA

Telephone: 715-845-7010
Fax: 715-845-7103
E-mail: museum@lywam.org
Online: www.lywam.org